The Way of Freedom

Conversations with

Salvadore Poe

Edited by Seth Colby

The Way of Freedom

www.liberationis.com
www.salvadorepoe.com

Published by: Liberation IS Publishing

Paperback:
ISBN-13: 978-1-7321411-0-0
ISBN-10: 1-7321411-0-X

eBook:
ISBN-13: 978-1-7321411-1-7
ISBN-10: 1-7321411-1-8

Edited by: Seth Colby

Photo of Salvadore: Elena Skaya, www.elenaskaya.com

Cover Design: Cade Siemers

Contents

Acknowledgments

Many friends helped to bring this book to life and each of them did so with care and love.

Thank you to:

Ryan Cramer for proofreading and providing valuable suggestions on clarification.

Christine Deluca and Vanya Green for offering wonderful suggestions and clarification.

Olivier Maguire for beginning the transcription process that got the book started.

Eva Raud Adamson, Marie Anderson, John Burke, Steve Gibson, Irene Kendig, Al Kuehn, Hazel Long, Robert Middleton, George Morgano, Erica Mulford, Matjaz Perme, Friedrich Roelli, Sandra Turner, and Eric Witt for transcribing, reading, organizing and offering suggestions.

All the friends who fearlessly engaged with this work through dialog and with their questions.

This book was created because of the great work of my editor, Seth Colby. Without him it would not have been.

Much love and gratitude to Dolano, and to all the other beautiful teachers and masters I have known - U.G. Krishnamurti, Sivasakthiammaiyar, Ajja, Douglas Harding and Toni Packer.

Editor's Preface

For many years of my life, I felt a sense of unease, restlessness, and discontent. Early on, I spent a lot of time using alcohol and doing many activities to avoid and quiet this internal turmoil. I engaged in many physical activities (marathons and triathlons), and I threw myself into college, law school, and then my career. I believed that by doing all of these things, I was going to get somewhere, achieve some sense of success, and obtain a feeling of peace and well-being. Nonetheless, it never worked out.

In 1995, I attended my first personal growth seminar. It was revolutionary in the sense that I resolved a lot of psychological trauma and saw myself in a new light. I felt great and I started "working on myself." I now believed that if I did more in terms of keeping my word and living a particular way, it would create a certain persona that would eventually lead me to the goal of peace and enlightenment.

Working on myself, however, didn't get me to where I thought I should be going. So, I began actively seeking in other venues to get answers and to resolve the continued feelings of dissatisfaction and unease. I became a workshop junkie, traveling around the U.S. and even to other countries, doing a wide range of retreats with many teachers.

Not surprisingly, the results were similar. I'd have an exceptional time at the retreat while learning new things and gaining great insights. (Some of the retreats transformed my life dramatically—a 10-day vipassana meditation course, for example, assisted me with ending a long-time addiction to alcohol.) But, for the most part, after each retreat ended, I found myself back in the same place I'd started, with the same nagging sense that there was something more to get and something else to learn.

After almost twenty years of attending retreats, I figured that my mind was getting trickier and smarter at keeping me stuck. So, in an effort to resolve my core issues without the mind blocking me, I decided to start working with psychedelics and other medicines.

Like all the other avenues of exploration, I jumped in with both feet. I attended numerous Ayahuasca retreats and even traveled to Peru for a two-week stint. I also worked with several shamans who employed medicines such as iboga, 5-MeO-DMT, marijuana, etc. As you can imagine, I had many mystical, magical, wonderful, and terrifying experiences as a result of working with these medicines. But, despite all of these experiences, the underlying goal always seemed to be the same—I was using the medicines in an attempt to heal, purify or resolve something that was obstructing the realization of my essential nature. As with all the other work, I was back at the same spot where I started.

In early 2016, I attended a non-duality meeting, and someone mentioned Sal's first book. The title hit me like a ton of bricks, reverberating to the core of my being. An unspoken "YES" flooded my consciousness—I wanted to be done! I was completely fed up with continually seeking, and I wanted it to be over.

I immediately bought the book, watched Sal's interview on Buddha at the Gas Pump, and arranged to go through the inquiry sessions, where I quickly recognized my essential being and realized the truth of many platitudes I'd heard and misunderstood along the path. Platitudes such as, "What you are looking for is what is looking," and "Unless you change and become like little children, you will never enter the kingdom of Heaven." I'd always attempted to understand these and other teachings experientially or intellectually. For the first time, I recognized that liberation had nothing to do with any experience or intellectual understanding.

After completing the inquiry sessions, I began attending group meetings with Sal and other inquirers. The purpose of these meetings is to assist people with being doubtless about their recognition and being completely finished with seeking. Another inquirer explained it best when he said, "Sal holds our hands as we go through this process until we no longer doubt our recognition."

As a result of this work, it is now clear that my essential being is the most obvious thing, and this realization has had a profound impact on my life. The incessant searching has stopped, and in its place, peace and stillness have taken root. I know myself as aware, free, and all-inclusive, and that is becoming the default resting place for my mind.

I feel blessed to have found this work and am eternally grateful for Sal's patient and loving assistance. This book was a complete labor of love for me, as I can think of no greater gift to give than that of assisting people with recognizing their own freedom and being reconciled with the fact that their essential nature is always aware, here and now. May it serve you well.

Peace,

Seth Colby
February 2018

Introduction

This book, a follow up to *Liberation IS, The End of the Spiritual Path*, is a collection of conversations and Q&A sessions taken from group calls with people who have completed one-on-one inquiry sessions with me. Its purpose is to answer questions you may have, clear up any remaining doubts, and help you to be truly finished seeking.

The first book is a book of inquiries that needs to be read in a linear way from beginning to end so that the entire recognition is clear. If you have not yet read that book, I recommend that you read it before proceeding with this one so that you will be clear about your essential being and will recognize—in your own knowing—everything that is presented here.

This book differs from the first in that it is more of a reference book. It's helpful to read it from start to finish; it will be powerful in that way. But, since each chapter stands on its own, you can also read them in any order you choose.

If you have read the first book or worked with me directly, you know that holidays are the foundation of this work. Because they are essential, I have interspersed them throughout this book as well. Holidays help you have a shift of knowing so that you come to see that who you are essentially is free. When I share a holiday, I suggest you read very slowly, stopping between each line and recognizing for yourself what that particular line is revealing. This, along with the Q&A and conversations, can help you to truly come to the end of seeking.

When engaging in this work, it is best to come with a clear and open mind, which means to leave all of your spiritual concepts, books, and practices behind for the time being. Otherwise, there is the tendency to compare what you recognize now with whatever knowledge you attained from other books and practices. Freedom is not found in your mind of philosophy and information. To find out what is true, in your own knowing, you have to stop comparing it to dead ideas and concepts from the past and see with fresh knowing what is actually true, now. Truth is not found in the garbage heap of past. It is alive, here and now, no-thing, no knowledge, no philosophy, no religion, no past, and no future. Freedom is free of all of that.

The Way of Freedom

There is no way of freedom that is truer, more resolving, more immediate, more absolute and more doubtless than the way of *freedom itself*. The way of freedom is to know truth and be free, now.

We've all heard the phrase, "The path and the goal are one." So, what does that mean in reference to the work I share? As you can see by the title, I do not say, *The Way to Freedom,* but rather *The Way of Freedom*. This is because when I work with someone, the first thing I do is help them come to know, for themselves, their free essential being. That is not something that takes time or is a goal to wait, hope, and dream for in the future. It is known, now.

This knowing is already the end of seeking, it is already freedom. But because of a lifetime of the habit of ignorance (which simply means ignoring truth in favor of all of the programmed and conditioned input in the mind), it takes time for doubt and the sense of lack (caused by the belief in a separate self) to be resolved. The way that happens is by knowing your essential being of freedom and remaining true to it at all times. In that, there is nothing you need to do. You just become more unshakable in the truth of your free essential being until there is no longer any doubt.

The way of freedom is to know truth and be free, now. The way to resolve doubt is to know doubtless freedom, now. The way affliction is resolved is to know what is free of affliction, now. *Knowing* the truth of your essential nature, and *being* that truth is the goal and it is the way. It is the goal in that you come to know your essential being, now. This is called Jnana. And it is the way in that by living free, in devotion to truth, all doubt is resolved. That is called Bhakti.

The most direct way I can say it, for those who have a clear recognition of their free essential being, is simply—Be free, now.

The Positive Way vs. The Negative Way

There are two ways people engage with self-inquiry work—the negative way and the positive way.

Psychological therapy is the negative way. The focus is on "going in there" and analyzing, dealing with, sorting out, fixing, correcting, etc. All of these methods assume there is a problem, or that something is wrong with a "me." This "me," however, is not substantial. To a person truly seeking freedom, all of that has to be seen for what it is—a myth. Once we get on the carousel of mind, there is no end. Round and round we go, forever. Of course, not everyone is ready or willing to be free and some need a therapeutic means for healing deep trauma and other suffering. There are many such therapies, and I support them.

The negative approach is also used on most of the so-called spiritual paths where there is still the belief that there is a problem or something wrong with a "me." Here, it is labeled as vasanas (tendencies), which have to be released or destroyed, or the mind has to be purified of all thoughts, or behaviors have to be corrected to avoid doing certain things that are against "spirituality" or "enlightenment." By doing this, we again wind up on the carousel of mind—fixing, purifying and correcting. As with all paths, it is an endless ride. Again, not everyone is ready or willing to get off of that ride, and for them, there are many paths to pursue.

But these avenues, while serving their own purposes, never get down to the essential truth of your being. The reason for this is that there is no "path" to knowing your essential being; you will not come to know it progressively. You either know or you don't. The negative way is both endless and ultimately never "arrives" at truth.

The way of freedom is the positive way. With this way, we are not trying to correct, fix, analyze, or purify anything. We don't even set one little toe on that carousel of mind. We stay off the carousel completely. Why? Because we have come to know our essential being, and that is what we value. Of course, a person first has to come to know their essential being in a clear and doubtless way, otherwise, it doesn't work. You can't pretend or fool yourself; you need to *know*.

The good news about the positive way is that you know freedom, immediately. No path and no more endless rides on the mental carousels. You simply know and be free, now. The other good news is that most of those things you spent a lifetime trying to resolve with the negative way get resolved automatically, on their own, without you doing anything at all. By continually remaining true to your essential being, things resolve on their own over time (some quicker perhaps than others), and you begin to know more and more peace and freedom.

Why would that be? Because you have turned off the power switch. What is the power switch? Belief. As long as you believe in vasanas, there they are. As long as you believe in afflictions from the past, there they are. As long as you believe there is a self/ego, there it is.

Some people will complain that this approach is too radical and does not properly respect or address past afflictions. Perhaps they do have real trauma that needs to be addressed through therapeutic means, and so, this work may not be for them. I do not think this work is for everyone. If someone feels they need a more therapeutic approach, then I encourage that. But, for someone who hears this message, resonates with it and feels that they are ready to be free, it is essential to first come to know who you are—free of afflictions. It is the beginning of living the way of freedom.

In coming to know there is no past, no future, and no self/ego, it is seen that you are essentially free of it all, here and now, and that you always have been. Continuing to know this and continuing to stay off the carousel of mind means that you continue to abide as truth, as freedom, and as peace. I call this having holidays. This is the positive way—being who you are, being free, now.

Come to know who you are and continually be that knowing. You have spent your whole life trying to fix and get rid of the afflictions in your mind, but it is endless and ultimately fruitless if you want to know freedom. Be free. Be who you are. See that everything is already resolved, here and now. That is the way of freedom.

Sat Chit Ananda, Sal

Sat Chit Ananda

You do not exist in time.
You exist now.

Sat Chit,
Being Knowing.

Believing in time is believing in self.
Knowing there is no time,
is knowing who you are, free of self.

Abiding in no time,
is abiding as your essential being.
It is being who you are, knowingly—
Sat Chit.

What do you want?
A myth?
Or truth, freedom, peace?

Who cares if there were so-called events in a so-called past?
Where are they now?

They are not, clearly!

So, why admit them into now?

Why let them disturb the peace of now?
The peace of your essential being.

The one who cares about past and future,
with all of its myths, is self/ego,
a thought, a non-existent "me."

Introduction

The only you, Sat Chit,
has no interest in,
or need for,
or places any meaning on
any of those myths.

That one is the only existence.

The only reality.

Know who you are,
in no time, now.

Sat Chit Ananda,
Being Knowing Peace.

Be who you are.

Holidays

A holiday reveals the truth of your essential nature—it is the way of freedom.

What A Holiday Is

A holiday is knowing.

Consciously knowing that you exist.

See that now.

And consciously knowing that your existence is:

Free of time.
Free of the stories of mind.
Free of psychology, philosophy, and spirituality.
Free of culture, politics, and religion.
Free of the myth of self/ego.
Free of seeking.
Free of becoming.
Free of doubt.

It is
ease of being.

It is
peace.

Who you are essentially is not the body-mind.

The Way of Freedom

Who you are is:

Being Knowing Peace,
Sat Chit Ananda.

Look for yourself, now.

So,
The point of a holiday is to *know that*.
And the point of repeated holidays is
to make that knowing doubtless.

So that, no matter if
the ocean of your being is still,
or there are ripples on the surface of you,
or there are huge waves on the surface of you,
you *know* you are free.

Waves come, of course,
small, huge, hot, cold,
pleasant, unpleasant and neutral.

That is the nature of ocean,
the nature of life, isn't it?

Why argue?

The secret is,
they all come and they all go.

And yet,
You remain.

So then, who are you?

Clearly, you are the knowing of it all,
Sat Chit Ananda.

Existence, consciously knowing itself as peace with
all the ripples appearing on its surface.

Now,
it is quite natural that by having more and more holidays
it will become more and more your default condition,
and in that, you will find yourself naturally
abiding as yourself,
Sat Chit Ananda,

while walking
while talking
while eating
while doing anything.

And if so,

enjoy the eternal sunshine of your natural human condition!

Is This Enough?

*When I am having holidays now, it does not have the
same excitement it had at the beginning. So, it feels like it
is not enough.*

When you first recognize your essential being, free from struggle,
strife, past and future, self/ego, and all the afflictions inherent in
that ignorance, there is quite naturally relief, which feels good. But

because the mind has been programmed with so many countless ideas about enlightenment, liberation, spirituality, non-duality, god, the divine, etc., very quickly expectation rears its ignorant head and then the thought appears, "There must be more to it than this." We are so habituated to expecting and wanting more, that at first, you may not realize the value of this nothing.

It is very natural to feel the way you do and to want something more. It takes time to reconcile all those ideas. And the way to reconcile them is by simply continuing to have holidays and be who you are. The more you continually know this simple truth, the more you will realize its implications and the more you will know it as the peace and fulfillment that it actually is. Let's be on a holiday, now.

HOLIDAY

There is only now.

No self, no past and no future.

Where are all of your cherished spiritual ideas, now?

Where are all the stories of past sufferings and future fears, now?

There is only this, *no*thing, no past and no future.

The question is, "Is this enough?"

For most people, it is clearly not enough. It is enough for someone who is very mature. It takes maturity for someone to recognize their essential nature, but it takes a far greater maturity to be reconciled (finished). That is because it is the end of you—the one that seeks, idealizes, hopes, and fears.

This is a whole new way of being in life and it takes some getting used to. We have had a lifetime of being engaged the other way, always wanting and needing to be *some*thing. Here we are *no*thing. Freedom is the natural human condition.

> *Even words like "free" have some meaning to me. My brain has some idea about what freedom should look like.*

Okay good, let's get rid of that word too. Be on holiday. Just jump. There are no words, here. Just *this*. Is it enough?

Wanting Something from a Holiday

> *Sometimes it seems easy to have holidays, then there are other times when it seems hard. It is almost like holidays are nothing but tiny little shifts of knowing, yet it seems as though we are all wired up to think that it will be something profound.*

Yes, the idea is that a holiday should be a profound *experience*. The reason why we think it is sometimes easier to have a holiday is that, in those moments, there is nothing challenging going on. Feeling good is not a holiday. When the shit is hitting the fan, you can still have a holiday and know who you are. Holidays are not about feeling any particular way.

Having holidays is profound and life-changing. Yet, a holiday is not necessarily a profound *experience* when it occurs because it is not about changing your current experience. Experiences are constantly changing. One moment the experience feels good, and maybe the next moment it feels not so good. Tell me one experience that has lasted the entire time you have been alive? There isn't one.

When you are feeling confused or not feeling good, *just for a moment*, see that everything is included here, including the confusion or the "bad" feeling. See that everything is equal, even the feeling that *seems to be* more important because it feels personal. Be honest and see that everything else is here as well. Let's be on holiday.

HOLIDAY

On holiday, all objects are here in knowing.

There is only one thing happening, now, and that is only *this*.

Mind divides this one moment up into countless things,
but if you don't refer to mind,
you will see this moment as one appearance.

It is like looking at one painting.

All the apparent separate shapes
and colors are just one painting.

In this moment, everything is equal, even the feelings.

They are all just various colors in the open field of you.

Get real about this.

Don't value one object over another.

In this way, it is always just this.

One appearance.

The mind fragments the one experience. Nevertheless, everything that seems to be separate, here and now, is just one appearance. Where is the separation between objects, really? I will give you an example. This cup I am holding appears solid, and there appears to be some separation between my fingers and the handle. However, if we looked under an electron microscope, we would see space with a few atoms floating around. There would be no line to show where the cup ended and my fingers started. There is no line. There is no line even between my skin and the air at the microscopic level. All there is, is space.

We are seeing one thing with different colors and shapes, which our mind then breaks up into countless, separate things, including feelings. It is natural to put more weight on the objects that appear to relate to this body-mind. But feelings are just one of the countless, separate things appearing, now. Seeing this shifts the concept of a holiday from being an experience to simply knowing— knowing, which includes all of the seemingly separate appearances.

> *It is almost like I am using a holiday as a technique to handle unpleasant feelings, like anxiousness. When an unpleasant feeling is there I think, "Oh, I should have a holiday." I seem to be expecting something from a holiday.*

It's completely understandable to try to use a holiday as a means of escape. That is fine actually because whatever triggers a holiday is good. The point is not to change your experience; your experience may or may not change in the short term. Whenever a holiday happens, whatever the trigger, just be sure that it is about *knowing*, which means, I know I am, here and now, and all objects are included, here and now.

To be clear, continuing to live the way of freedom does bring about more and more peace and ease of being. It is inevitable because, in the absence of the conflict and suffering caused by the habitual engagement with thoughts and feelings, peace is your natural condition.

Holidays Seeming Vague

Over time, it seems that holidays have become vaguer. Maybe, I'm hankering for more powerful experiences. There's a doubt that it should be more.

A holiday isn't a big thing. At the beginning, it can be because it is a shift of knowing and it may surprise you.

I see it's important to value holidays, and if it's vague, it's vague.

Okay, but let's look now, let's have a holiday.

HOLIDAY

Relax the focus of attention.

Don't attend to anything.

Nothing.

No objects.

What is here is open, aware, right?

Is that clear? Is it vague?

Kind of vague.

You say that because you're expecting some bliss or something to feel good.

Yeah, okay. Busted.

Yeah, exactly [laughing]. Let's have a holiday.

HOLIDAY

Relax the focus of attention and look, now.

Knowing is here?

Open knowing?

Yes.

Is it obvious or not?

Yes, it's obvious.

Good, it's not vague, it's obvious. If you continue to have holidays, you will find that it is *by far* the most obvious thing. You have a lot of ideas and expectations about what should happen, and they are tied to a state of feeling good.

Yes, okay.

You have to be honest with yourself. A holiday is knowing. It's not feeling good, it's not being in bliss. It's knowing, I am. Have a holiday.

HOLIDAY

I know I am, here and now.

Do you know you are, here and now?

Yes.

Is there a past or a future?

No.

Is that vague, or is that clear?

It's clear.

It's known. It's very obvious, isn't it?

Yeah, it's known.

The mind comes in and says, "This can't possibly be it. This is not it. I'm not in ultimate bliss. I'm not having a mystical experience. This can't be it." But what if it is? This knowing that's you, *nothing*. Keep having a holiday and what do you notice? There's the absence of any story right now, isn't there?

Yes.

In the absence of any story, there's nothing to cause suffering. Is that true?

Yes.

In the absence of story, in the absence of suffering, what actually is, is peace.

There's a sort of neutral-ness.

You call it neutral, but you're calling it neutral because the mind is saying it should be bliss. It sounds something like, "Well, it's not bliss, it's only *no*thing, so that's neutral."

It's a bit boring.

Compared to what? You're looking for something based on what you think it should be. What is, is and it's not what you want, so you call it "neutral" and "boring." Actually, it's peace, and truth— nothing boring about that. You have to see it again, and again, and again... Then you begin to see the value in that. You have to get real and jump. You can call it neutral if you want, but it's the absence of afflictions. Is it true, now?

Yes.

What if this was it? What if it was always like this, the absence of afflictions? Wouldn't that be pretty good?

That would be pretty nice [laughing].

See the value in this, now. If you continue to see the value in this and continue to value truth, this will become the most obvious thing for you. It is the most obvious thing, but right now, it's being overridden by your desire for an experience of some particular pleasantness or something. That desire is a filter that's not allowing you to fully enjoy this—*no*thing, with the absence of afflictions. In that absence is peace. And, when you value freedom, that peace becomes more and more obvious; more and more your default condition. That valuing is the way of freedom.

Be honest with yourself and see that you still want something. There's still a desire there for something that feels good, that's exciting, and that's not boring. If that desire is not being met, you're going to be disappointed. Even with the most beautiful peace, you will think, "This peace is boring."

Just see that the reason you say it's boring and neutral is because you have the expectation for something else. This is not going to match that expectation. It's going to blow it out of the water once you start valuing it. Your desire for something more than this, *no*thing, makes you overlook the incredible beauty that this is.

Been There Done That

Sometimes, I don't do the holidays as much because when it occurs to me to have a holiday, I think, "I have already done that before and I know what it is going to look like." So, I really don't do them.

Okay. First of all, with a holiday, we recognize our essential nature is free, here and now. We recognize there is only now. Recognizing this truth is what will set you free. In now, your essential being, there is no self. There are no stories of a past self or of a future self becoming enlightened at some point. None of that exists here, now. There is only this moment, and we see there is no self. This moment is Sat Chit Ananda.

When we have a holiday, the so-called goal is already attained. We see there is nothing more to attain. This is it. Freedom is already the case. Liberation is already the case. The title of the first book is *Liberation IS*. Some of you have heard that the "path and the goal are the same." Well, this is what it means. The goal is already attained in a holiday. And having a holiday over and over again is what liberates the mind from seeking, from thinking there is anything lacking, and from believing there will be enlightenment in the future.

Having a holiday takes no time. There is the immediate recognition of truth, but the mind is slow. There are many doubts and beliefs that take time to resolve. The way they resolve is by continually having holidays and recognizing what is true. Ramana Maharshi said, "Abide as the Self." This is exactly what he is talking about— just be on a holiday. It doesn't mean to stay here for hours by the use of will. You can't. Thoughts come in and attention focuses on them. And then again, have a holiday.

In a holiday, you recognize you are free. Slowly, over time, the mind gets relaxed as doubts resolve. Many people on the path have a belief they will have one experience of awareness and they will be enlightened. However, when they have this experience and it goes away, they wonder what happened to their enlightenment. I had this happen to me when I was a seeker. The fact is that one holiday, ten holidays, a hundred holidays are not enough. It has to be the way you live.

If you say you already know what holidays are because you did them before, you are only being a philosopher. If you say you know something, that is incorrect because you really don't know anything. Even if you know something intellectually, what good does it do you? When I say, "know what is true," I don't mean some intellectual knowledge, I mean know the knowing, now, in this moment.

So, do I need to have as many holidays as I can all day?

There is no doer. Holidays happen whenever they happen for you. I don't ask you to attempt to have holidays. A holiday happens spontaneously whenever you recognize you are attending to something. There's no right or wrong way to do it. The more you are tired of the suffering caused by focusing on thoughts and stories, the more holidays will happen spontaneously because you are sick of it and you just want to be free. It happens by itself. The way this happens more is by seeing the contraction when you focus on self and by seeing the peace of being free.

That is why I place such a big emphasis on valuing what is true in the inquiries. Seeing the value—that here and now, I am free—is very liberating. Also, it is very valuable to see that here and now, I lack nothing, and I am complete and whole. There is nothing more to attain than this. It is always good to go back and review the section in *Liberation IS* where the value of the recognition of truth is covered (Inquiry Two - Valuing What is True).

The more you see the value and the more you become sick of suffering, the more holidays will happen spontaneously by themselves. I want to stress there is no doer. Just continue to have holidays, hang out with us and ask questions when you have them, and it will happen by itself.

> *Inquirer 2: For me, having holidays clears things up. The analogy that comes to mind is lifting weights. Lifting weights once will not do much for my body but lifting weights over time will have an impact.*

Holidays happen spontaneously, but I put in your mind the intention to have holidays often. If you are not doing anything, just sit there and be on holiday. It is not a doership. Now, the seed will just appear in your mind spontaneously, as do all thoughts and intentions. What we are doing here is simple. It is not like you have to sit in meditation for two hours or something.

I used to meditate eight hours a day. Having a holiday is just taking a break from attending to objects. It is not *doing* anything, nothing is required. You are not trying to stop anything. It is very relaxed. Sit with your eyes open and recognize there is only now. Past is an illusion. Future is a fantasy. I am that I am, now. There is nothing more to become. The desire to become more in the future takes you away from truth and peace, which is only, and always, here and now.

Going into Story or Being on Holiday

I hear you say that no matter what my thoughts and feelings are, even if they are incredibly cruel, they are just like a wave in the ocean.

Yes, what is, is. There is no fault if unpleasant thoughts and feelings show up. Is there any fault if you get angry when your caregiver shows up late?

No.

From speaking with you, I know that you are concerned with the emotions that are appearing for you. Regardless of how they are being elicited, is there any fault on your part that anger appears?

No.

Is there some judgment that you should not be angry, and you have to fix yourself, or do something to get rid of the anger?

Well, I just don't like it. It doesn't feel good.

Of course, and sometimes anger is justified. Anger (as with any emotion) can elicit a story in your mind which can attract your attention and cause the anger to grow and stay around longer. It is very normal for this to occur.

It seems like it is harder for me to deal with anger after doing this work with you.

Why do you think that is?

Because there is a contrast between when I am on holiday and when I am in a story.

What solution is there? Obviously, your circumstance is what it is. One alternative is to keep having holidays and see your essential nature and the end of the story. The other alternative is to continue on with the story, being angry and feeling justified with the anger.

The habit for a majority of people is alternative number two. Now, you see there is a different option. What I hear you saying is now that you know there is another way, the old habit is clearly becoming very painful to keep. In a holiday, there is relief. Now, you know that relief. Of course, the suffering is now more unbearable. So, what is there to do? Stay the course.

I noticed recently that I have some resistance to being on holiday. I notice that I don't want it.

Yes, because what you want in that moment (no judgment) is to be in the story. If that is what you want, that is what you will get. If you want freedom, that is what you will get. If you go into a story, just notice with no judgment that that is what you wanted.

There is no one doing the wanting and yet, wanting is there. There is no one choosing it or creating it. You either want something or you don't. You can't choose. In the moment that a story is coming, you don't choose to want the story or choose to want freedom. That is why I say there is no judgment. If in the moment, you go into a story, it is clear that is what you want. You did not choose to want it. The desire or interest to be in the story and to be justified just appears.

A moment later, maybe a holiday appears, and you will see the value of that. You will then naturally want that. You don't choose to want that either.

Suffering can be considered grace because you can see the difference between going into the stories or having a holiday. That is why this work takes time. Clearly, the solution is known to you because you see the difference. Knowing the value of a holiday is very important because once you know the value, you will want that.

> *Inquirer 2: I had a point of clarification. I have times when a strong thought or emotion comes up and I have the thought to have a holiday, but immediately another thought comes up "Fuck that, I am NOT having a holiday!" My question is, am I having a holiday when I just have the thought "have a holiday?"*

The holiday already occurred. That is why the thought to have a holiday appeared.

> *Inquirer 2: So, in the moment when I am telling myself that I am not going to have a holiday, that is a holiday.*

Yes, you are aware of yourself in that moment. Knowing is present. Let's say you are wrapped up in thoughts and then the thought "have a holiday" appears. Why would that thought appear? It appears because you know that you are aware of only thoughts in that moment. That is the order of things.

> *Inquirer 3: One of the disadvantages of taking holidays is that it requires you to give up the story and all of your righteousness about it.*

That is right.

> *Inquirer 2: I recall someone mentioning that it was a huge loss for them to give up prayer and meditation.*

What I also notice is that there is a loss by giving up the misery and depression I have been holding on to. I see that it has been my default habit to gravitate towards these emotions and thoughts.

It is a habit. This is a lifestyle basically and it has been going on for however long it has been going on. It takes time to resolve these lifelong habits. A new habit is being created (no one is doing it). The habit is being free. This new habit will outshine everything else.

Senses are not Needed for Knowing

Without my senses there would be no knowing.

That's not true. Close your eyes so there is no visual sense. Is the knowing still here?

Yes.

Let's say you were floating in a completely black, soundproof, anti-gravity chamber where all of your senses were cut off, including smell and taste, would you still know that you are?

Yes, but my mind would also be thinking.

Yes, but let's say you went into a state of no thoughts for a moment. If there are no thoughts, don't you know that you are? Do you need thoughts to know that you are?

No, but I have emotions to know that I am.

Emotions and bodily sensations are objects as well, they come and go. You are the knowing of those sensations and emotions. And if there are no emotions, knowing is still known in and of itself. Have a holiday.

HOLIDAY

Just know.

Know that you are.

You can't deny it.

Just keep knowing that you are.

Be that knowing.

Being and knowing are one.

When thought, or any other object, is attended to exclusively, you are not knowing that you are the knowing. You are knowing the object. Then the object passes, and you know that you are here. And here, there is no past, no future, and no time. There is only knowing that I am here, now. All the stories in your head are gone. Nothing ever happened in this knowing that I am here, now. Here and now have no past and no future.

Your mind may say, "It can't be this simple," but it is. It is the simplest thing. Of course, it is because it is you.

Prerequisite for Holidays

I can't do holidays the way you talk about them. I have to sit down and think about them.

Okay, hold on a second. Look now and say, "I am consciously aware that I exist."

I am consciously aware that I exist.

Is it true, or are you just saying it?

It is true.

How long did that take? Look again, "I am consciously aware that I exist." Look. It does not take any time. That is a holiday. You are still trying to get into some state, it is much easier to just jump. Recognize, "I know I exist." You see this?

Yes.

A couple of seconds later, thoughts come and when you recognize you are thinking, say, "I know I exist." This is all it is. "I know I exist." The more you *know you exist,* the more you do it, and the more it becomes your default condition. It reveals what it needs to reveal. Do you see this?

Yes.

If, for now, you want to say those words ("I know I exist"), you will immediately recognize that you are here, you are this knowing. Is that clear and easy for you?

Yes, I can do it this way.

Thoughts can come in right afterward, like "No, that can't be it, that wasn't a holiday." But yes, it was a holiday. You are not trying to get in any state or elicit any feeling. You just know that you exist. When you know that you exist, you see that everything is here.

> *Inquirer 2: So then, do you really need to relax the focus of attention? I hear you say that when you ask us to have a holiday, but that seems to imply an effort.*

That is a fair question. When I first introduce people to what a holiday is, I say that. For you all, who know what a holiday is (which is when attention is no longer focused on an object), I am being more direct. I don't need to say, "Relax the focus of attention." I sometimes still do, but now, I would rather say to everyone here who knows what a holiday is, "Look. Do you know that you exist?" You see this relaxes the focus of attention. That statement, "I know I exist," *is* the relaxation of attention from objects.

I found that it was a very easy way for people to recognize Sat Chit Ananda. "Sat" is existence or being, and "Chit" is consciousness or knowing. Sat Chit = I consciously know that I exist. And the essence of being that knowing is peace, Ananda. This is who you are. You are Sat Chit Ananda—I consciously know myself as peace.

Who Am I?

Until you have come to know your essential being, you will be forever trying to change something about your mental and emotional experience, and you will never come to know the peace of freedom. Why? Because freedom is not an experience. Freedom is in, and as the result of, knowing. Knowing is both the way and the goal. It is the goal in that knowing is not separate from who you are—it is you, essentially. Therefore, you are already free, the goal is already attained. But for all doubt to be resolved, it is essential to continue valuing the truth of your essential being over experience. *Worship* truth! Come to this knowing more and more, until it is completely natural and doubtless. That is the way of freedom.

Know Thyself!

> *Could you say more about "all-inclusive?" Sometimes I just don't know what you mean by that. It feels like I get a little intellectual with it.*

Okay. We will take it from the beginning. Have a holiday.

HOLIDAY

Don't focus on anything in particular.

Let attention be open.

In this work, we are not attempting to find any objects.

We are knowing the knowing itself.

The Way of Freedom

You know that you are here, aware.

You know—I exist.

I am this knowing that is before, during and after
all thoughts and all appearances.

Are you separate from this knowing?

This knowing is your source, your essential being.

It is you.

If you are a meditator, you may focus on the breath (an object). In that case, you never come to source. You may be stilling the mind, and becoming "aware of awareness," but you never get the final little bit, which is, this knowing is who I am. Know thyself!

Have another holiday.

HOLIDAY

You know the knowing, which is here, now?

All the objects, which are appearing, are equal.

Whatever is in your room—sights,
sounds, smells, sensations, and thoughts—are equal
because the knowing knows them all.

That knowing is you.

You are the one who knows all the objects.

Know yourself as the knowing,
not as an object, like this body-mind.

Who Am I?

You are the knowing of this body-mind.

In this knowing, everything is included equally.

Usually, when we are focused on an object such as a thought, attention is exclusive. You are knowing only one object. This is duality, subject/object, and is not all-inclusive. You, this knowing, are all-inclusive.

To go a step further, none of these things are separate from this knowing. These things are the manifested form of this knowing, just like a wave is a manifestation of ocean. You are ocean and all the forms are waves on the surface of you. This knowing includes everything, which means the knowing knows everything and is everything. There is no separation.

> *This second part is not easy for me to realize. I know you say there is no witness, and it feels like there is a witnessing of everything.*

A witness is a thing. It is an object. Someone separate is needed for a witness. Knowing is not a thing or an object. This is why I don't call it awareness. I just use the words aware/knowing. These are not objects. You can't find aware/knowing as a thing.

> *There is a sense of being stuck on this. I don't feel separate from everything and yet, I don't feel part of it all. That is not clear.*

You are not part of it all. It is not like that. For something to be separate, there must be a you here. Let's be on holiday for a minute.

HOLIDAY

Go beyond the limited sense/feeling of "you" that is here.

See that knowing is not exclusive to this body-mind organism.

There is the sense here, "I am the body."

This is the first touch of ego,
this notion, "I am here in the body."

We all have this sense of "I am—I am here in this body-mind."

That is fine.

Now,
notice that you know the sense of
"I am here in this body-mind."
You know this, don't you?

You know it.

The felt sense of "I am here" in this body is no different than anything else in the room—objects, sounds, and smells. It is very habitual and subtle to associate with this felt sense of being in a body. You have to see that you know this felt sense. Like Nisargadatta says, hold on to the feeling of "I am" and go beyond the feeling. Well, this is beyond the feeling because this is the knowing of the feeling "I am." This knowing is not an object that you can find. It is just knowing. Don't stop at the feeling of "I am." Know, *I know that I am.*

Then everything is equally known and what is important is the knowing, not any of the particular objects. We have all been conditioned to think this sensation of a body-mind is the most important and special thing, and it is separate from everything else.

Of course, it is only a thought. When we step a little bit beyond that, we see that we actually know the sense of "I am" as well as everything else. Then there is less self-focus happening. Less self-importance. It is a relief.

In having a holiday, we are being the knowing. Knowing equals being. So, be the knowing itself. That is who you are—the knowing.

> I recognize "be the knowing" a lot. It seems like I was attempting to make something more out of the idea of "all-inclusive." Maybe I was looking for some experience or something.

The reason I talk about *all-inclusive* is to get people out of the limited attention to self. The sense of self is claustrophobic. So, I show people that actually everything is here. The term *all-inclusive* assists with opening people up to this realization.

To take it as far as we just did is the real point. To know you are the knowing of everything, and everything is equal and not separate from this knowing.

God

> I am fine with letting go of the concepts of Santa Claus and the Easter Bunny. I am having a hard time letting go of God. Who's to say there is no God?

Let's take a look. For a moment, assume that Santa Claus did exist, and you saw him. He would be appearing within you because you are knowing itself. You are all-inclusive without any separation.

Santa Claus is not appearing somewhere outside of you. He is within you because you are this, which is aware. It is your nature.

Let's say God exists and you see him. He would be appearing within you, knowing. You are not in God. God is within you as well.

Let's find out what God is. According to the Bible, God has some qualities. Have a holiday.

HOLIDAY

You know your nature is aware.

This,
which is aware,
is not separate from who you are.

It is who you are, essentially.

Another word for aware is knowing.
Whatever is appearing in aware is known.

Aware and knowing are synonymous.

Within aware, your nature, all things are known.

They say God is omniscient, that he knows all.

Knowing knows all, right?

We see that this aware/knowing includes everything.

Knowing knows the closest objects,
like thoughts and sensations,
and the farthest, like other galaxies.

Who Am I?

It is omnipresent, everywhere at all times.

They say God is omnipresent.

Knowing is your essential being.

So then, what is God?

This concept of "a God separate from me" is a fantasy for adults. Just like Santa Claus and the Easter Bunny are fantasies for children. When Moses asked God his name, God said, "I am that I am." You can also say, "I am that I am." God is telling Moses that he is it.

There is no difference between Santa Claus and God, they are both appearing within you. As Nisargadatta said, "God is my devotee." He did not say he was God's devotee. His point is that we have it backward. God is not something apart from you and greater than you. If there is a God, then it will appear in and as *you*. So then, you are the ultimate. God is only an idea. And even if he appeared, he would be an object known to you. You, aware, are the one that knows either God or no God.

Let's look at beliefs. Do you know for a fact there is a God apart from you?

No.

Do you believe there is a God?

Yes.

What we are doing here is coming to know what is true. What that means is knowing only what we can actually know for a fact for ourselves. There is only one thing you can know for a fact, and that is I am, here and now—I exist, now, and everything is known to and within me. God, apart from you, and Heaven, apart from here, are beliefs. Those beliefs have appeared in the human mind for security and comfort to allay fear and to offer hope. If you want to be mature and know what is true, you have to see that those beliefs are just that, beliefs, and as so, are false.

A mature person, one who wants freedom, does not need the teddy bears of God and Heaven anymore. True freedom is not knowing anything, and not needing to know.

You only know one thing, and that is NOW. This work, if you embrace it, ends all your beliefs, and you become reconciled with what is. You have to be ready for it. When people ask about my beliefs, I say I have none. Beliefs are childish. The brain is good at cooking a meal, but it can't figure out what this is all about and what happens when we die. For security, we take for granted a bunch of beliefs about what happens, and it is all nonsense. No one has any idea. Just realize that you don't know and be reconciled with that.

Recognize! You don't know, and you don't need to know. Recognize! This is it!

> *I have some fear and sadness about letting this go. I used to have something to grasp on to or strive for. Now, there is nothing. There used to be a framework, but now I am free falling.*

That is good—free fall. The sadness you are experiencing is no different than the sadness a seven-year-old girl feels when she loses her teddy bear. All concepts have to go, because, by their very nature (mind created), they are false. In truth, there is nothing.

> *It seems like many people and cultures have very deep-seated beliefs about spirituality and God. When we are with them, it feels like there is no reason to confront them about their beliefs.*

That is right. You know who you are, and you don't have to prove a thing to anyone. Who are you to question anyone's beliefs? I don't confront anyone about their beliefs except for people who come to me wanting to know liberation. If someone does not ask me to assist them with liberation, I go along with whatever they believe— crystals, tarot cards, gods, after-life, reincarnation. It's not my concern, and I don't hassle people about their beliefs because that is what they want.

> *In my work, I use sound tools, essential oils and things of that nature. How do I be with that?*

Do they help people?

> *I believe they do.*

Fine. What is wrong? You know who you are. The things you are doing are helping the person's mental and physical makeup. There is nothing wrong with that; just know those things have nothing to do with liberation, period. You are helping people's mental and physical conditions, and that is fine. It is beneficial and good.

The new age movement says those things have something to do with enlightenment; that is nonsense. We know this for sure because nothing leads to liberation. It is your natural condition. Your nature is liberated already. You are free.

Free of What?

> *When you talk about "free," what exactly am I being free from?*

That's a good question. Free from the past. Free from the ball and chain of culture which has, in a sense, created you. Look, the mind that is in your head is not your personal mind, it is culture.

This is like being nothing.

That is right. It's being *nothing*, as there is *nothing*. When you recognize your essential being and see there is no self here, you see there is *nothing*. This is something that can't be explained. Once you get it, you get it. There is no past. Nothing ever happened. We are getting real here.

Also, what seems to be appearing here is not a solid thing. Nothing here is solid; it is all ephemeral and insubstantial. It is constantly changing at the molecular level and is gone as soon it appears. There is *nothing*.

Inquirer 2: How do you prevent yourself from freaking out when you see that?

Don't prevent yourself—freak out.

It seems that the fear pulls me back.

If there is fear, it means there is the recognition, which is good. There is nothing to do. If the fear pulls you back, it pulls you back. So then, just recognize it again, and again, and again...

What is it that is fearing? It is only this sense of a separate self here. There is no actual self/ego here. Let's be on holiday.

HOLIDAY

This Sat Chit Ananda,
this knowing,
does not fear anything.

Who Am I?

The fear is conditioned
thoughts and ideas.

Of course, it is self/ego.

When the fear is there,
it is an object you know,
along with everything else.

Believe it or not, it is also equal to everything else.

It may not seem that way in the moment of the fear,
but it is just another appearance that comes and goes.

You are the knowing of that appearance.

If there is fear, have a holiday. And if it is really intense fear, you may not have a holiday. I had a crazy experience during my first vipassana retreat when I first began seeking. I was sharing a room with three other guys, and after a few days, this unbelievable fear started happening. It was sheer, abject terror. This went on for several days, and I was unable to meditate. At one point, I thought I was going crazy, and I actually had to leave the meditation hall. I have thought back on that experience and wondered what would have happened had I stayed. Maybe everything would have crumbled down. I don't know.

Anyway, there is no doer and that is just what happened at the time. If you have fear, it is good to have a holiday. If the fear is too intense, maybe something else will appear. If you can just sit with the fear, it is good. It is only fear.

Sometimes it feels like I am going to lose the freedom.

Well, the *nothing* is the freedom, so it can't be lost. The ego does not get freedom. *Nothing* is free from the ego, free from self. The sense of self is just culture, just the thoughts. There is nothing really. There is no ego. There is just programming in the mind that we believe is who we are. Freedom means you know that is *not* who you are. Actually, you see it doesn't even exist.

> Inquirer 3: Freedom is also free from all the psychological baggage. I remember hearing a teacher say he was "tired of all his bullshit." I related to that for a long time, and as I was doing this work, there was space for all of it and it was not personal anymore. So, you get free of your past, your notions, and all your beliefs. Then, there is just the "isness" of it all. All of my idiosyncrasies are still here, and I just don't take it personally anymore.

Freedom is a hard word to describe because we all have these ideas about what it is. We think it is some experience or something like that. Freedom is not a perfect word. No words are perfect and that's just how it is.

> Inquirer 4: For me, the big freedom was from seeking. I spent a lot of time reading and going to seminars and now, that is all gone.

That is great and really, we should not get stuck on a word because we are trying to live up to some ideal. No words are needed. Let's be on holiday and see if any words are needed.

HOLIDAY

What word comes in to describe anything here?

It is just adding something on to *nothing*.

Can we just be in this unknown?

This *nothing*?

Who Am I?

Can we not need to understand and find meaning?

Who would need the words anyway?

Does Sat Chit Ananda need those words?

Does your essential nature need words?

Ego is the only thing that would need anything like that.

You, essentially, don't need that.

You are it!

Inquirer 5: For me in a holiday, I need to use words like "I am that" in order to have the recognition.

What do you need that for? If you are saying, "I am that," then you are not recognizing yourself. You are having a thought. The phrase, "I am that" is just a pointer, and it has to be dropped.

Inquirer 5: When I say, "I am that," I am saying "I am existence."

In that case say, I am *this*. I have to use some words so you can recognize, but I don't want you to be holding on to those words. A holiday is about knowing. This does not mean knowing words. It just means knowing, period. In a holiday, look, now.

HOLIDAY

Do you know you exist? Are you consciously aware that you exist?

Yes.

Do you need words to know this?

No, but I was looking for words because I thought they would assist.

When you first start having holidays, it is good to consciously notice some things. Notice there is no past and no future. Just notice. Also, notice there is just this knowing, it is now, and all-inclusive. In the beginning, words are okay so that you recognize. Once you know these things, then you KNOW. Then forget the words.

A holiday is simply about knowing. What is it that I know? I know that I exist. You don't need any words. Just know that you exist. Another way to say this is, "Be who you are." Be yourself. Being is knowing. Now, of course, you can say, "I am that. I am the knowing." But forget those words or else you are stuck thinking. Just be, period.

Bliss

I get thrown by the word bliss or anything like that; happiness, joy, etc. I seem to be asking myself, "Where are those states?"

What I do "get" from doing this work is a subtle sense of this nowness. I see some peace in knowing there is nothing behind the curtain, but it is nothing particularly good or bad.

When we come to this work and recognize that our essential nature is free, it has huge implications as far as dropping the seeking, being okay with whatever is appearing in life and no longer arguing with what is. This is freedom.

Who Am I?

In my experience, if I am not doing anything, I am mostly on holiday. It is just how it is. When you are really on holiday a lot, which is being the knowing (Sat Chit), you will know peace (Ananda). When you are on holiday, everything else falls away. There is just less and less stress. Your natural being is just relaxed and at ease. Imagine, if you were on holiday all the time, you would be your natural essence which is peace—the absence of conflict.

In an experiential sense, your essential nature is peace. When you are on holiday a lot and not stressing, naturally your essential nature is very peaceful.

> *I am starting to get it that the words are not really important, and the idea of having some celestial experience is not it.*

Right, the words are not important. Also, this work is not about celestial experiences. Those are mystical experiences which are not truth. The bliss of Sat Chit Ananda (being, knowing, peace) is just complete relaxation and ease. The more you stay on holiday, the more you will recognize this. Even when "crazy" stuff is going on, there will be an ease because you just know your essential nature, and you don't stress the comings and goings. This work is about knowing your freedom and knowing what is valuable. And that elicits peace.

The more you are on holiday, the more beneficial it is. You can recognize your essential nature in one meeting, but the benefits of staying free are endless.

> *Inquirer 2: What I notice in doing this work is that the work is starting to "do me." What used to be in the background is now in the foreground.*

It is the most obvious thing. There is nothing more obvious than you, your essential being. It is not subtle or deep. It is the most obvious thing possible. It is not possible for it to be more obvious. Before coming to this work, we just did not recognize it. Now, the more you come to realize it, the more you recognize that it is the most obvious thing. It is not great or grand. It's just obvious.

The more you recognize your essential nature, the more these ideas that something should be a certain way just fall away. The ideas are just gone, then the mind is not looking for anything. It is just here, and you really start seeing the Sat Chit Ananda of the moment.

Just be on holidays. It is already the end. Thoughts still come of course, but you recognize there is no value in there. It is just the rehashing of impressions.

Is it Right to Say, "I Am Consciousness?"

Would it be accurate to say that I'm consciousness, or is that adding something onto this?

Saying you are consciousness or awareness makes you a thing. I don't say I'm consciousness or awareness. I don't say I'm *anything*, except knowing. Knowing is not a thing—I know, I am, I exist, and I'm aware. There's no "ness." There's no *thing* in any of that.

To say, "I'm consciousness" can become a bit philosophical and then, it's just some*thing* else to believe you are. You are not a thing, but you are conscious, aren't you? Clearly, you're conscious. But as what? Not a thing. We don't know what. The most we can say about ourselves is, "I know, I am—I exist, here and now."

Who Am I?

In past audios, there are times when you say, "I'm just Sal. I'm Sal." I get a little confused and yell at the recording, "But you're not Sal! You can't find Sal!" Can you say what you mean when you say, "I'm just Sal?"

I call it "full circle." First, we start off thinking, "I'm this body-mind organism." That's who I am—*only* that. I am an island unto myself. This very limited view creates a lot of fear and insecurity; a lot to protect and defend; and a lot of desire to accumulate more and more for myself.

Then we go on the spiritual path, and maybe we have some spiritual experiences and get some philosophical understandings. From this, we may start thinking, "I am consciousness. I'm not Sal! You silly stupid earthlings, thinking you're the body-mind. I'm consciousness, I'm awareness. The body-mind doesn't matter. It's nothing. Cut off the arm, who cares? Ha, ha, no problem. Kill someone. It doesn't matter. It's all consciousness." That thinking is pathological, and it can be a big part of the spiritual scene. That's halfway there.

Essentially, I'm aware; I'm aware of the body-mind. But at the same time, I am not separate from the body-mind. Full circle says, this body-mind is not separate from essential being—*nothing*. It's the ephemeral appearance of the absolute. It's how the absolute, you, appears in the world, like how the ocean appears as a wave. Wave is not separate from ocean, it is an appearance of ocean. This body-mind organism called Sal is like the wave in the ocean. It's the absolute, or whatever words you want to use, appearing now as Sal. It's not separate from that.

In the Play of Life, I don't walk around saying, "I am the unitary movement" or some other such silliness. I speak in normal dualistic language. This is the Play of Life, and what is appearing now is Sal. When I say, "I'm Sal," what I want you to realize is that there's nothing special going on here. It's very ordinary. Sal is not special.

Sal doesn't think he's awareness or something like that. As Sal, I am ordinary. Sal has his own preferences, his own likes, dislikes, and opinions.

It's just part of the play. Nothing is wrong with any of that stuff. When I say, "I'm just Sal," I'm saying there's nothing wrong with Sal. He doesn't have to transcend himself or become the Buddha, or anything like that. This appearance is Sal and can only ever be Sal. I can only be this. It's not possible to be anything else. I'm not going to be Ramana, the Buddha, you or anyone here. So, I say, "I'm Sal."

One Knowing

Inside/Outside

*In your first book, there is one experiment called
Inside/Outside. Can you say something more about that?*

We believe we are located inside the body, and the world is outside. We think there's a "me" in here aware of what's out there. We think there is a line here at the skin where I end, and the world begins. But this is all simply a belief that we have come to take for granted. Our culture teaches us that we are separate individuals and that self is a real and true entity, and is the most important thing we should attend to. This ignorance is backed up experientially by the functions of the body—localized consciousness, thoughts, emotions, sensations, and the five sensory functions, sight, sound, taste, smell and touch.

Since we have not, up until now, come to know another possibility, we simply take it for granted and the assumption becomes a conviction that seems real and true. We feel limited to this form and it is quite a compelling belief. So, we need to know ourselves a bit differently than we have in the past. That knowing includes all of the above but is not limited to it.

Let's find out if you, knowing, are limited inside this form. Let's be on holiday together, knowing.

HOLIDAY

I know myself as consciously aware, now.

Are you clear with that?

This aware knowing, is it only inside?

I would say neither inside nor outside.

Yes, it's seamless, isn't it? It's neither in nor out. In and out are just concepts. In your own visual experience, do you have a head?

No.

So then, you see that this aware/knowing is not inside anything, it's actually free. If you are this knowing, then you are not only inside the body. The knowing is not anywhere. It simply is. Is that clear?

> *I think it's clearer, now that we are talking about inside and outside. When you're talking about touch, it's not so clear anymore because then you have the surface that you're touching. I'm speaking about the different senses, you know?*

Put your hand on something, like the table. There's a sensation there, right? Okay, don't describe that sensation, just be honest about it. Be on a holiday.

HOLIDAY

Recognize all the visual, auditory, and sensory objects,
and all the different sensations as well.

There's just a sensation, right?

Does that sensation say, "table and hand?"

One Knowing

How do you know there's a table and a hand there?

How do you know there are two things?

There's only one sensation, isn't there?

You need to use the mind to separate that sensation into two
things.

Have a good look and see that.

If you are really honest and don't use your mind at all,
there is only one sensation, and you don't even know what it is
unless memory comes in and describes it.

Mind says, "My hand is touching the table."

What if you ignore that, and don't have that knowledge?

Then you are not limiting yourself to a body
that is touching something outside of it.

Then it's just a sensation and it's happening within knowing, you.

It's not outside of you.

Have a good look for a moment, here.

You have no head now, and visually,
all the objects of the room, are within you.

There are also sensations, all within you.

Aren't they?

When you see this way, that you're not in here looking out there, the
experience of yourself is a lot more open, you're not limited inside

something. Your experience of yourself is more freed, open because there's no line. There's not you and a world, it's all just one big open, knowing. All that is, is included, here and now.

You now know yourself as more open than closed inside because of this, right? Before I came to this work (and I don't really remember), I am sure I used to feel much more locked inside the body. Now, my experience is far more open.

Where's my border? Do I end at the skin? No, I don't end at the skin. I don't end.

This knowing goes forever, doesn't it? I am the knowing and knowing goes forever. It goes to the galaxies, and the whole universe, doesn't it? I don't end here and then there's something else. I am this knowing, which is ubiquitous. God is everywhere, God is ubiquitous. When you know yourself as the knowing, and not an object, all of a sudden, you're not so limited anymore.

> *At some point, we were taught that there is an "I" in here with sensory perception that looks outside. If you really look at it, it's not like that at all.*

Correct, we all have that belief. When we come out of the womb, we don't know we are "stuck inside the body." Do we? We don't even know we have a head or two eyes, there's only a big open space and that's who we are. As a baby, you aren't consciously aware of that, but it is like that. There's no "me" that's separate; there's only this knowing. Then we learn, "No, no... I'm sorry, you're a puny little thing that's stuck inside the body." Then we see the world that way, as very limited. We see ourselves as very limited.

When we do experiments like this, we see there's no line. We see I am the knowing, not an object. I am the knowing of everything and everything is equally appearing. They all come and go within this knowing. This knowing is always the same. With this work, we shift from believing ourselves as limited to a body, to the knowing itself which is not limited at all. That's who I am. And all of a sudden, the universe is within me. The galaxies are right here. Right in my hands, so to speak.

Thanks, it's a great experiment.

That's what a holiday is, being that unlimited knowing, being who you are. Knowing is being. Knowing who you are is being who you are. A holiday is knowing, and you can also say a holiday is being. Being who you are.

Another's Experience of Aware

I know my essential nature is aware, free, and all-inclusive, and I think other people's essential nature is the same. However, how do I truly know that? How can I compare my experience with theirs?

You can't know this through someone else's body because you can only experience through your body. Your body-mind is the experiencer. Aware experiences this body-mind and other bodies, but only you know your body's experience. You can't know it as if you were in someone else's body knowing it. Nevertheless, let's have a holiday, now.

HOLIDAY

This,
which is aware and free,
is your essential being.

This aware knowing,
is all-inclusive.

All is known within aware.

Now, is this knowing personal?

It feels like it. It feels like only I know my experiences.

That is true. Only you know your own experiences. However, I am not talking about your experiences. I am talking about aware, knowing. That is not an experience. It is knowing, in which your experiences appear. When we look at aware, it includes everything. There are no boundaries or borders. There is no time. This is not personal, is it?

Right, it is completely not personal.

Exactly. Let's have another holiday.

HOLIDAY

This,
which is aware, free, all-inclusive,
is your very nature.

Does my aware, free, all-inclusive go and go
until it meets your aware, free, all-inclusive, and then stop?

Is there some wall where your aware ends and mine starts?

When we hear, "we are all one," we get the wrong idea because we see separate bodies and get the impression, we are not one. At the level of the appearance of bodies, that is true. However, when you recognize there is only aware, knowing, and all these bodies are included in this knowing, you see your body is included in this aware just like all the other bodies. When you refer to yourself as this aware/knowing, you see that everything is included, and it must be the same for everyone else.

This aware/knowing is *I*. You can know *I* without referring to this body-mind object. Have a look. Within this knowing, there is the sense of a "limited I," a "felt sense of I am," existing here. Most of us believe that the limited sense of I am is who we are, but let's look, now.

HOLIDAY

What is here is aware.

All the objects in your room are included,
all sounds, all thoughts, all sensations.

Everything outside your window, the sky, the sun,
the stars, the galaxies, are included in aware.

This is what aware includes everything means.

If your body and my body appear in aware,
then isn't aware just one?

When I talk about this body-mind, I recognize that it is an aspect of me, the changeful aspect. I don't deny I am this body-mind. I don't walk around referring to myself as space or something. When I say, "I am hungry," I don't mean aware is hungry. I mean this body-mind is hungry.

However, in the true knowing of who I am, *I* refers to aware, knowing. This must be true for everyone. I can't know this in your body because it is your experiencing mechanism. The knowledge is in your mind, and you can't know the knowledge in my mind or my experience.

What is looking out of everyone's eyes is aware, knowing—hence, One. This is so because the *true I* is not referring to a body. The *true I* is aware/knowing.

If you still need some validation or verification by experiencing someone else's experience, you are going to fail because you can't have that.

> *I think what you just said helped break the personal sense of "I."*

There is a personal sense to it though. Of course, because there is this body-mind which is not excluded from aware. The personal sense is part of the impersonal. There is form here and it is seemingly separate and limited. This is the experiencing mechanism through which consciousness knows the world. This could be said to be personal, but in truth, it is not personal. This personal sense does not have to be negated or transcended. We are not attempting to get to a state where this personal sense vanishes.

> *I see that and what confuses me is the term "appearing within aware."*

Words are imperfect. It is not really "within." I don't mean that aware is a big container which holds everything. "Within" is an imperfect word because nothing is actually separate from aware. Aware is not a container or a space which holds things. It has no form. It is simply aware, and aware is not separate from the objects it is aware of. "Appearing within" is just a pointer so we can stop looking only through these eyes at the world, and the claustrophobia of being limited to this body can begin to fall away. It helps us to not feel trapped in this body.

This Is Where We Meet

We all know this aware knowing that is here, now.

This knowing has been here your whole life, hasn't it?

Even if you pick a previous event from your life,
before you heard this teaching,
you can see that if you had a holiday then,
this knowing would have been there.

If it is true for you, that this knowing
has always been here and it is always now,
then it must be true for me and everyone else.

Leave all the myths and stories behind.

This is where we really meet.

This one knowing, which we know, is true for all of us.

There is nothing here, only space for us to be.

Knowing Yourself as Other People or Things

Some people just walked by my window and I heard their voices. If a similar thing happened and you heard some voices, would you see those voices as being yourself? Would the knowing extend to the voices and be related to yourself? How do you have that experience?

We have this idea on the path that "I am everything." It's the notion that if I see a tree or another person, I know that's myself, in a kind of experiential way. However, that's not the way it works. It's certainly not my experience and I don't think it's anyone else's constant experience. That kind of mystical experience can happen, but it's always fleeting. All those experiences are fleeting.

On the experiential level, I don't really place much value on the idea, "I am you and you are me" because as a body-mind organism, I have my own particular unique experiences. I don't know all the experiences of your life and what's been recorded in your mind. There's no way I can know that because this body-mind organism is limited.

As far as I know, without this body-mind organism, as in deep sleep, or in death (which I don't know) there is no experience. This body-mind organism *is* the experiencing entity, and it is limited. It can only experience its own experiences. I have no idea about anyone else's particular experiences.

Although from another perspective, I do because there's only one knowing. The knowing that knows through this body-mind experience is the same knowing that knows through that body-mind experience. When you come to know yourself (and it's true of everyone), you come to know how you function as a human being. You come to know your essential nature, which must be the same for everyone, and you come to see how the misidentification with self has happened.

You see the ignorance you took for granted and have come to believe, and how that has caused this sense of lack, this sense that there's something wrong, and this sense that there's something missing. You see what caused it in yourself. Well, it must be the same as what caused it for everyone else. Another's experiences may be different, but the cause is the same: misidentification, ignorance. This recognition brings empathy and compassion. So, in that way, if you know yourself, you know everyone.

If I look at someone else, I don't know their specific experience, but I do know we were born free and then grew up in ignorance. So, there is compassion and empathy for others. But on an experiential level, no I don't hear the voices passing out there and think that's me. I don't actually think one way or the other. I don't think it's separate and I don't think it's me. It's not something that concerns me.

The reason the question comes up for you, and it is true of all philosophical questions, is because you heard an answer. In this case, the answer is something like, "When you get enlightened, you'll experience yourself as everything." That answer was put into your head. It was not there when you were born, and because it was put into your head, now the question comes up, "Sal, do you experience yourself as everyone?" The question is not even your own. It appeared only because the answer was already given to you. If that answer wasn't given to you, that question wouldn't appear.

A question like that doesn't appear for me because I don't believe any of those answers any longer. I don't have any interest in cultural or spiritual philosophies that have been programmed in my brain over the years. I've seen that it's all nonsense, and I don't buy any of it anymore. Those questions don't come to me. You see what I'm saying?

Absolutely. It is really helpful just to hear that.

Freedom is *knowing*. You come to know how you function and you come to know who you are essentially. Then, all of those questions stop because those answers no longer have any relevance to you. That's freedom and it brings with it an ease of being. It's just being who you are without needing to become something else in the future, or to understand something about life which is never going to be understandable anyway.

Those questions drop, and what you're left with is this, whatever is appearing, here and now. There are no questions like that any longer.

What is self?

Understanding "No-self"

I don't understand the concept no-self. I seem to be identified with self and I don't want to be.

Okay. First, we have to find out what the self is to see if there's no-self. What is self?

The body-mind?

Well, if the body-mind is self, how are you going to live and have no-self? That would not be possible because the body-mind is always going to be here until you die. So, the body-mind, in and of itself, cannot be the self that causes bondage. The body-mind is an object appearing to you which you refer to as self in the world, "I'm Sal, this body-mind."

There's nothing wrong with that. Saying, "I am Sal, this body-mind," doesn't cause suffering, in and of itself. It's just a simple and practical reference in the world of form and a way of speaking and relating with others. The self that causes bondage and suffering is the belief that I am limited exclusively to this body-mind and because of that the story of this body-mind is truly who I am—the Sal with all the past regrets, losses, traumas, etc., and the Sal with all the future hopes, fears, and desires. This self is assumed to be true, and therefore, causes suffering.

Let's be on holiday, now.

HOLIDAY

There's only now, right?

In truth, be honest,
the only thing that actually is,
is this, here and now.

In truth, is there a past? Or a future?

Where's that story of self?

You have to go into the mind,
into the past and future,
into the story, which is not true.

Is that story of your past actually true, now?

Is it actual, now?

Are the stories of future hopes and fears actually true, now?

Do they actually exist, now?

What is true then?

What's true is this, now—this knowing.

I am, now.

That's the only thing that's actual.

The only thing that's actually happening is this, now.

So, is there a self?

No.

Self needs time to exist. In no time, there's no self. Yes, of course, there are feelings in this body-mind, and that feels like "me," here and now. But again, that in and of itself does not cause suffering. What causes suffering is the belief in the time-based self. However, that self does not exist. There is no actual self.

This work is about knowing what's true—past and future are not actual. The more you're convinced of that, the less you suffer. Conversely, the more you believe in your story of the past and your future projections, the more you suffer. What happens if you don't believe that at all? They can't cause you to suffer any longer, can they? I want you to hear that really clearly. If you don't believe that past stories and projected futures are true, then they're impotent. Even if stories occasionally appear, as a habit of mind, they have no power to make you suffer.

Belief is what causes suffering. Belief is what creates your world; the whole world, actually. Your past and future world is belief, and with it all the suffering it entails. Don't believe any of those stories. Know what's true—there's only this, here and now. That's the only thing we can say truthfully.

Just keep knowing that. Keep having holidays and seeing what's true—there is no self. You know the self story is a lie and it can't fool you anymore. It's like when a child is in bed screaming because they think they see a ghost. You go in their room and turn on the light and they see there's no ghost. Then, they're no longer scared. It's exactly like that. We turn on the light—a holiday is the light. It's turning on the light of truth. This is the light, and it outshines all illusion.

Darkness is the belief in past and future; that's ignorance. You turn on the light and have a holiday and no longer can you be scared of the past and future. That ghost is not real. There's enough in life happening in each present moment that can be unpleasant. There are going to be things that are unpleasant, and there are going to be things that are pleasant. We don't need to go back in time or into the future. Leave that alone. We don't need to predict pleasantness in the future or rehash unpleasantness from the past. Life will provide all of it in the moment, now.

Knowing No-self Conceptually

I like your distinction between knowing and seeing. Does that apply to knowing there is no self and seeing it? I know and see there is no Santa Claus, but so far, I only seem to know intellectually that there is no self. I still function as though this self is real, whereas I don't act as though Santa Claus is real. Does it matter at all, since it's all conceptual and the question doesn't arise during a holiday?

Knowing there is no self conceptually is not true knowing. Anyone who has been on the path and who has read enough books will say, "I know there is no self." But what good is that? It's just another concept to add on to the garbage heap of concepts.

I use the word *knowing* in two ways (not the way mentioned above). One way is knowing there is no Santa Claus. Once, you believed there was a Santa Claus because your culture gave you that idea. Of course, in your innocence, you did not question it. The "authorities" said it was so, and that was that, it was so. One day, you found out that, in fact, there is no Santa Claus. It is clearly true, and now, you know it. You don't need to remind yourself or look up the chimney anymore. You know there is no Santa Claus.

Similarly, your culture has convinced you that you are the personal self with a history of experiences and stories. In your innocence, you did not question this because again, the "authorities" said it was so. One day, you came to see something different—here and now, I am aware, free, knowing. You found out there is no self, and you realized that you previously thought this personal self (the amalgamation of beliefs and ideas, based on input recorded in the mind, all of it ephemeral, none of it actual) was the actual *I*. Now, you see this self is clearly not true, actual or existent.

What is true, actual, and existent is I, here and now, being, knowing, Sat Chit. This is the only I. This is clearly true, and now, you know it. You know the truth—I have been here before, during, and after every experience of this lifetime; everything comes and goes including the changes to this body-mind, yet I always remain, even if I am not aware of it.

Who I am essentially is—Sat Chit, Being Knowing. You don't need to remind yourself or look up the chimney. You know it now, and you know self is a myth. Now you know, just like you know there is no Santa Claus. NOW YOU KNOW because you have seen.

The second way I speak about knowing is: KNOWING IS WHO YOU ARE. You are: here, now, existence-being-peace, aware-knowing—Sat Chit Ananda. Knowing is your nature. All things are known in, to, and as YOU. You are the knowing that knows it all. This aware knowing is, in real time, completely obvious, unchanging, and eternal. When I say, "Know who you are," what is really being said is, "Be who you are." Knowing is being, Sat Chit. All that is needed is to be who you are. This is the way of freedom—to *knowingly* be free, here and now.

As far as acting as if there is a self, the so-called self is simply an ephemeral appearance. When thoughts appear and attention goes to them, it is the apparent birth of a self. But every appearance of self is different from every other appearance of self. It never appears the same way twice. There is no "one self" that is of actual substance. The idea of a continuity of self is based on a belief that this thought and the previous thought indicate a "me" here—the "same me." But this thought, and the previous thought don't indicate a "same me" here. We collate the thoughts together conceptually and believe it indicates a "real self."

There are simply thoughts, recorded data, being replayed from experiences, appearing, here and now, in, as, and to, YOU: aware, knowing, open, spacious, all-inclusive, free. Yes, we believe thoughts indicate there is a me here. It is all we have known and all we have been taught by culture and the authorities, which are ignorance.

IGNORE and see that all thoughts come and go, are never the same twice, and in fact, do not indicate a self. IGNORE. However, because we have been taught that thought is so important and valuable, we don't ignore. We think it means so much, so we value it and give it undue importance. That is why this work takes time and authenticity—the interest and intention for truth and freedom. The habit of ignorance is a lifelong habit, and it takes a new habit to break it.

That new habit is: Know thyself, Be thyself.

Continue to know thyself and continue to value what is true—here and now, I am, aware, knowing, existence, being. Don't know it as a concept. BE IT. Knowing is being. That is the way of freedom.

Being Human, Here and Now

At times during the day when I still believe I am a person or have a personality, I get wrapped up in that. I know it doesn't mean I am not aware, but you seem to be taking that further and saying you don't believe in a self, ever. Is that right?

Let's look at the first statement. Yes, you are always aware, even in deep sleep, although you are not consciously aware, or don't remember it. You know you are aware in deep sleep because when the alarm goes off, you wake up. Obviously, you must be aware of the alarm. But, in the waking state, which is the state in which we can inquire, you are always consciously aware, usually of some object such as a thought, emotion, sound, sensation, etc. Also, in the waking state, we can, through this work, become consciously aware of nothing in particular—aware, knowing itself, here and now, with all the currently appearing objects included.

In the second part of your statement, you ask if I ever believe in a self. Let's say some thoughts are appearing in your mind now, and you are aware of those thoughts. Why do you take those thoughts to indicate an entire self? Why isn't it just one thought appearing in the moment, and then another thought appearing in the moment?

I guess there is not a good reason for it.

There is only now, right? There is no past hidden somewhere. If there is only now and there is no past, where is the self, this story character created with its background and history, and whatever psychological things that have allegedly happened? Where is any of that stuff that you seem to remember and hold on to as a self, a me? Where is it now?

It doesn't exist.

Right. Actually, that is why I say there is no self. There is only the belief that the amalgamation of thoughts and ideas that appear in the brain refer to something in time called a self. You create a continuity of thought that is, in fact, not so. There is only one thought, now.

We see that here, there is only now, and self doesn't exist. It is a myth, it is not true. Is that clear, or am I just making it up?

> *No, I get that. What happens to me sometimes is that I will get wrapped up thinking I am a person, at the same time, knowing it is just a fleeting appearance. So, I feel it's not a problem that I am a person, but you are saying you never think of yourself as a person.*

Okay, I see. I never said that I don't think of myself as a person. I am a person. I am a human being, here and now. That doesn't have anything to do with the story of self that is a myth. The character, Salvadore, with his whole history and afflictions, and his future hopes and aspirations, is clearly not an existent fact, is it?

> *Not without using your mind.*

I will go a step further than that. In truth, it is *not*, at all. You base your belief that there is a self on some very insubstantial and questionably remembered events from this life. These events are not present now. You put it together into a life-sized character in your mind now, and believe it means there is a self and it is who you are. I simply say that character is not real, or *actual*. It is mythical. However, that doesn't mean, here and now, I am not a human being. We are called human beings. We are not called human self-ings. I am here now, being human with no history.

What is self?

Really, all we are doing here is being honest. If I am very honest and truthful, I have no history. If I want to lie and tell a tale of a mythical character named Salvadore, then I can say, "I have a history." If you are here feeling like a human being, good because you are one. However, if you are here reviewing your very sketchy past story, your poor-me or great-me story, and going into descriptions of a character, then you are really just believing a myth that is not true.

> *Maybe there was a bit of an issue because I was thinking there were two ways to look at it. I could look at what is here right now, and then I could look at memories of the past, etc.*

One way to see (the way we are seeing here), which is the same for all of us, is that there is no difference between any of us. We see this on a holiday. Let's have one, now.

HOLIDAY

Relax the focus of attention.

Allow attention to be open and free.

There is only now.

I know I am, here and now.

Where is this story of self, now?

I say it is the essential truth of who you are. The other way is to buy into the story, the myth of a self, and by doing so, suffer along with it.

So then, would it be true to say, I am a person with a past, even though it's not really here? That is where I get hung up because I feel like it depends which way I am looking at it.

If you say you are a person with a past, you are identifying one thing that is actually appearing now and one thing that is not. "I am a person," is true in that it is appearing now. "With a past," is not true because where is this past, now? You don't have to equate being a person with the story of self. Why can't you just be a human BEING appearing, here and now?

You are the absolute, being human, here and now. Where is the self, the past, in that? It is not. It is the ocean looking like a wave in the moment, that is all. It is ocean, being a wave, here and now. The wave appears, moves a bit and disappears. It's in constant change, never stagnant or solidified. That is your actual experience as well.

Now, you can buy into a story of self. There are plenty of memories to work with, which are very vague and questionably accurate anyway. If, because of habit, you put together those memories into a story character, like Romeo on stage, and you believe it, you suffer.

If you want to be free, which you do because you are here, and if you want to be honest, which is all we are doing here, then you have to get real. Those stories are not true. Your brain hears this message, and over time, if you stay authentic, you will stop believing. That is because the strongest intention in you is for truth, freedom, peace, and happiness. You can't create that intention, but if it is so for you, then that intention will prevail. The strongest intention, whatever it is, prevails. If it takes time because of the momentum of taking for granted the belief in a self for so long, then that is what is. It takes time for everyone.

What is self?

All that matters is if what I am saying is true or not. I am not interested in being a philosopher. Is it true or isn't it? See for yourself if anything I say is true or not. If it is true, you will know for yourself.

The Sense of self

Merging Felt Sense of I Am with the Infinite I

I recently saw a Nisargadatta video and was wondering about his teaching of holding onto the felt sense of I Am, and then going beyond or prior to it, into the universal I. The video seemed to instruct people to hold on to the felt sense of I Am until they merged with the infinite I. Could you talk about that?

Yes, he said something along the lines of, hold on to the felt sense of I Am and then one day, you will recognize what is prior to that. With this work, we go directly there. We go beyond that felt sense of I , immediately. There is no way to describe it and have someone understand it philosophically. People have to see for themselves, and that's what we do with this work.

Something else Nisargadatta pointed out was that even when you recognize your essential nature, there is still going to be the felt sense of I Am. This is true. This personal feeling comes and goes, and sometimes it's not present. The felt sense of I Am is just another appearance, another feeling, which *you* know! You know that feeling. It's not you, essentially.

What I'd like to do is just see for ourselves, what he's actually speaking about when he says, "Go prior to the I Am and merge with the universal I Am." I call it a shift of knowing. What we believe now is this feeling here—this limited and claustrophobic feeling—is essentially who I am, and I need to escape it. Most people go through their whole lives believing they are trapped here and limited.

The felt sense of I Am here, is different from the belief in the story of self (past and future), which is easy to immediately jump off of in a holiday. Nevertheless, even without the story of self, there's still the *feeling* of location here. It comes and goes, it's an appearance.

So, what is Nisargadatta really speaking about? Again, the answer is not found in words. The answer is—let's find out. Let's be on holiday together.

HOLIDAY

First, I'd like us to see the opposite. You can keep your eyes open or closed, whatever you want. Now, say to yourself, "I am here." Nisargadatta says, focus on the felt sense of I Am to the exclusion of everything else, thoughts, desires, etc. Just focus on the felt sense of I Am; it's very localized and limited. Now, go in there and do that for a few moments.

See, there's a real feeling of I Am, here. Now, relax the focus of attention. That feeling is still here, but so are all of the other objects, aren't they? What is here, essential to all of it, is this knowing of everything. This knowing is here, and in this knowing, you can still have the sense of I Am. It's not, "I Am here, separate and claustrophobically limited in this body." It's just, "I, knowing."

I is all-knowing and all-inclusive. Even those words can go. No words are best. Just, *knowing*.

The Bible says God is all-knowing, all-inclusive, eternal and ubiquitous. This knowing has no location; it's just knowing, isn't it? In truth, nothing happens. There's no merging with this knowing. You already are this knowing; there is no other you to merge with it, it is you already. What shifts is, you now know yourself as you truly are, not limited to this body-mind.

I have feelings just like everyone, but now, I don't feel claustrophobically trapped like I used to. I don't feel myself "out" either. Out implies an in, but there is only one seamless knowing, neither in nor out. Knowing, the limitless knowing, which has no form and no location, is obvious. It's most obvious for all of us, it's not subtle.

> *Inquirer 2: Somehow this relates to the thought of not being spiritual anymore because I really don't pay attention to anything like that anymore. To me, it's not important if I see this knowing. This shift of knowing gives me so much safety because I know that everything's alright. I can just be a normal interacting person and act normally. Why not?*

> *I don't have to seek for merging with the knowing or merging with a tree and seeing it's me or something. It just doesn't interest me anymore because it's clear to me. This knowing just relaxes everything.*

> *Before this work, I was always trying to be in the now. There was this urge to see or be something. What a straining thing to do! Now, I don't have to. I don't need to see it for weeks. I just don't care if I see it or if I have any spiritual experiences. Actually, just being normal, that's the biggest relief for me.*

You've just written the whole first book right there.

> *No, Sal, I've read it!*

But you got the message. That's a very mature recognition there. Once you know there's no Santa Claus, you don't have to keep looking up the chimney anymore. You just go about your life. You know there's no Santa Claus, and that's great. You come full circle and you're finished.

Like I say, "I'm Sal, I've got no problem with Sal. I have no argument with Sal. Sal is Sal, he can't be anyone other than Sal." I'm very happy to hear that from you. That's wonderful. That's exactly what I hope to share with people.

Sensing vs. Knowing

For a long time, I have felt that I was aware and I knew there was knowing. This weekend, I was having a holiday and I was definitely trying to confirm that understanding. What I could see was sensing: I could see objects; I could hear sounds, etc. There was sensing and I was wondering, is there a difference between sensing and knowing, or are they one and the same? Is knowing happening through the senses? Also, is this a small point or a bigger issue?

It's a crucial point.

First of all, knowing is not known because of the senses. The senses are known to you, the knowing. Let's say you were floating in a hermetically sealed, pitch black, soundproof, anti-gravity chamber, so that you had no tactile sensations, no sounds, no sights, no smell and no taste. In this situation, none of the five senses would sense any objects at all. Nevertheless, you would still know the felt sense of I Am. The knowing would know the object, the felt sense of I Am.

Knowing needs none of the senses. It is prior to the senses. Let's go further and make it more recognizable.

You are saying that the senses are known too, they are experienced?

Yes. It is through the senses that you know the so-called world. The world is not separate from the senses or the knowing. Knowing is not separate from the senses or the objects that it knows. If we think, "I know because of the senses," then we are not knowing Thyself, which is essential. We have to come to know the pure knowing that is prior to the senses, including the felt sense I Am. Let's be on holiday, now.

HOLIDAY

I know I exist.

There are no senses involved in that knowing, are there?

This is extremely important, and this is the key. So, let's take our time with it. This is the whole shift of knowing.

See now that knowing is not objectifiable. It is not an object. It is not a sense. It is just knowing. It is just self-effulgent or self-knowing. Have a holiday and see this.

HOLIDAY

That is clear, right?

Yes. So, nothing that is known could be the knower.

There is no object that is known that can be the knower. The first object is the felt sense of I Am. That is actually an object. You are prior to that, and we will explore that further in a moment. But the first object is the felt sense of I Am, which means the sense of being here in a body. It is not an object known by the five senses. It is just the felt sense of a self (localized consciousness) in the body. This is an experience that you know—you, the knowing, know the felt sense of I Am. When we relax the focus of attention from the felt sense of I Am, then knowing knows itself. It's just I knowing I. That I (knowing) is not localized.

This is where we see that knowing is ubiquitous. Let's have a holiday.

HOLIDAY

Within knowing, all objects are included.

When you look in the night sky, even all
the stars and galaxies are included.

It is all happening *here,* in knowing.

It is not anywhere in distance.

It is here in knowing.

The primordial, or essential knowing,
which is prior to the felt sense of I Am,
is who you are essentially.

Is this clear?

If I say I don't know, that probably means no.

Here's the thing about this. You do recognize this, but the mind has doubts, that's all. There are a lot of ideas about what should happen or how it should be. The mind has many "buts." This is true for everyone. However, the more you have holidays, the more it becomes obvious that you do in fact recognize this.

Nisargadatta said to hold on to the felt sense of I Am, which is the first sense of self/ego, until that falls away and you go prior to it—

to the true I. But I want to go directly there. Let's be on holiday. Don't attempt to figure anything out.

HOLIDAY

Just know.

Just be.

Being and knowing are the same.

Sat Chit.

Be the knowing.

Be who you are.

The way of freedom is to be who you are, knowingly.

Knowing is not confined to this body here, and you are the knowing whether you know you are it or not. The more you have holidays, the more you will be reconciled with that truth—you=knowing.

> *If I could formulate this, there are things that are known to me.*

Yes, everything is known to you. Knowing includes everything. That is why they say God knows everything. God knows all because God *is* knowing. Sat Chit is God.

For a moment, don't attend to any objects. That does not mean to avoid them or pretend they are not there, or anything like that. Everything is still here, but I want you to know yourself, which is essentially knowing. Don't bother with anything that is. Just be knowing itself (pause).

For our entire life, all we have known are objects, gross and subtle. And everything we have learned on the spiritual path suggests that we are going to gain a new object: a specific state of consciousness (bliss), or an experience (the great silence). Guess what? Any particular state of consciousness or experience is an object that you know. They are all objects.

For the purpose of this work, ignore all of the objects and don't place any value on them. I don't care what the object is. Just know. Be the knowing. You *are* the knowing.

> *Inquirer 2: I am confused about the I before the felt sense of I Am. Could you talk a little more about that?*

I don't like to talk *about* it. I prefer to assist with finding a way for you to recognize it yourself. Let's have a holiday.

HOLIDAY

Have this felt sense of I Am, here.

It is not a sight, sound, taste, touch,
smell, thought or emotion.

It is none of those.

It's a felt sense of I Am—located here.

There is a felt sense of I Am somehow in this body.

Be aware of that for a moment.

Feel yourself limited here within the body—
the feeling of I Am...

Is that recognizable?

Yes.

Okay. Recognize the feeling of I Am, which is clearly limited to this body. Is that true?

Yes. It seems like looking out of these eyes.

Yes, it can be like that and just have the sense of being in a body. Just a feeling sense of I Am, here in the body.

When you say feel within the body, I feel the body, very strongly.

You feel that there is a me—I Am this body. Not using any of the five senses: sight, sound, taste, smell or touch. It is the feeling of life or consciousness that is here in the body. It is a felt sense of I Am, here is this body. Obviously, this is limited; and it is what Nisargadatta wants you to hold on to—the felt sense of I Am. Now, ignore that. Just allow attention to be open, completely.

HOLIDAY

Recognize. Knowing is not limited to the body. Knowing is ubiquitous. It pervades everything. It knows everything. It even includes galaxies that you look at in the night sky that are ten billion light-years away. Those galaxies are within knowing.

Yes. Everything is within knowing.

So, knowing is not limited to this body, is it? The felt sense of I Am or feeling of I Am is limited to this body, but knowing is prior to that. You see what I mean?

No, because knowing always seems to be physically located in this body.

That is not my experience. If you are looking at the moon, the moon is in knowing. It is not in the body, but it is in knowing.

It is a little easier for me with sounds.

Fine. As an example, the sound of a car going by outside is happening within knowing, right? But the sound is not located inside the body. The source of the sound is not located in the body.

No.

It is all within knowing, but it is not within the body, is it?

The sound doesn't even seem to have a location. It is just here.

That's true. If you are really identified with the felt sense of I Am, here, limited, localized, then you can hear where a sound comes from in relation to the body. If you are not identified with the limited sense of I Am, then within the knowing everything is *here.*

Yes, I get that.

So then, knowing is ubiquitous. It is not actually localized here. The conscious aspect, which is the body, and which is limited here, you can't deny. And the knowing is not limited, it goes in all directions...

Could another way of saying that be that it encompasses everything that appears as an object?

Yes, knowing is all-inclusive, all-encompassing. Knowing is ubiquitous, it is everywhere. I also say that knowing permeates through all the objects. It permeates the body. It permeates everything. There is nothing that is separate from knowing. Nothing is separate from the knowing of it. That is why they say that God is within everything as well.

When you read this section again, don't attempt to figure out, get or attain anything. Just keep being on a holiday and ignore the felt sense of I Am located here. Go prior to that, which is just to be the I, the knowing.

It is easy to do. Just ignore the felt sense of I Am. I don't mean to deny it, get rid of it, or change it. Just don't attend to it. Nisargadatta says to attend to the felt sense of I Am and keep holding on to it until you go prior to it. I say, "Why wait?" Be the knowing, now.

This makes sense and I may be trying too hard.

Yes. Don't try at all. Don't look for anything, try anything, get rid of anything, or expect anything. Just have a holiday and for a moment ignore the felt sense of I Am. Just know yourself as ubiquitous.

There is still going to be a subtle sense of being here in the body because this is where the function of consciousness is. To deny this or think that there is going to be no localized sensation of being here, is inaccurate. It will remain, and you know that localized sensation, as well as every other appearance.

You are not the felt sense of I Am. You know the felt sense of I Am. You are knowing.

HOLIDAY

Nothing to do...

I, knowing, can't be reduced any further.

The senses can be reduced to the body.

The body can be reduced to the felt sense of I Am.

The felt sense of I Am can be reduced to knowing.

That is as far as it goes.

Knowing includes everything.

Knowing knows everything,
including the felt sense of I Am.

Knowing the self

*With a holiday, there is still a sense of a separate self here
and all of the five senses conspire to confirm this sense of
separateness. When I get really clear on a holiday, the
sensations don't really point to a separate self until my
mind enters into the picture.*

Correct. This is because of the habitual patterns of the mind. This is
a lifetime habit of the mind, and it is why what we are doing here,
even though it is simple, is not a trivial matter.

Remember, whatever and wherever the feelings are, you know
them. They are just feelings appearing, and your mind says, "There
is a self here because there is a feeling." In truth, it does not mean
there is a self. What is true is that you know the feelings. Therefore,
you must be *prior* to those feelings because you know them.

*I am getting this knowing more and more, and I think
about the Zen quote "first there is the mountain, then there
is no mountain and then there is the mountain." If am*

looking at a rainbow, I am wondering if it exists. In one sense, I see it exists, and in another, I see it is just a play.

The rainbow appears. It is apparent. Everything appears now, which means it is apparent. Because they appear, however, does not mean they are substantial, nothing is substantial.

The feelings in the body that we have come to identify with are not going to stop happening. What can end is the belief that those feelings indicate the existence of a self, which is the cause of suffering. The *feeling* of separateness is really the first basis for the belief of self. This idea of self is not time-based, because feelings are happening now. The body is always now. From feelings of a self, comes the time-based belief in self, which is psychological. The psychological, time-based aspect of self causes suffering.

When I am on a holiday, my mind comes in and says, "I am still experiencing a separate self." I have been trying to figure this out.

That is your problem right there, your mind comes in and describes. That is why I say, "Jump off the carousel of mind." Don't try to figure it out. Does the Bible say, "Figure it out, and figuring it out will set you free?" Of course not, it says, "Know what's true, and truth shall set you free." Have a holiday and know you are free. Don't figure it out. Just have a holiday.

These conversations get me spinning in my head sometimes, and I see I'm attempting to grasp what is going on.

All I can say is have a holiday and be finished, now. The question you have about the sense of a separate self here is just another thought in the mind. So, what do you do? Just ignore. Jump off that.

There is only this. There is only freedom. What do you want? If you want only freedom, then you have it.

Seems Like a "Me" Here

During this call, there seems to be a me that is doing something. However, I now see the thing that seems to be me is not doing the being. Knowing is just knowing. This is the only thing going on, and I am not doing it!

You are just telling the truth, aren't you? That is all we are doing here.

Yes, then I go back into daily life and there certainly seems like there is a me.

Well, it depends on what you mean by there is a "me." There is a belief that I am this self which has a past and a future and is an amalgamation of stories. Until we come to this work, that is who we think we are. That is the "I Am" we are taught we are. I am my name, ethnicity, etc.

When we come to work like this, we see there is no past and no future, and we recognize this knowing is just here. Then, we recognize there is a felt sense of I Am here. There are the feelings of the body, which are appearing now as well. Essential to all this, and imbued within, is the knowing of these feelings. That knowing is the only I.

We used to believe we were the amalgamation of all the stories and myths. Now, we know we are only now, knowing, with this felt sense of I Am included. There is this feeling sense of I Am. Do you know this sense of I Am?

Yes.

You know this feeling sense, don't you? That means you are actually prior to it already. Even without the words, the knowing is still here. That knowing is I. The only thing you can know is what is appearing now, which includes a felt sense of I Am. This is still an appearance, which you know.

Let's have a holiday and just drop it all.

HOLIDAY

Don't attend to anything.

Ignore everything—
all thoughts, feelings, emotions.

Leave them all behind.

Knowing is here and everything is included.

Even the felt sense of I Am.

Whatever you are looking at, hearing, or smelling
is equal to this felt sense of I Am.

Because you know all of them.

This is very important. I want to make this very clear because we are speaking about this felt sense of I Am. I am saying this felt sense is an object that you know. It is no different than any other object in the room. Be on holiday now and notice that.

HOLIDAY

Everything in the room you are seeing,
everything you are hearing, and
everything you are smelling.

You know.

You also know this felt sense of I Am.

This felt sense of I Am is no different than any
of the other objects you are knowing.

They are all equal.

See, you are the knowing. To use words, you are prior to the felt sense of I Am. You are the knowing of I Am. Until we do work like this, we think we are the amalgamation of the experiences of the time-based self. Then we see something that is not time-based and is just a felt sense of I Am. In a holiday, we see that this felt sense of I Am is known just like all the other objects and is equal to all the other objects. In a holiday, you recognize the essential I, knowing itself.

Nothing Behind the Curtain of Now

Coming to recognize and reconcile with the truth that there is no past and no future has big implications. If you want freedom, you have to see that you have no history. This means your poor me and great me stories are myths. And, if they are myths, they are meaningless and hold no sway over you, now—you are free. And it means your fears and hopes for salvation in the future are fantasy and have no basis in reality.

When I say, "All there is, is now," it is not a spiritual platitude, like "Be in the now." It is true. There is no past, period. There is no future, period.

Time is a mind-created concept appearing in the eternal here and now. The only thing you actually know, the only thing you cannot deny (and needs no thought at all to know), and the only thing that actually is, is—here and now. I am this knowing that knows itself. This knowing is not a "self," the time-created myth of me. It is simply what exists here and now, knowing all the appearances coming and going. It is no-thing.

The Knowing That Is Aware

Here and now, knowing is.

This knowing is synonymous with aware.

Synonymous with who you are, your essential being.

All things are included within this.

It is not knowledge.
It is not information.
It is not concept.
It is not philosophy.

It is none of those at all.

It is knowing, which is aware.

Here and now, only.

It is the unknown
because it is not knowing anything in particular,
descriptive-wise or philosophy-wise.

This moment is simply known, unto itself.

And,
since you are not separate from this moment,
meaning you are not "in" this moment,
you are this moment,
then it is known by, to, and as you.

Getting There

*You were making a comment on one of the old audios that
there is only now, and everything appears and
disappears, moment to moment. I said to you that I had
read that the universe arises and disappears. You agreed
and mentioned that you had an experience and recognized
that reality. My response was that I could only*

understand the concept. What was that experience like and how does one get there?

One doesn't get there; it just happened spontaneously. But that experience doesn't matter. Clearly, there is only now, and everything is just appearing, now. If you get the mind out of the picture for a moment—the mind that thinks this now has something to do with the past and is heading into the future—then the only thing actual is now. All else is thought. The mind is using concepts called past and future, painting a picture that is not actual, now. So, don't do that for a moment. Really, don't do it at all and just look here, now. What do you actually know about what is here and now?

The only thing you can truly say, the only thing you actually know, is that here and now, what is, is. If you are honest, the only thing you can say is, "What is appearing now, is appearing now." Anything other than that you need to use some type of concept based on time. Is that clear?

Yes, that's clear.

If you jump off the carousel of conceptual philosophizing, then what is appearing must only be appearing now. It is the only thing you can honestly say is true. It's a big step for most people because it is very stark. There is nothing. It doesn't give you anything to hold on to as far as knowledge or philosophy, like knowing where you came from or where you are going. In this way, it is the unknown and can seem like a very insecure position. But, in fact, the concepts of past and future are not secure because they don't exist and cannot be depended upon at all. The only thing that can be known and depended upon is now. In truth, it is the only actual security.

Another way to say it simply is—what is, is. Not what is, is because it came from the Big Bang fourteen billion years ago. Not what is, is due to something that happened in the past, karma, etc. What is, is—PERIOD. No past—PERIOD. No reason. No meaning.

There is nothing behind the curtain of this moment. There is no past. There is no future. If you say there is, where is it? In the Play of Life, concepts like time appear to exist, here and now. But they have no empirical truth or fact. There is nothing to substantiate your so-called past, except some vague thoughts that are not even dependable. Also, there is no proof of any future, there are only our projections of desire, hope, and fear—imagination.

However, *this*, here and now, is clearly known and cannot be denied. It does not need the concept of time; it does not need thoughts or memories; it just is. The Play of Life is an appearance. Just like images on the movie screen. They appear real, but there is nothing substantial to them. The only thing substantial is the screen.

Now is the screen. Knowing is the screen. What is appearing now, including ideas of past and future, is an insubstantial image. Just like the movie, it appears and dissolves now, not coming from anywhere and not going anywhere.

The reason you would want to know there is only here and now is because you want to know what is true and to be free of time-caused suffering. In coming to know this, you see that the story of self is not true. If it is clear to you that it is not true, then it becomes clear to you that you have no history. If it is clear to you that you have no history, the past-based ideas (the poor me stories, self-judgments, blaming of others, victimhood, etc.) lose their power to cause suffering or seeking, now. Similarly, if it is clear to you that there is no future, the future-based concepts (hope, fear, longing, becoming, and comparing your current unsatisfactory state with a better state) lose their power as well. Being thus reconciled is freedom.

Most nonsense falls away when you are reconciled that *what is, is*. And it gets reconciled by being brutally honest about what you actually know. What is actually true? Know what's true, and truth shall set you free.

The scientists say the Big Bang occurred fourteen billion years ago. I disagree. The Big Bang is now. This is it, here and now.

Future is an Issue for Me

Recently, I noticed that I'll be walking down the road having a holiday, and then a thought about the future will come in. You know because life is scary with illnesses, and physical, mental, and emotional problems. All sorts of stuff. This sort of messes everything up for me, and I find myself thinking, "Well, it's all very well, having these holidays, but what about…"

I think one of the most challenging things to take on board is that what we're calling liberation is only now. This is all sort of weird because I want it to be in the future as well. I want to be absolutely sure, especially when the shit hits the fan and something happens to me, that I'll be cool, man. I'll be on holiday and it won't matter.

I've got friends who have been doing this stuff for years and who I know have profoundly recognized what you're talking about. Then, shit has happened in their lives and they seem to have fallen apart. I am thinking, "What was that all about? I thought they've seen this."

I don't know what I'm saying exactly. Past, no problem. I don't have much trouble with that. It comes up every now and then, but I'm okay. The future is more of an issue for me.

Of course, and especially as we get older, you know. We get older and the body starts falling apart. Shit is going to happen, but I know who I am, now. That's the only thing I know. Maybe many bad, horrible, terrible things will happen. Okay, if so, that will be the way it is.

There's that funny old "Be here now" thing we used to all say when we were hippies. But it's kind of true because this knowing is only here, now. To hold yourself to that.

Well, you don't hold yourself to it. The seed to have a holiday is in your head, and you just continuously come back to having a holiday and knowing. It happens all by itself. It may seem like you're holding yourself, but what is happening is that you have the intention for freedom, for whatever reason. You didn't create it, but the intention is there. That intention will create the action of a holiday. That's how it goes.

Like the issue of free will that we've looked into before, the intention to be free creates the action of coming and doing this work. The intention for holidays creates the action of a holiday. It has nothing to do with free will or doership. When a holiday happens, you know liberation is only now. Liberation is not in the future.

And somehow, that's the trickiest little thing in the corner of my mind to negotiate. It's kind of like, "Really, you mean it's only now?" God...

Just keep coming to know what's true. It's very helpful. Just keep doing it. Why? Why do I say keep having a holiday? Because a holiday is freedom and the goal is already attained. The way of freedom is—be free, here and now. That reveals freedom, now and resolves any afflictive or other habitual tendencies that keep you in the ignorance that causes suffering.

> *Immediately, even just in saying this, I want to say, "Oh, so you're saying it's going to make things okay in the future?" I can't help going there.*

Of course, it's just a habit. There's a whole lifetime of this habit. It isn't going to stop rearing its ugly head immediately just because you know who you are. It's not realistic to believe that. Whenever that habit appears, have a holiday. Don't worry about the outcome, see that the outcome is already attained, now. The goal is already attained, now. And the way to the goal is a holiday. A holiday *is* the goal, and it's the way as well. It's already finished, now—liberation is. Know what's true and remain true to that.

Your question is very valid for all of us because there's the momentum of habit to worry about the future, especially as the body gets older. It's natural. When you were a teenager, you didn't care about all that stuff.

> *Yes, nothing bad was ever going to happen.*

In reality, bad things happen. Maybe, it appears that a person has fallen off their knowing. I don't know your friends but let me just say something. Last week, I had a massive toothache, which was caused by an infection, and this led to some type of virus in my stomach. I got very sick and for four or five days, I had severe stomach pain. For forty hours straight, without a single break, it felt like ten knives cutting into my abdomen. It was horrifyingly painful, without any break. Finally, after forty hours, it subsided to only terrible pain and I was like, "This is amazing, only terrible pain, wonderful!" That's how severe the original pain was.

Believe me, when I was in that pain, I wasn't walking around saying, "Oh, I have transcended pain." No, because it was painful, man.

Does that mean I don't know who I am because I'm not in bliss like the Buddha? ("Oh, my stomach, there's ten knives in there digging around, but ha, ha, ha, I am in bliss.") No. From the outside, someone might say, "Well, he's so unenlightened because he's moaning." But that doesn't mean a damn thing. It came, and it went. The body had pain and the body responded to the pain. It doesn't mean a thing, and it doesn't mean anything was "fallen off of" or anything like that.

The whole time it was going on, I knew it was going to pass because everything does pass. That's where the benefit of knowing your essential nature comes in—knowing that the changeful always changes and the changeless never changes. So, I didn't worry. I knew that one day it was going to pass. There wasn't anything psychological about it, I was responding like an animal because it hurt.

Your friends, I don't know what they went through.

> *This particular friend I'm thinking about went through an emotional thing after a divorce. There were a couple of years where he found life difficult in many different ways. But, from conversations I had with him, I also think that he knew who he was during that time. That period passed, but he had a hard time for a couple of years. I made conclusions about it, like, "That was a bit weird. I thought he was really liberated."*

Well, there can be things still stuck. If something like that happened, maybe it was beneficial that it happened. The divorce may have been the thing he needed so that he could be finished.

> *Maybe somehow, he had to find some kind of new level of doubtlessness.*

Yes, that is very possible. If he saw it that way, it could have been very beneficial. It's all going to come, it's all going to go, and nothing's changed essentially. If I look back on all the years I've lived so far, I could say that many things, good and bad, happened. Let's have a holiday.

HOLIDAY

Where are the painful things that happened, now? They never happened. They never happened. Nothing happened. I'm free. I have had painful things happen, of course. The stomach pain that was horrifying, where is it? Why would I dredge it up now?

The worry about it coming back might be there for a few seconds, or whatever.

It may, and I don't think there's anything wrong with anything. I realize worry about the future is just a habit. We have no idea what's going to happen in the future. I may walk out the door and get slammed by a truck and that's it, I'm over. We believe in this idea of a future and think, "I'm going to be seventy and I'm going to get some type of cancer." How do you know? You might die tomorrow. There's only now.

Worrying about a future is a habit that we've had our whole life. You learn it through culture, which is relentlessly focused on the future, the future, the future, the future. We are terrified of the future. You weren't thinking about that when you came out of the womb, but by the time you grew up, you were like, "My future, my future, my future!" Culture is ignorance. Religion is ignorance. It's all ignorance and it causes ignorance in us and so we worry.

There's no fault and no blame. It's true for every one of us, without exception, until we're fully reconciled with the fact that there's only now, that's it. I refuse to admit that there's a past or future because I refuse to be victimized by a myth or a fantasy. I'm not going to be victimized by something I know nothing about and that will never come out the way I perceive or fear it will anyway. So, I refuse to admit there's a future.

This all has to do with suffering. The reason we are reconciled that there's no future and no past is because it has to do with suffering. If you think, "There's no past, but okay, maybe there's still a past," then you can be a victim again. If you think, "I know there's no future, but okay, maybe there still is a future," then you can be a victim again. I'm not going to admit it, there's only this, now.

In a sense, that's kind of holding yourself to it.

Be reconciled that there's only now. There's no doership in being reconciled, you are only reconciled. You've come to see that this is true—there's only now—and it's just reconciled for you.

I admit I don't know much. I only know this. Why would I want to believe something, for what purpose? Does it give me some sense of security to believe that there's life after death? Well, that's why people believe there's life after death, for some sense of security—a life never-ending. That's a gross level belief, of course, but I don't care to have that sense of security. I don't want to believe anything I don't know. And I know very little—just this.

This work is all about being ready and mature. Being reconciled with truth is what I call maturity. Maturity is not about owning a house, having kids, or how much money you have in a 401k. Maturity is being free, now. Why? Because this is simply true, isn't it? I don't know a damn thing about the future. I have no idea. That's truth.

The Past "Never Happened?"

I'm struggling with knowing that the past never happened. That's mentioned in the audios a couple times. I get that the past doesn't exist. When I take a holiday, there is no past, but to say it never happened... that doesn't seem to be true.

I'm currently editing a short video of some travels I took. When I have a holiday as I am editing, it's clear that there is no past, now. What's not clear is that what I'm working with "never happened." It seems like it did. I see it and it doesn't seem like I need thoughts or a story to see it.

Am I mistaking the wording or missing something?

It's a good question and one that many people have. I realize I am quite radical when I say, "nothing ever happened," but there is good reason for it. The point of reconciling the fact that there is only now is not a philosophical one, at all. The point is, the belief in and valuing of past, and future causes most of our suffering. When we see what actually is, what actually exists, it is clear that the only thing actual, the only thing true, is what is now. This is where freedom lies. It is where the end of time-based psychological suffering resides.

Yes, things can appear that cause suffering. Those things are unavoidable. But the suffering that most people hold on to, like remorse, blame, regret, guilt, acrimony, worry, fear, hope, and desire, etc., is completely pointless and is based on a myth called "my story." It is a myth because it is nonexistent, now. And those afflictions serve no purpose, except to cause you to suffer or perhaps feel self-righteous about something.

Also, it is not only the "negative" things from the past that cause suffering. I actually find too much sentimentality and nostalgia to be suffering as well. The longing for the "good old days" and wishing things were as they used to be—knowing full well that everything changes—is just comparing this, here and now, unfavorably to days gone by. Of course, all of this applies to the future as well—future longing, hoping, seeking, etc. All of it is suffering, in my opinion.

Freedom is now. Freedom has no past and no future. In fact, YOU have no past and no future. You are NOW. If the raw truth of that seeps in and is reconciled, then all of those time-based causes of psychological suffering have no power.

I am radical about it. But it is not actually radical because it is true. There is only now; there is nothing behind the curtain. In the Play of Life, appearing now, we have something called time. We *play* time, we *play* past and future. But where is it now? It is not. And, if it is not, then nothing ever happened, including the Big Bang.

If you want to edit a movie about some travels, of course, enjoy. It is the Play of Life. But get real about what actually is true and be free from time-based suffering.

Parameter of Now

In a holiday, there is the recognition that I am, and all of this is appearing, now. However, what has been niggling at me this week is the parameter or edge of this now. Right now, I recognize that I have no head and I am looking out of one big view. I know the sensations in this body and I am aware of words coming out of my mouth. Also, I know I am in a room in a house. However, right now, I am not aware of my children, yet I know they are downstairs in this house. So, the thought of my children feels like a concept.

It is a concept. You don't actually know it right now, do you?

No.

Let's make sure we understand what knowing is. Knowing is only the present, known now. Knowing is not the information in the mind. Knowing is not even the senses. All the senses are objects. All the thoughts and memories are objects as well. Knowing is that which knows all of that.

The thought that you have children is an object. You don't have to deny you have children, but in your direct knowing, right now, they are not, are they?

No.

That is not really the main point. It is true that you still have children, but we want to know the knowing itself. What knows that you have children? You. What knows all the objects in this room? You. One of the objects is the idea that you have children. There are the physical objects in the room, there are sounds and there's the thought, "I have children." Those are all objects. They are all equal in that you know them.

In a holiday, don't know the objects. Ignore them and know your essential being, the knowing. This is the most important part of this whole work. This is what Ramana Maharshi, the Ashtavakra Gita, Dzogchen Buddhism and all the highest teachings point to—forget (ignore) all the objects whether they be physical objects, like a cup or a chair, bodily sensations, sounds, or thoughts in the mind, and just know yourself, the knowing. That is what a holiday is.

There is mindfulness meditation which is being mindful of the moment and what you are doing with the objects. This is not like that. This is something different. Let's have a holiday.

HOLIDAY

Ignore the objects.

Ignore the body-mind, just leave it behind.

Ignore the thoughts.

Just know that you are knowing, here.

I am.

I know I am this knowing.

This is non-dual.

It is self-evident.

I know myself.

A Garbage Can

If we start to think about yesterday, should we stop?

It depends what you want. If you want to think about yesterday and be nostalgic or review your poor me and/or great me stories, that's fine. But if you want freedom, then yes, stop.

I was just thinking that there is something to get in there.

What are you going to get in there? It's a garbage can. There's nothing alive in there. Is there anything living in there? What are you going to get in a garbage can? Garbage. What do you get here and now in *nothing*? You get the precious jewel of freedom.

Valuing Truth

There are two essential parts to the way of freedom. The first part is to have a shift of knowing. (The previous six chapters were about that.) It is called Jnana in Indian Vedanta. It is Self-knowledge, coming to know who you are essentially. Most people consider the recognition of essential being, or Self-realization, to be the end. They believe that perhaps after forty years of meditating they will realize it and it will be over, but that is just the beginning of the end.

In this work, we come to recognize our essential being first, not after forty or more years. Nevertheless, in almost all cases, it is not the end because there is the habitual tendency of the mind to doubt, and this needs to be resolved for the mind to be at rest in freedom. There is a lifetime of cultural impressions (samskaras) in the mind that we have come to believe are true and have taken for granted. Those impressions continue to play themselves out, and because we believe in their truth and validity, doubt is created.

So, just coming to recognize your free essential being is not enough. While what you come to know ends seeking, it is not yet liberation because of the habitual, reflexive habit of believing and valuing thoughts. This habit needs to be shifted to the habit of being free, now. That is the purpose of a holiday.

This takes time for everyone. There is no specific amount of time. For some people, one in a million, it happens immediately. But for the rest of us, it takes as long as it takes. And, for everyone, what it takes is dedication to truth. This is where the second part of this work comes in, which I call valuing truth.

In India, it is called Bhakti, worship. However, what most people consider to be Bhakti is worshipping something other than oneself—God, the Guru, the deity, etc. If you worship something other than yourself, you never come to the end because you are worshipping what is false, not what is true. All of that is mind only.

True Bhakti is the same as Jnana. By knowing your free essential being, who you are, Jnana, you are worshiping yourSelf, Bhakti. Remaining devoted to truth is true Bhakti. In valuing truth, all doubt gets resolved and it is finished. Without both Jnana and Bhakti, the reflexive habit of believing the mind never ends. So, *knowing* and *valuing* truth is the way of freedom. The way of freedom is to know thySelf and to worship thySelf. Know you are free and value that knowing until it can no longer be doubted. (For an in-depth inquiry into the value of truth, refer to *Inquiry Two* in *Liberation IS*.)

The Momentum of Ego

> *So, ego is the belief that I am separate from the flow of life, right?*

Yes. I is free; the belief, "I am separate" is ego. And from that "I am separate" idea the entire world of self is created. If you remove that "I am separate" card, then the whole world is gone as well.

> *And that card can be removed slowly?*

No, that card is not removed slowly, it's removed in no time. Have a holiday, now.

HOLIDAY

Know who you are.

Valuing Truth

Free, open, knowing.

That's it.

I know who I am.

I am here and now, knowing.

It takes no time to know who you are.

Freedom is immediate because it is already true.

There is no path to it, you just look and here I am.

Do it now.

Sat equals existence.

Chit equals knowing.

I knowingly exist. True?

It takes no time, how can it?

It takes time to stop falling for the lies. It takes time to stop biting from the apple of knowledge because that apple is very tasty, isn't it?

And it feels like there is a certain momentum behind it.

Yes, there is the habitual momentum of taking for granted what the mind is saying is true. We've been told that that is what's true—our thoughts, our stories are true. We say, "Don't tell me my story is not true damnit!" Of course, we take it for granted because no one ever showed us what truth is.

So, inherent in this contracted I am is a sense of lack. And
I have a desire to be special so that maybe I won't feel
lack.

Yes, that's why we seek, to try to make that ego sense feel complete.
But it's never going to be complete. What is complete is *you*. Have
a holiday and look, now.

HOLIDAY

When you have a holiday, you are turning off the power switch to
suffering. The on switch to suffering is belief—belief that the stories
of the mind are true and that you need to suffer because of them
and do something about them. When you come to know what is
true, you come to see that the mind is not true, it is myth and
fantasy. You have been believing your whole life that the mind is
true and is everything. It is the god you have been worshipping, but
now, you see it's not true. When you have a holiday, in that moment,
the switch of belief is turned off, and there is no more power going
to story. However, the momentum of that lifetime of belief keeps
compelling you towards itself.

Am I wrong in saying that the power will never be on
again once I know who I am essentially?

Yes, that's wrong. The momentum of a lifetime of belief is like a
speeding locomotive. Just because you apply the brakes once does
not mean the train will stop. The brakes need to be applied
consistently until the train is stopped. The habit of belief is not a
trivial thing. It comes from a lifetime of being conditioned by the
entirety of culture. So, although this work is simple, it is not trivial.
It needs to be known many times. In fact, it needs to be lived. The
more you know who you are essentially, by having a holiday and
turning attention away from mind to truth, the more that becomes

your default condition, until one day it is doubtless. You know, I am free.

What exactly is a belief? Thinking something is absolutely true?

Right. Your whole life you have believed you are the wave, the personal story of your life, all of the things that have happened to you. The belief is, "I am this character, called Sal, and I am the past stories and future hopes and fears." Look how it is, especially in western culture like the USA. They say, "I know who I am. Don't tell me my beliefs are wrong. They are MY beliefs, and that is who I am. I believe strongly in my beliefs. And if you don't agree, you are wrong!!" It is really a constricted and limited idea of oneself. That is believing. It's believing a myth and a fantasy. Have a holiday now, and see if any of that is true.

HOLIDAY

Is any of it true now? Just be honest.

Does This Work "Work" for Everyone?

Something occurred to me recently. I figure with work like this, there is no guarantee it will "work" for everyone. Knowing there's no free will, this leads me to wonder about the possibility that I am one of the instances where this doesn't work completely, and just sort of facilitates my life, but not in the ultimate way I want.

This work shows what is true. Let's be on holiday and see.

HOLIDAY

Any genuine inquiry work, like what we do here, shows what is true. There are other types of work that resemble a journey on a path. And the critical question to ask is, "Does the path lead to the goal?" I say, no, it doesn't, regardless of the nature of the path.

This work is not a path that leads to a goal. This work shows what is already true. If someone recognizes what is true from this work, then the first aspect of this work has worked. It has shown what is true. The other aspect of this work is showing how to resolve all doubt so that liberation is known. For that, one's own authentic intention and commitment to truth is what will make it happen. The work itself cannot do that. Only you can. Not that you have the free will to do that, but if that is your intention, then that is what is.

If you are ready to recognize, then you recognize what is true. If you are ready to have the recognition fully resolve all doubts, then seeking will be finished and you will live more peacefully with less struggle, strife and suffering. Yes, life carries on, and sometimes things will clobber you over the head and you will feel it. That's fine, but overall, your experience will be one of ease.

The original question, "Does this work work for everyone?" implies, "Will seeking end and liberation be realized for everyone who engages in this work?" And the answer is, no, not necessarily. The work isn't about you being ready to be finished/reconciled, that is different for everyone. If you are ready, you are ready. If you are not, you are not. For whatever reason, some people are ready right away to be reconciled after having recognized what is true, and some people are never ready. Most people fall in the middle and need time before they are ready to be reconciled. If you are looking for a result—the realization of peace and the end of seeking—it is not guaranteed. How can it be?

However, does the work "work" for everyone who recognizes what's true? Yes, because the recognition of truth is now. In that way, the work is already complete. And it is good to see it this way because then you are not expecting something else to do it for you. You are not thinking something like, "The work is going to do it for me."

The work isn't going to do it. What does it is your intention for freedom, which is not self-created. That intention happens to be, and that is what does it. Your intention for freedom is why you are reading this. You would not be reading this without it.

I always say, "Keep knowing what's true, and keep seeing the value of truth." In doing this work and seeing what is true, you see that this recognition of essential being is the most valuable thing to come to know. It's more valuable than E=MC². Why? Because from the recognition, you see that you lack nothing, and are already complete and whole, here and now. This, Sat Chit Ananda—existence knowing itself—is peace. That's what it is—peace! And, by seeing this, you see its value.

The value is no longer needing to compare yourself with anyone else, whether they appear to be more or less "spiritually advanced" (Ramana, the Buddha, et al.), whether they have more or less money, or whether they have more or less "success," etc. The value is not needing to find fulfillment (more money or more enlightenment) in the future because you see you are already fulfilled. The value is not feeling the lack that creates the afflictions of greed, lust for power, and control.

In comparison, when you are struggling, striving and seeking experiences, you can easily see that there is suffering involved. Yes, you may get some kind of high out of certain experiences, but there is always the backside of that. Of course, experience has value, relatively speaking (birth of your child vs. changing a flat tire), but placing an inordinate level of value on experience creates a lot of suffering.

If you clearly see the work for what it is and clearly recognize how valuable it is, you realize that this is what you ultimately want. This alone will finish it.

Benefits of Knowing Liberation

It is interesting to me that knowing my essential nature seems to produce goodness. There is something about this knowing that is essentially benign, and I was wondering if you could comment on that.

It is resolution of the filters you express yourself through and as. What are those filters? The sense of lack and the need to get more for myself all the time (greed); the sense there is something wrong with me; the sense of inferiority or superiority; the sense of the need to be right; the sense of the need to control others; and the sense of the need for power. It is obvious that those filters cause a lot of the malignancy in ourselves, our interpersonal relationships, and in the whole world. So, when we are expressing through those filters, the expression may not be so benign.

Why would someone need to have a lot of power? Obviously, they feel they are lacking something and need something to make themselves feel better, whole or more complete. In your own relationships, you can see how the need to be right shows up and how you want to be in control of the situation or the other person. This all stems from the sense that there is something lacking in you.

Also, the notion that I am a doer compounds things. There is a basic belief that there is a substantial, actual, separate self here. This is not true. The self is not actual and was not here when we came out of the womb. It is a belief that we have taken for granted and lived by, unquestioned. When we came out of the womb, there was pure essential being, aware-knowing, with no programming or filters. When we took the birth of self, suddenly there was a belief in a me, separate from everything else, limited and lacking. From then on there was a growing sense of incompleteness and fear and desire, which created the constant drive and seeking for fulfilment.

As you know, when you come to recognize your essential being and you realize there is no past or future and self is a myth, you see that this self never existed. All of the need to control and to be right, and the desire for power, arose from this non-existent self mechanism. In our essential being, when we are on holiday, we see there is no need to control others or have more power. The illusion of a self is a great burden, on ourselves and on others.

Going through life, we develop many afflictions, fears, desires and needs. This is not who you are essentially though. Coming to know truth and valuing it reconciles these issues. There is no doing, just see there is no basis in truth for any of these pathologies.

The knowing is you. You are free. Knowing yourself to be so is beneficial to you and to others.

Morality and How to Live

> *When I have a holiday and think about this work, there is nothing. I don't see anything coming up in terms of how to live. I know this work makes you more benign, and I've already experienced that. It's taken away a lot of beliefs and judgments, and arguments with people. But I feel that I really don't have any footing in terms of a way to live, and sometimes I feel guilty and uncomfortable.*
>
> *I know you say there's no right way to live, and you don't tell people how to live, but there's sort of a rootlessness with this lifestyle and how to relate to people.*

We all have a habit of believing we should behave and live in a particular way. When that is gone, it can feel like there is no footing and nothing to hold on to. But all of those ideas about having to live or act in a certain way are just conditioned thoughts in the mind. Those ideas or concepts (called morality or right behavior) were created by the human mind in response to its own pathological behavior.

The pathology of the human mind is based on the sense of separation, which leads to the sense that there's something wrong with "me," and there's something lacking that "I" need. The sense of separation and lack are the birth of the so-called seven deadly sins.

However, when you value what's true—that you lack nothing, and are complete and whole already—why would greed appear? Why would the need for power over others appear? Those things wouldn't appear in a mind that knows it's complete and whole already; it doesn't need those things. However, because we've gone astray, so to speak, and have come to believe that we are separate and alone in this world, and the outside world is against us, these pathologies have emerged. Because of that, the concepts of morality and right behavior have emerged as an antidote.

Now, of course, all those concepts, like the right way to live, the Golden Rule, etc., are all good. However, why do we need to even say that stuff? We only need to say that stuff because we've "gone astray" from the natural human condition, which is goodness. When you come to see for yourself that you lack nothing and your essential being is goodness, then, for the most part, pathologies like greed, lust for power and control over others, no longer arise. You no longer need morality, right behavior or rules about living; you just live.

Because of a lifetime of conditioning, you think, "I must 'do' right behavior and if I don't think about those things, I'm doing something wrong. I'm going astray again because I don't care about that stuff anymore." I say, "No, you're not going astray." You've come home to your natural human condition, which no longer needs those rules because the natural human condition is goodness. It's a habit of the mind to continually think there's something wrong. That will fade; that will just go away because as you said, with this work, you recognize there is nothing.

Most people don't really get that "there's nothing" because there are still objects coming and going. "There's nothing" just means that all the concepts you've had about yourself, the world and spirituality, are gone. There's nothing. That's all empty. There's nothing to any of that. All the conditioned thoughts of how to behave and how to live are moot and no longer necessary. That leaves you nothing in that way, and it can be a little disconcerting perhaps because we hold on to those things as the sense of who I am—I'm a good person, I'm a good Christian and abide by the rules, and so on.

When all those ideas are gone and no longer needed, there can be a sense of guilt— "I'm obviously being bad because I'm not being a good Christian anymore." Well, now you are actually being a good

Christian in my opinion. The real Christian, the real Christ, or the real Buddha doesn't need rules. You're free. You *are* morality. Morality is your essential being. The natural human condition is moral.

Yes, we're human, which means we're not perfect. I don't mean for this work as a path to be perfect. For the most part, as we do this work, we become benign, and things like greed, envy, lust for power and control, disappear, as does the need for all the teachings on right behavior and morality.

> *I think that whole thing about not having any sense of lack makes a lot of sense because I find lots of times when I am feeling angry at the world—it's because I feel that lack. I use this to measure how I'm doing and I tell myself that I'm not there yet because I still have that sense of lack.*

It's beneficial to stop believing you are not there yet. Let's have a holiday, now.

HOLIDAY

Be here, now.

This, now.

There's nothing, right?

Look now.

Know the nothing you spoke about.

Know it now.

Right now,
without referring to thoughts or feelings,
is there any lack?

The idea, "I'm not there yet," is the only obstacle. There is no, "Thou shalt do this," or "Thou shalt not do that." And it's not a healthy habit to think, "I'm not there yet." Have a holiday and see that you are here, now.

HOLIDAY

This work is always about: here and now is freedom. It's not in the future. You're not going to be more perfect or something like that. There's no *state* you're going to attain that's always stagnant and never changing—no state of perfection, where nothing negative ever rises. The goal is already attained, here and now. The goal is here. The goal is now.

Instead of saying, "I'm not there yet," just look again and see that you *are* here, now. You are already finished, now. That's what this work always has been and always will be about—seeing what's true, now.

Doubt

No Words Needed to Know This

Here we are, here and now.

There is nothing behind the curtain of this,
which is appearing here, now.

To deny that this is appearing now is philosophical, isn't it?

And to what purpose anyway?

Right here,
where are any of the apparent stories
that have to do with time?

They are not.

There is not a single self here, now, is there?

There is only one essential being,
this, which we all are.

No one is more or less enlightened,
or awakened or anything like that.

In fact, no one is enlightened at all.

There is no one to even jump.

Who is to jump?

The Way of Freedom

This knowing is here,
and it is true for everyone.

This knowing is all there is.

This knowing, being here, now, in this *no*thing.

If we start having philosophical conversations,
what is it going to add?

To this, *no*thing.

We are just here, what words are needed?

What questions can survive in this, *no*thing?

In this *no*thing, all the questions are gone.

Isn't *this*,
here and now,
the answer to all of the questions?

If freedom is the main intention,
you can't fail because it is already true.

You are not going to get
it in the future.

If freedom is the real
intention, then it is not possible to fail.

All that is needed is
to clear up some doubts.

Self-Doubt, The Final Obstacle

Could you talk about Ramana Maharshi's statement about "self-doubt being the final obstacle?"

In truth, there are no obstacles. I just say that doubt is what keeps the belief in bondage alive. Doubts eventually end and when they do, what is there? Let's have a holiday.

HOLIDAY

This aware knowing is here.

The countless things are just what is.

Now is just what is.

I am here, now.

I am.

You see, it is already doubtless.

There is no doubt in this knowing.

Doubt is only the remnants of ignorance coming and going. Just disregard, it does not matter. See that it is already over, then whatever comes is what comes. See that any doubt is not real, and it has no power and no validity. It is just like a cloud in the sky. The blue sky does not care if a cloud goes by. You are the blue sky.

Thoughts and feelings have no meaning. If you believe they are real, they will stick around. If you ignore them, they will disappear. Belief is the power switch that turns it all on.

I say to people who I do this work with, "Just know!"

Inquirer 2: I see that "just know" pulls the plug on all beliefs. I trained as a therapist, and I did my own therapy. I recognize that so much of it is aimed at modifying the story that is being believed. This is pulling the plug.

That is great you see that, and for some people, therapy is needed. Not everyone is ready to have nothing, to know nothing and to be no one. Many people do need therapeutic help, and that is fine. For you, that's over. You just know. "Pull the plug" is the same thing as "jump." Just be finished. You can't "do" finished. You are finished.

The End of Doubt is Now

When I look now, everything is clear and there is no doubt. But what about tomorrow, or next week? Sometimes I do still doubt. When will that end?

Don't project into the future. Don't predict your un-enlightenment tomorrow. There is no future. Let's have a holiday together, now.

HOLIDAY

There's only now, right?

Isn't that true?

Is there a past or a future?

There is, in truth, only now, right?

Yes.

You sound pretty doubtless to me. Do you have any doubt?

No.

What if you have a doubt tomorrow? Why do I say that? Let's find out. There's an important reason I say that. Let's be on holiday, right now.

HOLIDAY

This cup that I am moving across the computer screen from one side to the other is coming into the screen on one side and is going out of the screen on the other side. As the cup is passing across the screen, has it affected you at all? Are you here before, during, and after that?

Yes.

If a doubt comes and goes (like the cup passing across the screen), aren't you here before, during, and after it?

Yes.

There's the idea in your mind that it will "become" doubtless, and you're projecting that hope into the future. I do say that it takes time, but I have to tell you to get real, now. Have a holiday, now.

HOLIDAY

See if it's doubtless now, without projecting into the future. Is it doubtless, now?

Yes.

Right, there's nothing to attain in the future, even though I say it takes time for doubts to resolve. Just look, now, and don't project that you're going to be finished at some point in the future. It's very hard to speak about this because I have to say doubts will resolve, but in truth, there's no future. Just know again, now, that it's already finished. Know again, now, and don't be concerned that you're going to be finished in the future. Just get real and see, now, that it's finished. Do you see what I'm saying?

I am speaking words and it sounds paradoxical. I understand, but forget that it sounds paradoxical, and just look again, now. If you believe you're going to be finished in the future, then you're going right back on the mental carousel, aren't you? It's the spiritual carousel that says you're going to be finished in the future sometime.

Be authentic now because it's only going to happen now. The recognition that it's doubtless is now. For me, it's doubtless without any possibility of doubt, now. For you, it's doubtless now, with the *idea* that *maybe* it won't be doubtless tomorrow.

Oh, okay. I see, I see.

I can't doubt, it's not possible to doubt. I don't even care anymore. It's over. See now, it's over for you as well. You may have the thought, "Well maybe, but perhaps I'm going to have a doubt, and it's going to be finished later." The answer is jump again, right? If I could say to you, "Be finished, doubtlessly, now, forever," I would say it. In fact, I am saying that, but I'm realistic. There is a momentum of beliefs that occasionally appear, now. One day, they won't appear anymore, but don't worry about that. There's no goal to attain—there's nothing to attain in the future. There's only—get real, and jump, now. That's all. It's not doing anything, but you see, that's it.

If there was no habitual mental activity, I could just say to you, "Be finished, now," and that would be it, wouldn't it? It would look something like this: I say, "Be finished," and you respond, "Okay, thanks, see you later, nice to meet you!" That, however, is not how it works because there is a momentum of beliefs in the brain that continue to play out.

You can call it the karma of the mind or whatever. There are beliefs that there's some future you're going to get finished in, or beliefs that the doubts have some meaning as they appear. It's all about believing the nonsense that just appears. It always appears now, doesn't it? Nothing's going to appear tomorrow because there is no tomorrow. What is, is, now; and if there's a doubt now, then jump, be finished. You see?

> *Yes.*

Just keep knowing what's true. That's it. Forget what happened and what's going to (or not going to) happen, that's all nonsense. What is true, now? Have a holiday.

HOLIDAY

Is it true that you're here, now, this knowing?

> *Yes.*

Is there any doubt?

> *No.*

Okay. It's already doubtless, you see? Who cares if doubts appear; it doesn't matter. They come, and they go. Doubts—no big deal, nothing happened. Where is the cup you think you previously saw moving across the screen? It never happened because there's only now.

> *Got it.*

Just keep staying authentic. You have a true recognition. We worked together, and your recognition is true. Just keep knowing what's true, that's it.

> *Inquirer 2: One of the things I used to think was that once I was finished, there would be no more unpleasant thoughts passing by. That is not the case. What I notice is that they pass by less frequently and when they pass by, I don't pay attention to them. That makes a big difference.*

Yes, and I can say the same thing. I don't care if they pass by or not, and therefore, they have no power.

> *Inquirer 2: But I did think, at least in the beginning, that being finished meant those thoughts would never show up again. Now, what I recognize is they show up, or they don't show up. So, I don't give them power anymore.*

Yes, that's perfect. That's freedom because you can't control what comes and goes. So, who cares what comes and goes? We're living in the world with work, relationships, stresses, politicians cheating you, and they sometimes trigger unpleasant experiences. There's nothing you can do about it. It comes, and it goes. I don't give it much value, and that's freedom.

Freedom isn't dependent on having no thoughts, or no unpleasant thoughts because that's never going to happen. With some teachings you have to always be in a state of "awareness," and if thoughts are there, you must be unenlightened. What? All of a sudden, you're unenlightened because there are thoughts! Come on! That's not freedom, that's bondage. Freedom IS. Liberation IS.

Not worrying about what's coming and going is freedom because you can't control it anyway.

Am I Missing Something?

I've been listening to the audios quite a bit these last few days, and there's one point of confusion that keeps arising. You ask me, "You know who you are, right?" and then, you tell me, "I know you know because I'm with you every week, and I see that you know."

The way you talk about it, it's like once you know who you are, then you can never not know. Is this what you're saying, or have I misunderstood? It doesn't seem to happen like that for me. Sometimes I know, sometimes I don't know, and sometimes I get misidentified and it's just not clear. A memory of knowing isn't knowing, it's just another thought.

You've said to me, "Yes, of course, you'll get misidentified in the beginning, and it's totally natural." This I also find confusing because in the moment I'm misidentified, then by that very fact, I can't be clear on knowing who I am, right? If I knew who I was, then I wouldn't be misidentified.

Looking forward to getting this cleared up!

If you have come to clearly see that who you are is not separate from this which is aware, then why deny it? This does not mean you will never misidentify again. Maybe you will. After a lifetime of identifying with "self," doubt is unlikely to end with one knowing. What I ask you to do is to come to this knowing as often as possible by having holidays.

If I am engaged in something, I am not consciously aware of myself as freely aware. But, of course, if I am not engaged in anything in particular, it is so obvious. Keep having holidays. Don't be concerned when you become misidentified. It does not mean you do not know. (Read that again.) It just means that, in that moment, you are not consciously aware of it. No problem. All we are doing is gaining certainty. This happens, over time, the more and more you relax the focus of attention and see what is true.

> *There's one other thing that's not quite clear. I see that all there is, is this, and there is nothing else. It's clear and obvious, but doubt creeps in that "this" is what I am. It doesn't feel like there's a separate "me" knowing there's just "this." But I start to wonder if there is a subtle sense of duality at play that I'm being blind to. It's like I don't quite believe that "this" is what I am.*

> *Okay, as I'm writing this, I think I just answered my own question. I see that the thought, "I don't quite believe that 'this' is what I am," is just a belief, and I'm valuing this belief. I'm valuing the doubting.*

> *What you're saying it that this belief is just another appearance, nothing more. It has no value, it's just an object. It has no more (or less) value than the tree outside my balcony. In fact, it's equal to the tree, in the sense that it's also just an appearance.*

> *When the doubt/disbelief creeps in again, I just have to remind myself that the doubt/disbelief is just a thought, nothing more. Then, all that's left is "this!"*

I'm happy to hear you recognize this. It is really very simple and that is why most people overlook it. See how this recognition happens more and more all by itself, and see that it begins to happen more and more even in the midst of emotional appearances and doubt.

Also, keep having holidays. When you recognize that who you are is free already, know the inherent value in that. This is freedom, here and now. Value this at all times. When an emotion, confusion, doubt, or question appears, don't value that appearance by believing in it. Value what is true. This is what will liberate the mind from all doubts, all questions, and all seeking. Here and now, you are free.

Am I Fooling Myself?

I have come to the realization that holidays are very simple, but very difficult to integrate into my life. I think, "Yes, a perfect time for a holiday," then before I know it, I'm off doing something else before I've barely paused.

Yes, I frequently catch myself being identified with something, and when I am self-aware in that moment, I end up not going down that path. But I keep wondering, is that it? What does it look like to have holidays all the time? Am I fooling myself?

A holiday is not for integrating into your life. A holiday is about knowing. Knowing what? Who you are is: knowingly aware peace, here and now, and is not the myth of self you have believed your whole life. You know that all appearances, pleasant and unpleasant, come and go, yet you remain, before, during, and after each one. When you stop valuing appearances, there is less attachment to outcomes and less fear of loss.

A holiday is about knowing the value of your essential being—you lack nothing, you are complete and whole, and you are the natural human condition of health. Your ordinariness is a huge relief from the need to be special, and you are not higher or lower than anyone. A holiday is about coming to see again, and again, and again… that you are already free, finished, and it is doubtless.

What difference does it make if you are caught up in work or any other activity, even thinking? It doesn't because you know something—you are free, you are fine.

Keep having holidays. Not to attain a specific state, but to know what is true, and to be finished.

Is This It?

Sometimes I'll have the thought, "Am I doing it, is this it?" I know it's just a thought passing through, but it's kind of confusing because I think, "Was it a holiday before I was thinking that?"

Does anyone want to answer that?

Inquirer 2: I had that, "Is this it?" experience for a while, and it was because I had different pictures associated with what enlightenment was going to be like. Then, as time unfolded, that disappeared, and I saw, "Yes, this is it." So, after a while, that questioning stopped, and it was just apparent.

Thank you.

Let me ask you, why would you ask, "Is this it?" This is a real question, and there's an answer for it.

Inquirer 1: Because I'm assuming it's not it.

Yes, and where did you get that idea?

Probably one of those Zen books or something, I don't know.

Exactly. Is the idea true, though? It's really a very loaded question— "Is this it?" Why does it appear? Because of all these ideas we've gotten from reading books and listening to spiritual teachers. Okay, but let's have a holiday.

HOLIDAY

Is there anything behind the curtain of now?

If we're honest, in truth,

there's only this knowing, here, now.

I'm not separate from this knowing,
which is here, am I?

This knowing and I,
we're not separate, we're one.

I am this knowing.

What more would there be to this?

What would you add on to this?

Some experience?
Some thought?
Some philosophy?

This knowing is *no*thing, isn't it?

This knowing is not a thing, it's *thing*less.

Why add something on? Because we want something, and we only want something because we have heard there's something to want.

> *I think I latched onto the holiday thing, and I thought using the holiday would somehow break the thought patterns or something. Something along those lines, like there's something to do.*

There's no goal with a holiday. You just recognize what's true—here and now; it's already finished. This needs to be seen and heard many times; it's just the way it is. It's a tenacious belief. I'm saying, have a holiday, and there is nothing more to do. There is nothing other than this, here and now. Let's get real. If there is something else, where is it?

If you want truth, the only thing you know that's true is this, now. Anything else is an idea or a belief, isn't it? The only thing you actually know is this. If you want to know truth, just be finished.

I know nothing, I have nothing, and I am nothing! I'm not a spiritual teacher or a guitar player. In truth, I'm none of it. I'm not enlightened, nothing. You get nothing, and it takes time for that to really reconcile. What you've been seeking your whole life is this. This is it. What a relief, no longer needing to want, want, want... more, more, more all the time.

Again, there's a seeming paradox because it takes time. Now, forget I said that, and recognize it's true, now.

Let me just talk about the apparent contradiction of time a little bit differently. The movie screen metaphor is really good, and it's a metaphor so, take it with a grain of salt. The movie screen represents this knowing, now. The knowing, the essential background, is who you are, essentially. Upon this movie screen is appearing a movie, but is the movie actually going anywhere? Isn't it just staying right here, appearing and dissolving right here, right now? It's not coming from anywhere or going anywhere. It's just appearing, now. It's not even substantial. This—what is—is just appearing and vanishing, now, now, now.

There's no future where it will be reconciled—it is reconciled now. When things appear, they appear now, like on the movie screen, appearing and going, now. There's only now, there's no future. Just keep knowing what's true, now, and see, manifestation is a constant flow of appearance. Just keep knowing what's true, now—that's it.

> *I pretty much keep making things up, that's what is going on.*

It's just a habit, and we all do it. It is normal. We've read many books and heard many teachings. By the way, you're not making anything up. There's no doer. We all know that, that's clear for everyone. We worked together, and your recognition is true. Just stay with it, that's all I can suggest to you. Just know what's true, that's it. Nothing to do. Everything is as it is.

Seeking

What is the cause of seeking? Clearly, it is the sense that you are lacking something. Without a sense of lack, why would the urge to seek appear? And what causes that sense of lack? Was it there when you came out of the womb? It happens because of the samskaras (mental impressions) recorded in your brain through experiences and immersion in cultural, religious and societal ignorance. For spiritual seekers, a big impetus to continue seeking forever comes from reading, listening to and/or attending spiritual teachings. In doing so, you obtain more samskaras, compare it with your current condition, and once again, you find yourself to be lacking. So, seeking continues forever.

In my view, when you come to know what is essentially true through a teaching that resonates, and you intuit that the teaching can help you to be finished, it is very important to stop with all of the spiritual promiscuity that continues creating new mental concepts and ideals. Otherwise, you will stay on the seeking carousel forever. At some point, you need to stop, get real and be dedicated to truth. For many of us, we are only ready for this when we are exhausted and frustrated, and willing to jump off of that spiritual mind carousel forever.

Dedication to Truth

What does being dedicated to truth mean?

It doesn't mean
I'm going to find truth in the future.

That's not being dedicated to truth,

that's being dedicated to seeking.

Being dedicated to truth means stopping, now and seeing the truth that's here, now.

Truth is only now.

Dedication to truth is only *now*.

Seeking Energy Has Returned

The seeking energy has come back and it doesn't bother me, but I guess I wanted to get your thoughts on this because I thought it was done. Nevertheless, I still have this impulse.

What's the impulse to do?

Read other things and look at videos. I feel like someone has an answer for me. I guess I feel bored and a bit restless. Also, I think I am missing something.

Are you getting anything out of the material you are reviewing?

It's the same as it was before I started working with you. It just adds confusion. Also, there is a sense that the seeking feeds itself like an addictive cycle. It feels like something is missing and something's not right. I feel restless.

It is good to see that it adds confusion and makes you feel like something is missing. Those were the reasons why you started this work in the first place.

It is good that you see this for yourself. We have only been working together for a short period of time, and I won't tell you or anyone what to do. However, if you are seeking for answers in anything except your own recognition in real time, you are comparing *no*thing with something. By that I mean, knowing your essential nature and being finished seeking does not need anything other than itself. It is not intellectual, not descriptive, not a state and not information at all. It is no-thing. But, when you seek, you are obviously seeking for something.

What you are reading or watching is only the words or comments of someone else. Is there truth in those words? You have to stop and come to see what is true for yourself again, and again, and again... Then, you come to see that seeking outside sources is not where the answer lies and in fact, it only makes you think you are missing something. But who said any of what you are reading is true? Just because it is in some book or said by some "teacher," does that make it true? All the spiritual books are in essence fiction. How could they be true? This, here and now, is what is true. However, we put veracity on the words of alleged authorities who we believe know more than we do.

You need to come to know for yourself! Who cares what I or anyone else knows? What is your knowing? What do you know for yourself? You know your essential being is free. That is paramount.

The process is fine because even after I was complete with my teacher, on a few occasions, when a doubt would arise, I would seek out and read some other spiritual books or do some meditation. Eventually, this passed. I just got tired of it as there were no answers there. I am sharing this, and I don't recommend that anyone do what I did. If you are doing it, it is what is. Just see for yourself how it goes.

> *I did come to this realization because even as I was viewing this other material, I was thinking to myself, "How do you know that?" So, I did not throw away my authority. I just thought it was interesting that all of a sudden, this seeking impulse arose.*

It is fine. We have not been working together for that long, only a couple of months. It does take time to resolve a lifetime of habits and to just be finished. For me, I can't do it anymore. Even if I try to look at spiritual stuff, I can only do it for a very short period of time. If I am reading, it's only a sentence or two. I don't need to know anything.

More importantly, I don't believe there is something more than this, right here, right now. I am home and at rest with this character called Sal, with all the imperfections. In that, it is perfect as it is. It can't be any other way. I don't need to look for something more. I know that I know very little. I just know this knowing, now. To me, this is ease, simplicity, and relief. This is being finished, and it is freedom.

I don't get anything from this recognition—no awards or concepts, especially not the great spiritual concepts I picked up along the path that I used to believe in. I only get NOW, *nothing*, not something. Liberation is being fully reconciled that *what is, is*. This moment can't be any different than it is now. It is not possible. It can only be as it is. The mind will argue, "There must be something more, there has to be something more." Well, look, where is it? There is only an idea in the mind that there is something more. If you jump off this idea, you see there is nothing more. This is true! There is no future and no past. Whatever is appearing now has to be it. It has to be true.

Seeking

Seeking in spiritual literature just propagates the belief that there is something else and there is something wrong. This is all it does. It provides no value. Just see this for yourself.

I don't compare the work I do with anyone else's teachings, even Ramana's, whom I love and respect. What I am sharing is that you are human. I don't have some lofty concept that we are transcendent awareness. The only thing I share is that freedom is the natural human condition.

This work stands on its own. It may have some similarities, but if you look into your own recognition and start comparing it to other teachings, it is going to be a big mess. The only thing I want is for people to look for themselves at what they know, then stand alone without any other authority. This is freedom. I want everyone to be a master, not a follower.

> *That is why I love this work, and it resonated with me so strongly. It showed me the way off the merry-go-round.*

You will just do what you do, but if you keep valuing truth, you will get tired of seeking because you will see it is not beneficial, and in fact, creates suffering. It perpetuates this belief that there is something wrong with you. In these meetings, we get nothing—utter simplicity. No one has the inside scoop on your knowing. No one knows more about you than you do.

After I was finished, I met a friend of mine who previously lived with me at an ashram. When I mentioned to him that I was done, he told me I had to go back to the guru of the ashram and get confirmation. I said, "No! If I have to go to some other person to get their approval about what I know, then obviously, I don't know." If you know, you don't need anyone else's approval. You stand alone. You are a master.

To be clear, I don't think I am Ramana or any other person. I am me.

Attending Other Satsangs

I am again watching too many satsangs on YouTube.

Why?

Because I think I am missing something. I am listening a lot because I still feel there is something to find. I still hope I am going to change.

What's going to change?

I don't know.

It sounds like you are looking online at satsangs because you are hoping something is going to happen.

Yes, I'm still hoping something will happen, like enlightenment or awakening, or just getting rid of myself. There is just dissatisfaction about my life and about the search. I'm just hoping something will change.

It sounds like you are hoping something will change circumstantially or feeling-wise, or that some final and permanent experience is going to happen.

It's not even that it is so bad. It's just the "I," the "me," that is fed up with itself, you know? It's like the searching that was always there was gone while I was working with you, but now... again, I am looking.

What I am sharing takes time for everyone. That is why I say, "You have to continue being devoted to truth." Even after you have recognized what is true (which you have), you have to stay with it. That means going through the inquiries again, and again, and again... And that means listening to the group audios again, and again, and again...

If you do that, it will work. If you don't do that, however, you give your mind a chance to start doubting. And again, it will start comparing this work with what you heard or read in the past about perfected states, transcendent consciousness, non-dual realities, or any other *ideas* about "enlightenment."

When you are not regularly having holidays, the mind starts doubting, and it just falls into its old seeking habit, and you fall with it. Why? Because, for your whole life, you have had these habits of seeking and being dissatisfied. It takes no time to recognize what is true, but it takes time and dedication to truth for those habits to be resolved.

And why shouldn't it? There is a lifetime of momentum that has made these doubts and false ideas linger in your conscious (and so-called subconscious) mind. Why would that stop right away because you had some recognition with this work? It won't. It is a very unrealistic expectation. It might happen for one out of a million people, although even that I doubt.

You mentioned that when you started this work, the seeking stopped from the recognition you had. If you had stayed with it and continued to do this work, the recognition would have become more and more obvious and doubtless. Instead, in the face of some dissatisfaction, you moved on and started listening to other teachers on YouTube. Then, once again, the old ideas got activated in your mind, and once again, you thought they had some value. You started comparing your current condition with some ideal state you heard about, and all of a sudden you say, "Nothing has changed."

If you go through the inquires with me or read *Liberation IS*, and then just go on to the next thing, you are like a window shopper, who never actually buys anything. You are just going right back into seeking. You are not being finished. If you feel this work has shown you something that is essentially true, you have to be finished and stay with it.

> *Inquirer 2: I have been with Sal for a couple of years. After I went through my individual sessions with him and completed my first group two, I just kept listening to the audios. Every time I was in the car, I was always listening to one of the audios. I immersed myself in only that for at least two years.*
>
> *It made a big difference. If I had just done my individual sessions and a group two and then moved on, I don't think I would have gotten it that clearly. With the constant repetition and being immersed in it, I noticed over time that more layers of the onion would disappear and things became clearer.*
>
> *Inquirer 1: Thank you. Yes, I noticed in the beginning, I was very much occupied with the work, and then I lost track and listened to my previous teachers again. People, like U. G. Krishnamurti say things like, "Nothing that you do helps," and "Whatever you do will not work," and "If it is a teaching, it will not teach you anything." I got totally de-motivated. It felt hopeless sometimes.*

That's fine because it is hopeless. What is to hope? Hope is nonsense. There is only now. This is it!

I have some issues on a personal level. It is so difficult for me to make decisions. These are psychological things. I feel stuck. I don't know what is good. One minute I want to go to Tiru and the next minute I don't.

What is now is what is now. If now, you want to go to Tiru, that is what is. If two minutes later, you don't want to go to Tiru, that is what is appearing. These are just thoughts going back and forth, and at some point, one of these thoughts will prevail as an intention. Then, the action or non-action will follow.

As you know, the work I do is not psychological work, it's not about purifying, correcting, fixing, or anything like that. You just have some ideas that are going back and forth in your brain. I don't see a problem with it. If it is, we are back in the realm of self-improvement and right behavior. Sorry, I don't do that, and I don't believe it ultimately works because there is this idea of some perfected mental state you are going to get into.

The mind is fickle, it's meant to be fickle. There are billions of bits of data constantly flowing by in the mind and circumstances and experiences sometimes trigger them to go crazy. This whole personal growth movement, which is about fixing the non-existent self, may be relevant on the path, but it is not ultimately effective for liberation. It is endlessly working on the carousel of mind and reifying the self.

I'm normal as myself. I just don't argue with what is going on. *What is, is.* I am me. I don't expect some ideal, perfected mental state to be happening because that is a ridiculous expectation. I just let the mind do its thing. There is peace, ease, freedom, and liberation in being finished with trying to correct a so-called self, which is just a myth. A myth that actually has no truth or power.

By thinking there is something wrong because you are indecisive, and then listening to other teachings again, you are right back on the carousel. That is exactly what we are jumping off of with this work. In the first inquiry, we jump off, and the point is to stay jumped. By staying jumped, I mean don't go back into spiritual teachings, don't go back into psychological corrections, and don't go back into all of your ideas and hopes about enlightenment. Jump off those carousels and stay jumped. Don't know anything and don't hope anything because there is no hope. There is only now. *What is, is.* Obviously, this is true because what is now, is. Hopes and longings for something different are a lie because they don't exist, now. Jump off all of that. Now is all there is. Freedom is now only.

Stick to the work. If you have seen that this work is pointing to truth, to not stick with it is not wise. If you digress or stray, so it is. It is normal, but know, in the back of your mind, what is true. If you recognize something that is so simple and so obvious—*nothing*; if you see the truth of this, simple, ordinary, no-thing; then to stray is foolish.

It is not what you thought, like some perfected, elevated, or transcendent mental state. It is just ordinary consciousness as it is, here and now. This is the only thing you can actually know. If you see that here and now is true (that there is nothing more than this; and that there is no past and no future), this knowing is only possible now. What is now is that you are here, now, aware. Is that true for you?

> *Yes, now it is clear. As I listen to you, I am back on track.*

You just told me it is true. So now, you KNOW it is true. Why do you question yourself when you just told me you know? If you see it is true, just keep listening to the audios. If you recognize it is true, don't stray.

> *Yes, sometimes I put on your talks and in just a few minutes, there is a direct recognition that what you're saying is true. But there is the mind with its resistance*

that says, "It is not good enough," or "Something bigger should happen." I know it is all mind games.

Yes, it is, but you see, we really don't hear what these other teachers (you mentioned U.G.) are saying. We just look at his so-called "awakening" *experience*—he had ashes on his body or whatever it might be. We overlook what he was saying, which is—nothing is going to happen; there is no such thing as enlightenment; all these ideas and teachers are wrong. We don't recognize the message. All we think is, "Oh, he had an experience with ashes on his skin, that must be enlightenment."

That is just one of many examples. What is he saying to you? He is saying, "Get real man!" Just stop, just jump and get off all of that nonsense. Especially someone like you, who has a clear recognition. Just stop! But it's very tempting to read U.G., Ramana or whomever because there is a lot of romance in that. If you are tempted, then you are just going right back into the known, which is all of the ideas you have already accumulated. A doubt happens, and you read Ramana because it is already in your conscious mind, so it is known and comforting, but it doesn't get you anywhere.

If you have recognized that your essential being is here and now, free, unchanging, eternal, and you lack nothing, just stay here. Keep recognizing that again, and again, and again... Soon these doubts and dissatisfactions will lose power.

Listening to Group Audios

I am spending a lot of time listening to the audios, and I am worried this seeking mechanism is still running. Nevertheless, I do notice that I feel like I have been on a holiday when I get done listening.

It is a good thing to listen to the audios a lot. When you do, you are not seeking, you are finding. This is the only thing to do. We have a habit of believing we are this body-mind. The new habit is to keep finding out that you are the knowing. This will become so habitual that it will eventually be over. This becomes your only habit after a while, then it becomes your default condition.

Listening to the audios is giving you a much better habit than buying into the stories of self all the time. When you are on holidays, you are finding. We are all on holidays here together. The meaning of satsang is, being together in truth. So, when you are listening to the audios, you are being in truth. These meetings are not about philosophical or spiritual concepts. If they were, listening to them would be a total waste of time.

The point of these meetings is to continually be fully knowing holiday for an hour. All this is doing is making the holiday a habit until it is finished. Just know it is already finished and keep knowing it. All is well.

Inquirer 2: I have thought that holidays are just like some other work I have done, and in a way, they are conceptual.

If I write it down on a sheet of paper, it is a concept. However, a holiday is not a concept. It has nothing to do with thought. Thinking that a holiday is just another concept is a concept.

Seems like I just have doubts.

Yes, but where is that doubt happening? It is happening in the mind. A holiday is out of the mind. Just jump. It is that simple. Just know. Know and jump mean the same thing. If there is a doubt, know it is just a thought. This is just a habit. We have this lifetime of habit of believing all thoughts mean something.

Doing Bodywork

There is this body-mind that exists, and I've heard the analogy of the body being like a vehicle. I know there are different things to be done to the vehicle to keep it running, like eating, sleeping, drinking, etc.

Also, I have been involved in car accidents and done other things to my body where it has needed "repair." What is your view on doing bodywork? In the past, when I have done bodywork, it has brought up different experiences and emotions from the "past." So, I want to know, is that continuing seeking, by doing that type of work?

If the purpose of the bodywork is to heal the body, then no, not at all. If the purpose of the bodywork is to look at the emotions that appear and analyze them and find out why, then I say, that's still the psychological model, and back on the carousel. If you're doing bodywork because you've been in a car accident, then that's what is needed. And if experiences or emotions arise, so it is. When they do, have a holiday.

Of course, bodywork is fine and yes, bodywork can elicit some emotions or some thoughts that supposedly happened in the past somewhere. However, for someone who wants freedom, and who is authentic, the resolution for that is to just jump. Authentically, if you want nothing, nothing also includes not analyzing or understanding whatever supposedly happened in the past. You don't get to analyze, figure out, straighten out or organize. You ignore it because it doesn't exist, and it's not true.

Anything we do with that, even witnessing it, is giving some credence or validity to something which, in truth, is not. Even if that emotion appears now, it's just a thought appearing now. If there is no past, then literally what is appearing now has no cause. If there's no past, then let's get real. Whatever is appearing now has no cause. It's only appearing now, period. There's nothing behind the curtain.

This may sound radical, but it's true. This moment is uncaused, it just is. If that's true, what's there to understand, analyze, figure out, solve, or resolve. Nothing! It depends what you want. If you want freedom, then here it is. Just being here now, you get nothing. And, if one still wants spirituality or psychology, those carousels are endless. Enjoy, they go on forever!

You Stand Alone

Holidays have dimmed a lot from what they were in the beginning. I know I am not supposed to focus on the feelings, but I'm just noticing that I think "what happened to that sense or experience?" Stress comes up and I think, "let me have a holiday and see if I can calm myself down," which again, I know is not the purpose of a holiday. My worry is that the seeking will come back after these meetings end. There is already the thought "this is not working?"

First of all, when you first start having holidays, there's often a big "AHA" along with them, and of course, it's going to bring some good feelings, relief, excitement and all that. Then, you equate a holiday with good feelings, excitement, and all that. You think, "That's what happened when I first started having holidays. Now, that's not happening anymore. So, I must not be having holidays." But that's not what a holiday is.

A holiday is just knowing: who you are; there's only now; and whatever is appearing is appearing, now and it's disappearing, now, simultaneously. In the moment, if there's something stressful going on, of course, it's not pleasant. A holiday is knowing you're fine in the midst of it all.

Also, a holiday needs to be the way you live, not only for the very short period that we've known each other. People who have been here for a long time will say the longer they have holidays, the more effective it is. Everything's fine.

> *Inquirer 2: I remember when I finished with Sal. He said, "that's it, you're finished, you're on your way." God, I was sick, it was just awful, and I thought, "How am I going to survive?" It's good practice to be off on your own for a while.*

That's really true. You have to stand on your own two feet. This work is about being your own master. Everyone here knows everything. It's up to us to walk this life ourselves, in freedom. Meetings definitely add support, but really, everybody takes the lumps of life as they come, and during those moments, just recognize freedom. Just do it. Because the more you do it on your own, the more valuable it is.

With my teacher, you went to her retreat and then you left. That was it. There was no ongoing support, and most people went back to their own country. At some point, everyone has to take the training wheels off. You'll fall, and you'll get back up. Keep having holidays, keep knowing what's true.

It's a good question you bring up. I don't want anyone to be dependent on me. I want everyone to be free. I'm actually kind of weird. Most teachers are very happy if people stick around forever. They get the money and whatever else they get out of it, I don't really know. I don't want that. I want everyone to be free.

The End of the Seeker

What would it be like to not understand anything?

To not know the meaning of anything?

To not know what anything is, or why anything is?

This work is not about *gaining* anything.

Not even peace, or well-being,
it's not about gaining anything.

It's about seeing that here and now,
there's no need for anything.

Seeking

There's no need to be fulfilled,
and there's no need to get enlightened
or understand anything about life.

All of that movement is the movement of the mind—all of it,

just thoughts conditioned into this mind.

None of that movement was here originally
when you came out of the womb.

None of it!

Freedom is not a state, condition, or experience.

It's not any of that.

Freedom is the end of the need for any of that stuff.

Because the "person" who needs any of that stuff
is only conditioned thought—an illusory self.

All seeking for answers
comes because there's an assumed problem.

That assumed problem is manifested
by experiences of the body-lifestream.

But look, now!

Those experiences are not manifesting, now.

All of the problems of seeking arise because of conditioned
thought.

The Way of Freedom

But, here and now,
we see that none of that is actual.

If you see it's true,
then who is here to have any questions,
or any issues, or any problems?

The questions, issues, or problems come from conditioning.

There is not a you that has those questions.

When the question appears, it *is* you.

If that question doesn't appear,
there's no *you* to have the question.

We have a lifetime of habit (it's a momentum)
of wanting something to hold on to.

We want an understanding of who I am
and to know something.

It takes time for all of that to just stop.

It's an ongoing momentum and it takes time.

Slowly and gradually, you start seeing what's actually true—there's
no one.

There's no one separate from the question, to have the question.

There is *only* the question.

The question *is* you in that moment.

Seeking

In the next moment, the question is gone.

And *you* are gone.

Is that ok?
Do we want that?
Is this *no*thing enough?

Is it enough to not know anything and
to not be anything special?

Is it enough that what appears, appears,
and what disappears, disappears?

That's it.

Reconciled.

That's freedom.

Freedom isn't like the image of Rumi,
jumping up and down in drunken ecstasy.

That's nice,
but that's not the freedom I'm speaking about.

Freedom means there is no longer any argument.

There's only what is.

You don't get to attain enlightenment.

"Oh no! I don't get to attain enlightenment?"

No!

The Way of Freedom

There's no you to attain enlightenment, is there?
That's just more conditioned thoughts.
The seeker is a thought, and that seeker goes.

The seeker doesn't get what it wants.

The seeker ends.

Being Finished

Being finished does not mean that you have attained a new state of transcendent consciousness and/or that you are "aware of awareness" every second of the day. Nor does it mean that there are no more thoughts or emotions, or that you always feel good. It simply means that you have come to know your essential being of freedom and it is doubtless. Your mind is at rest in freedom. Life carries on with its normal ups and downs, but there is no more arguing with what is, and in that there is peace.

Finished Already

There is only here and now.

Where is the future you are going to be finished in?

The only thing you know is now, right?

This is so simple, here and now, so no-thing.

Any doubt about that?

Then, it is already finished, isn't it?

This is a genuine question—
where is the self that is not going to be finished tomorrow?

That is simply an idea, it is not an actual self.

Don't believe in a self that is not going to be finished tomorrow.

In fact, who is the self now that is finished?

Is there one?

Since there is not,
will there be a self tomorrow that is not finished?

The question of being finished or not finished is gone.

Doubts may appear, but who cares?

Does a doubt mean that what you have come to know,
that your essential nature is free, is not true?

A doubt may appear, and then it will be gone.

Get real now, see that it is already finished, now.

Don't believe there is a person who is not finished.

Don't believe in a future where this person is not finished.
If you do that, you will never be finished.

If doubts come, ignore.

Just be finished, now.

See that it is finished, now.

If I Am Not on Holiday, "I Am Not Getting It"

When I hear you talk about being "finished," I hear you saying that when you are "finished," you are no longer concerned or worried about whether you are knowing yourself as the knowing in any particular moment. For me, I think that when I am not on holiday, I am not "getting it." It seems that for you, being on holiday has ceased to be an issue.

That is correct. That is one aspect of being finished, and it is a very important aspect. Being finished means you know you are free, period. Seeking is over. You know you are whole and complete, lacking nothing, and there is nothing more that needs to be found or attained. Being finished means you know you are free. There can be thoughts and it won't matter because you know you are free. The knowing of your essential being, Sat Chit, does not have to be in the forefront of your mind. Just like knowing there is no Santa Claus does not have to be in the forefront of your mind for you to know there is no Santa Claus.

There is just a habit of believing that there is more to find and more to attain. Your spiritual path may have told you that you have to get rid of all thoughts, purify all your conditioning, or achieve a state of awareness twenty-four hours a day. These are just ideas, and they keep coming back, over and over again. They may cause you to believe you are not finished because you were thinking for an hour. This belief has to be reconciled. And it is reconciled by just continuing to know what is true.

Is there a past or a future?

No.

Do you know that is true?

Yes.

That is finished, right?

Yes.

You did not hesitate. Why would you say that so quickly?

Well, it is the same thing as Santa Claus. I know it.

There is only here and now. Is that true?

Yes.

Why do you say that so quickly?

I have seen it so many times I know it is true.

Now, you know it is true. You know. Anything else is just a silly doubt and a habit. It is fine.

They will just carry on until they don't.

Exactly, and the way they stop is by you being authentic. Keep coming to meetings, listening to audios, and having holidays. "Abide as the Self," said Ramana. Just know. Be this knowing, now. Knowing is being. Being is knowing. There is no difference between being and knowing. So just be. That is all.

Inquirer 2: What draws one back into story and belief?

It is just a habit. We believe the ignorance and lack an authentic intention to be free, here and now. When stories arise, we are compelled to believe them, and we go down that rabbit hole of ignorance. We value the stories and emotions more than we value freedom. If there is a strong intention for freedom, that will end.

We are trained our whole life to value what is going on in the mind. We are trained to value how smart we are and how much we know.

A ridiculous example is the TV show *Jeopardy* where people know all this useless trivia. The people watching think the contestants are intelligent. They are not intelligent, they are just regurgitating information, like a computer. They are little more than trained chimps. Many people place a lot of value on this.

In many ways, we are trained to believe the mind is the most important thing and there is a lot of value in our life story and plans for the future. We are trained, and of course, we have a habit of believing it. So, why do we get lost in stories? Because that is what we have been trained to do our whole life—to believe there is so much importance there.

Now, we come to see something different—there is no intrinsic value in any of that. There is value in freedom. Of course, there is value in having a good mind to do your job. That is not the same thing as valuing your stories and continually reviewing and analyzing them.

It is good to hear that this is just a habit because what we usually hear on the spiritual path is that the ego is a great evil, it's the greatest demon and it needs to be killed—some say it will take fifty lifetimes. That notion is very daunting. If we hear it is just a habit, it makes it much easier to address. Actually, it's true and it's a lot nicer to hear it that way. You just have a new habit, which is knowing your true nature and seeing that there is no overpowering ego to slay. There is just continuing to discriminate between what is true and what is false, seeing the value in truth, and having that value strengthen the intention for freedom and truth.

No One to be Finished

I thought that once you are finished, you are finished, but there seems to be a process going on with me. I guess I heard you say there's a process going on, and that things get deeper...

There are a couple of ideas you have. The first is that if something so-called troublesome appears, there's further to go. The second is that you will come to a point where nothing's bothering you anymore. This body-mind organism experiences pleasant and unpleasant thoughts and feelings, the ups and downs. I know it. It's a fact. That's it.

There's a slowing down of the momentum of the habit of grasping. On the one hand, there's a feeling of being done, but I also notice the mental habits of wanting to attach and seek come up from time to time. Now, there's not the tenacity to follow them.

There's no one here to grasp anything and there's no one here to be enlightened. There's no one here to be finished, there's only being finished. If compelling thoughts are appearing, there's an idea that there's a "me/self" (so-called "I") grasping for them. In truth, there is no me here grasping for thoughts. There are just thoughts, and one of the thoughts happens to be, "I am here grasping for thoughts."

Being finished means knowing there's no one here grasping for thoughts. There are just thoughts, no matter what they may be. As long as we think there's a me here grasping for thoughts, we're going to have another thought that says, "I still have further to go." When we truly recognize there is no me here to grasp thoughts and there are just thoughts, then the problem is resolved.

All the thoughts and feelings in the body, which we come to believe indicate the sense of self, don't indicate an actual self. If you inquire, you can't find an actual solid self. If there was a self, it would be a thing or an object with its own substance. In looking, it has to be seen that the *experience* of self is in constant, never-ending change and movement. There's nothing stable objectively or experientially that can be called a self.

If the belief in a self is no longer here or cared about, then it's finished. Even though there are feelings in this body that seem to indicate there's someone here, you see in truth, those feelings are ephemeral. They're constantly changing and there's no substance to them at all. Instead of a self here, it's known that what is simply is. In this moment, what is, is and this moment is not something that can be grasped on to because this moment has no solidity to it. It's ephemeral and whatever's appearing now is already gone.

When this is reconciled, there are no more arguments. There's no one here that's going to claim it "has further to go." If there's no one here to claim it has further to go or that there's a problem with anything, then there *is* no problem with anything. And the waves of life carry on, sometimes small ripples, sometimes bigger waves, sometimes cold, and sometimes warm. That's the nature of living life.

Holidays Make Your Recognition Doubtless

*I listen to the audios of the group talks a lot. I've heard
you say that once you've seen your essential nature, you
never really have to have a holiday again. Could you talk
about the purpose of continually having holidays?*

Once you recognize your essential being, then you have recognized
it. You know who you are. But I always say that's just the beginning,
not the end. Most spiritual seekers seek for forty or fifty years and
never get to the beginning. They think they're going to meditate for
forty years, recognize their essential being, and that's going to be it.
For the vast majority of people, that will not be the case.
Recognizing your essential being is the beginning and most seekers
never get to the beginning.

The beginning is recognizing your essential being. Once you've
recognized, you've recognized. However, a lifetime of habit keeps
you occupied with misunderstanding and misidentification, and
with continuing to believe the concepts, hopes, and promises you
learned as a seeker. Those habits can die hard because many of
them are very appealing with promises of perfection, bliss,
happiness, etc. So, the reason to continually have holidays is to
switch that paradigm of belief, to the paradigm of knowing your
essential being, until it's doubtless.

What I have noticed is that everyone I work with does recognize
their essential being. But, in most cases, there is an immediate
tendency to doubt. Right away, an impression from something that
has been read or heard appears in the mind, some idea or ideal of
what enlightenment is, and the mind immediately compares that
ideal with the current completely simple and *nothing* recognition,
and says, "No, this is not it. It is *more!*"

Over time, by continuing the knowing of holidays, the truth of freedom outshines the ignorance of those beliefs and ideas, and you come to realize that what you have recognized has been it all along. And by continuing with this work, ease of being becomes the default condition.

The Way is the Goal

On a past group audio, you were talking about how maybe six months from now, something could come up and clobber me over the head, and then I'd think, "Oh shit, what happened?" Right now, I'm not doubting truth, but the idea that something could happen in the future makes me think that I should be doing something now. I know I can just have a holiday and it goes away, but that doesn't seem to be enough of an answer.

Okay. So, let's not be specific about that question. Forget there's an actual, specific question. It's fine there's a specific question appearing, and let's just say, generically, there's just *a* question there. Where did it come from?

From the assumption that there's something more to get.

Right. The solution, and it's a permanent solution, but it has to be solved many times, is to just not believe it.

That's the tricky part, that it has to be solved many times. Then, there's a future thing kind of there. Know what I mean?

I know, no problem. There are tenacious habits. Okay, now, tell me the question again.

Well, it's going to sound silly.

It's not silly. There's no such thing as silly questions. Everyone here is thinking, "Thank God he asked that, so I don't have to look silly."

It has to do with—I don't like the word enlightened—but with being finished, completely finished. There seems to be some kind of end to what's going right now. The idea of that is what makes me think that right now, there's something lacking because I'm assuming that at some point, I won't have any questions like this.

Where is your "problem" happening? In the mind, right? There are three carousels of mind: the philosophical, the psychological, and the spiritual (future enlightenment). What do we do with those carousels? The normal answer is, "I have to get in there and arrange them all, straighten them out, understand them and get rid of all my vasanas. That's the only way. Then, I have to achieve all of these specific experiences. It's the only possibility. Of course, it's endless and it will take fifty lifetimes, but that's just the way it is."

The hope of being finished at some point is clearly the future carousel, isn't it? It's obviously in the mind, isn't it? All of the carousels are mind. The only solution is to know what freedom is, which is here and now only, and to jump, now. That's what I always say. That's how strongly I feel about it, and I admit it takes time to be completely reconciled. The reason I say that is because if this work is about being finished and someone comes to work with me for a few weeks, and they're not finished, they'll say, "It didn't work."

Because I am respectful of the way the habitual human mind works, I say, "It takes time." But you see, you have to forget I said that. You have to get real, *now*. I only say that so you don't think there's something wrong with you if there are some doubts appearing, now. That idea that you will have a problem in the future is simply a doubt appearing *now*. So, jump, now. Now is all you have, and now is all you can deal with.

> *Deep down, I know that I can just have holidays over and over again; that's the only thing that's going to happen and that's it. I could stop coming to these groups and it would be fine. I mean, I'm going to keep coming.*

Yes, you could, and that is my intention. If you were finished, you would be finished, and you could stop and not come to groups anymore. But it's unrealistic with the momentum of mental impressions (beliefs, etc.) that it will be finished right away. So, therefore, I want to give support until it is doubtless.

Everything is only happening now, but that momentum is also happening now. That momentum is not thoughts or ideas. It is only one thing—belief. When the thought comes up that you're going to be done in the future, there's a belief that it is true. What if that belief wasn't there? You would only be here, now, knowing you're finished, that thought be damned. The on-switch to the momentum is belief. Does that sound, contradictory?

> *It does, but it makes a lot of sense. It's like the path is the goal.*

Right, and perhaps it's better to say that the way to the goal is the same as the goal itself. The way is to know yourself, here and now, and the goal is also to know yourself, here and now. Let's all be on holiday, now.

HOLIDAY

Is there a past or future?

We have to get real here, no hedging bets.

There's no past and there's no future, very simple.

There is nothing behind the curtain of now.

Know that you are, that you exist, here and now, *only*.

The knowing of yourself, here and now,
is the way to be finished with doubt.

And the knowing of yourself, here and now,
is already the end.

What more is there to recognize than this?

If there's no past and there's no future, then it's already finished because there's no future that it's going to be finished in. If a doubt appears, have a holiday and see again, that it's finished, now. Let's have another holiday.

HOLIDAY

This knowing—I am now—is known, isn't it?

What about the knowing that's going to be in the future,
do you really know that?

What do you actually know?

Be truthful.

You only know, here and now, I am.

The rest of it is concept and ignorance, isn't it? There's nothing that's actually truly known other than this knowing, now. There's a belief, "I'm going to be finished in the future." However, I'm not interested in beliefs. A holiday, as I say a million times, is not about relief or any particular state. It's none of that. It's about knowing something. It's about knowing the only thing you actually know, which is now, I am. That's the only thing you actually know. The rest of it is belief. Stop believing.

Let's start being honest about what we actually know. This work is just about being honest, that's all.

Impediments to Enlightenment

You've talked about how continuing to use drugs that alter your consciousness can possibly prevent the recognition from becoming doubtless. Also, you say reading other spirituality books can cause confusion. Are there other things that will make this never happen for me?

For example, I'm a writer, a storyteller, I make videos and I keep having thoughts related to what we're doing here. I think about creating a record of the process I'm going through, like a documentary of enlightenment for the world, or something like that. But I keep resisting those thoughts, and they are strong.

Is that something that could be dangerous? I know when I have started a blog or something in the past, it creates its own energy form that can really suck me in. So, I'd be terrified that I'm not enlightened, but I'm writing this little blog about whatever's happening. Is there anything else I should be wary of or that I should not be getting into?

The answer is only you will know that for yourself. You'll find out for yourself. If the blog becomes a thing about being special or trying to be someone, then you'll see it, no problem. You'll know for yourself. Only you can know it. Actually, freedom is not opposed to doing anything. Anything can happen. You can write your stories, make movies, or music, or whatever you are doing. The question is, what's behind the actions?

It took me a long time before I started teaching because I was aware of teachers teaching with ulterior motives, like power, sex, greed, fame, etc., and I wanted to make sure that was not the case with me. It's good to be honest with yourself about that, and it's good to be wary because yes, anything can take you out of a holiday and into becoming more ego/self-centered. There's nothing evil about it or anything like that, but you want freedom. You want to be no one. Freedom is being nobody special.

I find myself strangely in the role of a teacher when I am answering peoples' questions or when I am on these group calls. The rest of my life, I am not in the role of teacher, and I don't speak to people about this at all. Whatever's appearing in the moment is what I am. If in the moment I am making music, then I am a musician. If in the next moment, I'm hanging out with my girlfriend, then I'm a boyfriend. It could look from the outside that this guy, Salvadore, is a teacher, but honestly, I don't see it that way, that is simply a projection. In this moment, that's what's happening here. That's all it is.

You have to see for yourself, and your authenticity for freedom is the only guide that you need. You are in these meetings, and you've come this far, so your authenticity is there. The only thing that's needed is authenticity. The intention to be free is your guru. That's your guide right there, and you'll learn everything you need to learn. If there's intention of specialness and ego, you'll find out.

Thank you very much.

You are welcome. Do write your stories. That's your creativity. Of course, you should enjoy your creative talent.

Resolving Afflictive Tendencies

All appearances are equal because they all come and go, and they are all known to you. But some appearances are very convincing, and for most of us, it is not so easy to resolve or know freedom in their midst. These are afflictive tendencies, which may be caused by past traumatic experiences or may simply be very normal tendencies such as jealousy, worry, fear, anxiety, anger, etc. Although the resolution of afflictive tendencies is in truth no different than any other thought, emotion or experience, it is good to look into resolving these tendencies specifically, as it is one of the main concerns people have when coming to work like this.

For most people, a therapeutic approach is needed to deal with afflictive tendencies because they are not healthy, able or willing enough to stop the compulsive, obsessive, habitually reactive attention to afflictive thoughts that cause suffering. That is just how it is and there is no fault. But for one who hears this message and wants to come to know the peace inherent in freedom, I am unequivocal—the way of freedom is to be finished with that. That simply means, at the onset of any afflictive thought, attention is immediately withdrawn and a holiday IS. A holiday is simply knowing yourself, free of all of it, and BEING THAT, here and now— Sat Chit Ananda.

Holidays occur in the midst of afflictive tendencies when the intention for freedom is more dominant than the interest in following any train of thought. I want to be clear that this does NOT mean there is a doer of this intention. It either is or is not. Freedom either is the dominant intention, or it is not. If it is not, then there is suffering the whims of the mind. If it is, then it is over.

Dealing With Afflictions
Talk from Tiru Intensive, January 2018

Now, we know the way of freedom is to be free. We know what is true and we know the value of truth. In the past, we have dealt with afflictions by the negative approach, which means getting in there and trying to do something about them; to get rid of them, to anesthetize them, to change them, to replace them, to understand them and/or analyze them. Let's face it, that is endless.

Most good therapists never lose a client, and it's a good gig if you like that. Most spiritual teachers never lose a client either—they never lose a devotee. But I'm in the business of losing inquirers. We are all equal here and when people are ready to be done, they are ready. I do not have disciples, I have friends.

What would be a better way to deal with afflictions when they arise? We spoke about it a little bit the other day. We all have our own particular afflictions, so let's just pick one: jealousy. Maybe there are a few people who don't experience jealousy, but most of us are familiar with that affliction, it's very human. Usually, we berate ourselves when something like that appears, or we go to counseling, lash out at our partner, or have some other reactive response.

What happens if jealousy appears in the mind? This goes for any affliction that arises (we each have our own predominant ones). Everyone experiences jealousy to some degree, so let's assume that is one of our predominant afflictions. I think we all know the moment when jealousy appears, right? Is anyone fooled when it arises? No, we know, right? We know, it's easy. Okay, then be done knowing it. How much more do you need to know it?

When something like that starts appearing, what are you going to do? Immediately, you know it, it takes no time to know. You don't have to analyze it, and you don't have to acknowledge it, "Oh, there's jealousy again." If you do, you have just given it a whole life. Don't even do that, don't do anything. You already know in one billionth of a millisecond that the affliction appeared. Just have freedom— have a holiday instead. Don't witness it either. If you think, "I'm going to witness the jealousy," then you just created something to witness. If there is something to witness, then you are saying, "There is something there." I say, "Ignore it."

I've gotten in trouble for using the word "ignore," believe me. People who want to prove they're a separate self get mad at me when I say, "Ignore your ego." Their response is, "Me, ignore my ego?" (Sal laughs). I'm going to get myself killed one of these days. So, I don't say it anymore in public.

If jealousy or whatever affliction appears, ignore it and know freedom. Then, maybe, the jealousy is persistent and draws you back in. Then, again, in that moment, have freedom again. If you stay true to truth, if you value and worship truth, then eventually, it has to go. It has to go, it is scientific. If you don't give it power (the power of belief) and instead ignore, then it will slow down and disappear. Of course, because the light of truth outshines everything. It is so obvious, isn't it?

Okay, in the moment of the afflictive emotion, maybe it doesn't seem so obvious, but so what? Have a holiday. What do you want? You can see what you want in that moment. If you want freedom, here it is. If you want to get into that story because of jealousy, then you can. And maybe you will for a while. There is nothing to judge about that, that movement is a habit. There is no judging, "Now you've done wrong, thou shalt not do that." I don't do that kind of work here. We just know what's true and truth shall set you free. When you see you went into the story, no problem, have a holiday. You see?

It doesn't matter how many times this cycle happens either. Truth is going to still be true, so keep knowing truth. Then that episode of affliction will come and go in a very natural way like a wave. Over time, maybe that particular affliction will be resolved as well. Resolving the affliction is not a goal. I don't want to make that a goal because really the only thing to see is that you are free, now.

This is something very practical. Each of us have things appearing, no one is exempt here. For instance, the need to be right. We all have that because we think we have an ego. If we believe in ego and that our beliefs are important, or we believe that we need to be special and seen in a particular way, then we have the need to be right as well. That is an affliction, no problem. We don't judge the appearance of the affliction, instead we just see what is true. And then, in the moment of its appearance, we know it immediately, and can then return to knowing what's true. I'm planting the seed in your head so that it happens—know what is true, be free. The way of freedom is to be free.

Sarcasm is another thing we do, and it is based on insecurity and the need to be right. Sarcasm represents the need to put someone else down to hold ourselves up. Actually, sarcasm is not health, it is not real humor. In my view, real humor is silly, funny, harmless, selfless or self-deprecating. But I don't consider sarcasm to be humorous. It is based on a need to be right and put the other person down. It's subtle, and you have to see it for yourself. It is a protection mechanism. If that's a tendency for you, then see it, no problem, there's no judgement. Who's to judge anyway? Just know what's true and want freedom, that's all.

Envy is very common. We envy someone else who is more successful, who has more money, who is more "enlightened," or whatever. This is such a normal human affliction, isn't it? It's impersonal because everyone can be touched by envy. This is very practical if you see that envy is based on comparison. If I feel that a person has more than me or is superior to me, then obviously, there is a belief that I am a self that is lacking. Just know it. You see? It's very clear, very simple, no judgement. Just know what's true and, in that moment, immediately, have a holiday and see, "Oh wow, freedom. Nice."

And you know what? When we have a holiday, in the midst of jealousy, anxiety, or whatever the affliction is, that feeling isn't going to disappear immediately because although thoughts are very fast, feelings tend to linger. In the moment of a holiday, thoughts stop for a millisecond, a second, a few seconds, or however long. It takes longer to build up a feeling and it takes longer for a feeling to dissipate.

One of the most common things I have heard over the past six years is, "I may have a holiday, but I still feel bad, so that means I must not be on a holiday." No, that does not mean you are not on a holiday. A holiday is knowing, with everything included: the sun, the mountain, the objects in the room, and the feeling in the body. It's all included, isn't it? You are on holiday and by remaining on holiday that feeling begins to lose power—the power switch is off. Looping thoughts cause more and more story, more and more feeling—it's a cycle. On a holiday, these looping thoughts don't get generated.

Some people who are pathologically ill have one main story that they hold on to for their whole lives. It's even true on the macro level; some cultures have one story that they hold on to forever. And they use it as a means of control by playing the victim card. We do this on our own personal level, "I'm a victim, don't you see? Poor me, poor me, poor me." That poor me story is a means of control. "Don't you say anything to me, poor me. This terrible thing happened." Okay, fine.

> *Inquirer 1: Or we say to ourselves, "I did this terrible thing," and then feel shame and guilt.*

Exactly, they're the same thing. You're right, that's right. We all have this whole thing with regret, remorse, and guilt, especially

Christians, Catholics and Jewish people. Occasionally, a memory comes back of some stupid thing I did in my life and, of course, with that is the appearance of the feeling of regret. It's natural, isn't it? Because the memory appears, we think we have to feel remorse. And by ignoring it, we are being irresponsible and denying what happened, however many years ago. We think we have to hold on to that regret, "Oh, I'm such an asshole." What benefit is that? Is there any benefit?

You know it was stupid and you're not going to do it again. So, when the feeling of regret or guilt comes up, know it and be finished. Be free. This is important for all of us to see because, of course, we're all good, caring people. We want to be good and we've all done stupid things. I don't care, enlightened or not, if a painful a memory comes up, feelings of regret will come as well. That's okay, now you know it, be free.

This is the way to deal with afflictions—know them as they arise and be free. Guilt and remorse are afflictions. It doesn't benefit anyone to keep wallowing in them. You know that you did something stupid. Okay, maybe you won't do it again.

> *Not just stupid but bad, you know?*

Harmful, let's say harmful. I don't like the word "bad." Yes, you've done something harmful, and you know it. If there are amends to make, you make amends. Now, what's the point of holding on to the guilt? Does it do anything?

> *Inquirer 2: I think when I have an affliction it's just that I need to learn something about it.*

Do you need to learn something about the affliction?

> *When something happens, just accept it and learn something about it.*

I hear what you're saying. If you did something, you know if it was harmful. I don't think you need to know any more than that. We're all very intelligent. We know what's right and wrong; what's harmful and beneficial. We don't need to go into it, analyze it, and feel bad and beat ourselves up forever about it. It doesn't help anything.

Inquirer 3: What about the feeling of love?

In Vedanta, they speak about binding vasanas and non-binding vasanas. The binding vasanas cause suffering. Feelings of guilt, remorse, or victimization come up and there's suffering. A feeling of love may be called a vasana. I just call it a very natural human response. I don't even consider it a vasana. It's not harmful and it doesn't cause suffering. It's obviously a benefit.

We know what's harmful and what's not harmful. You know the actions you've performed that have been harmful, and you know the actions you've performed that have been beneficial. You know what I mean? There's really not much to analyze about it.

Often, love can turn into a romantic story of illusion and suffering, and of course, that's an affliction. But feelings of love, gratitude and openness, those are not afflictions, they are beautiful responses to life. They are appearances that you know. They're obviously appearances that come and go. They are objects that you know. So, they are not the essential you. But in a healthy person, there's going to be more love and gratitude experienced and expressed, more caring expressed, more kindness expressed, and more generosity expressed. Those characteristics are just naturally the behavior of a benevolent, healthy person.

Are afflictions natural?

Well they're normal. But what I call the natural human condition is prior to afflictions. The free consciousness of a human being is benevolent. When you are free of this constricted self, you're free to love, you're free to be generous, you're free to be caring, you're free to be kind, and you're free to be giving because you don't need so much for yourself. There is no need to hold on to an idea of self and have it as a wall between you and others. Of course, because you're happy, you want everyone to be happy. This is just very natural, isn't it?

I don't consider that an affliction or a vasana. I consider it the natural human condition. The natural human condition in a healthy mind is generous, kind, caring, loving, and benevolent. That's what Douglas Harding means when he says, "Can't you see, I'm just space for you to be." That's pure benevolence. A person with afflictions and especially with pathological afflictions is not space for others to be of course, because there's too much pathology and too much self focus. No judgement, it's just the way it is.

> Inquirer 4: It's funny because I never really realized that whenever an affliction comes up, there's a focus on it. There's either a focus on trying to solve it or trying to push it away. The continual focus is still on self. It's another movement of it, trying to move away from it, trying to improve it, or whatever. But it's always focused on self. Always.

That's right. Great, very good. So, instead, we have a holiday and know freedom. We know what's free. What is actually free from affliction? You essentially, the essential knowing. Who you are is knowing. If we want to say, "free from," we can, but I prefer to say, "The way of freedom is to be free." I don't say "free from," but if we want to use the phrase, then "free from affliction" is one good example.

> Inquirer 5: The thing I've noticed about regret is that there is this underlying assumption that the mind makes when it comes to regret. The assumption is that things

would have turned out better if I hadn't done that. I have no way of knowing that, but that's the assumption that the mind makes.

That can be one assumption. I don't know if I have that assumption, but sure that makes sense, that could be an assumption.

Yeah, it would've turned out better if only I had or hadn't done something. But things turn out the way that they turn out.

Things are as they are, right now.

That's right. Things are as they are, right now. So that's been helpful for me.

That's good.

Realizing this with regards to regret—to see that that's what the mind does—is a relief because then I'm really released.

That's all well and good, but I want to be even simpler than that. Now you know that, be finished. You never need to know it again. That's fine, good, and possibly very true, and there may be other responses to regret as well like, "I'm so wrong and I'm so evil," or "Some things may have changed differently," or whatever. All of these different responses may come from a feeling of regret, fine. I am just saying don't even go there. In my view, you know it, be finished—freedom.

What are you smiling about back there?

Inquirer 6: (Laughing) Just seeing that everything you say is true. I was doing the work yesterday and experienced something that I want to share. It's about all of the thoughts about people and I realized I was able to see everything (descriptions, illusions, desires) in my mind and was able to drop them. I felt some kind of sadness and grief like I was losing something. I know you told me it's normal.

Of course, it is. And that's a good thing to speak about because, especially in the new age communities, people believe that waking up is going to be nothing but peace and bliss. And it's going to happen on a spiritual retreat at the hot springs while servants fan you and feed you grapes. Guess what? Maybe there's some pain, suffering, and even fear and sense of loss. Why? Because you are waking up from the myths and fantasies you have believed your whole life! Realizing everything you have ever believed in the past is wrong can be shattering. So, of course, perhaps it is not pleasant at all. For some people, it's very unpleasant with tons of fear and a lot of sadness. Much worse than anyone here is experiencing. For some people, it is a major crisis—it's ripping those beliefs out of your head and destroying your world.

It's different for everyone. In my experience on the path, there was one brief period of intense fear, but when I finally recognized the truth, it was simple. I had already been through many impactful experiences and realizations. It's different for everyone.

Enlightenment isn't all roses and incense. It's ripping your world apart and seeing something completely different. You are losing every belief you have ever had. By waking up, you see that all the rest of it is a dream. This "you" that you believe is real is a myth, it's not existent, it's gone. Where is it? Show me. Go ahead.

I'm glad that you're giving all of this explanation. I don't feel that I'm nuts.

You don't feel that you're nuts? (Sal laughing) That's good, you're not nuts at all. You're crazy in a really good way if you ask me (everyone laughing). I think you have to be crazy to be at this intensive.

> *To take the risk and to lose my whole world—yeah. I was sharing with a friend yesterday that I realized all the thoughts I have in my mind about my friend and the people who are very close to me, including my children, are lies. All the thoughts are lies!*

Wow, that's amazing, that's big. Of course, you might feel sad about that.

> *Well, I feel regret that I wasn't able to see them in this light before.*

Okay, so you see that regret? Now be done. Have a holiday. This is a good example right now. You have a holiday and that feeling of regret is still going to be here, isn't it? Does it mean you're not on holiday? No. You are knowing—I am here, now and everything is included, the feeling of regret, my voice, the mountain out there, etc. Just keep knowing who you are. That's all.

> *I feel liberated; total liberation from all the lies. I will have new and fresh eyes that I will be able to see my family and friends with. In the moment, I will be with them and get rid of all those illusions, images and all of that. It's very powerful.*

> *Another thing I started noticing is that unconditional love is coming out. It's very interesting to see this showing up.*

That's very good. What is unconditional love? It means everything is included. Everything is included unconditionally, now, isn't it? Is there any condition for anything that's appearing, now? If there's no mind, no thought, are there any conditions? Everything is as it is, unconditionally so. That's unconditional love, isn't it? Your nature is that.

That's the beauty of it. I just realized that too. It's a totally new, fresh life. And at the same time, the heart and the love are still there.

Of course, it is and maybe it's going to be there more, in a healthy way—more benevolent.

Inquirer 7: The situation that came up with my ex-boyfriend is funny because the text messages are still continuing, and it's so nice to see that I don't have to feel like a victim anymore. Also, I don't have to feel like I have to be a certain way with him. It's like I can stand my ground because I see the dynamic and it's a relief. Before, I think I would put myself in the victim box of, "You've done this to me and blah, blah, blah." Now, the victim story doesn't even come up and it's just another event that's happening in this moment. It's not bad and it's okay.

Wonderful, that's great.

Also, it's different with my current illness. Before, when I would get sick, I would think, "Oh, poor me, I'm sick." It's so funny because I can see what that story was doing for me—absolutely nothing other than keeping an identity in place.

Yes, an identity and suffering. It was adding suffering on top of the sickness—psychological suffering.

Right, because if you're just sick without the story then it's just more sensations. You just feel more in the body and it may not feel great, but that's also just known. That's also just there.

Wonderful, great. Good share.

Just Know and Be Free

I want to go back to the call last week, which I found very useful, where you were talking about vasanas and when they come up. You said, "Just know it and then be free," or something like that. The "be free" part I get, it's "have a holiday" or a holiday happens. The "just know it" part I don't really get. I think you said something about "just impersonally know it." When I'm in the middle of something, I can't help but know it in the ordinary sense. I mean it's happening, I know it's happening, and I can have a holiday. But I think you meant something—or maybe you didn't—when you said, "Just know and then be free." I'm not sure what the "just know it" part means.

Okay, that's a good question. I'll see if I can make that a little clearer. We all have afflictions. Everyone has their own particular afflictions, whatever they are—anger, jealousy, anxiety. We all have them. Some are more troubling than others. We may have one or more that are very troubling for us. So, whatever it is for you (let's say it's anger), you know that's true, right? You know you have that affliction. You're not fooling yourself about it.

Whenever that affliction starts to appear, you know the affliction is appearing, right? You can feel it right away. So, I say, "Do nothing about it" because you know that's what it is. You don't have to deny it, you don't have to acknowledge it and say, "Oh, there's that anger again" because that gives it too much power. You don't have to witness it because if you witness it, that's admitting that it exists. It takes no time to know it's there because you know. The knowing of it is just in a millisecond, and in that millisecond, you get off and know your essential being, here and now.

In other words, by saying "know it and have a holiday," I'm saying don't give it one iota of juice.

> *Since it arises in consciousness, you know it by definition. You have to know it for it to be in consciousness. Is that all you mean, to just notice it's there and then have a holiday?*

Yes, and it's subtle what I want to impart here. It's true, you notice it's there. But I want to give it as little validity as possible. I don't want you to notice that it's there and keep noticing that it's there. Some people say, "Just witness it." I don't want you to witness it either because then you're saying there's something to witness. I don't want you to acknowledge it because if you acknowledge it, it's like giving it permission to be there. It's a little subtle what I'm trying to say here because, you're right, it's just to notice, but I want to say it as subtle as possible. The instant that it's noticed, get off and be free, immediately. You see what I'm trying to say? And in doing that, you're giving it no power at all. It's like you are immediately, saying, "No."

> *Okay, I still don't get it because it sounds kind of like a holiday. The "know it" or "notice it" part is almost automatic, and may or may not trigger a holiday, but it seems like whatever is enough to trigger a holiday is maybe all you're talking about?*

Yes, it's just have a holiday, basically. It's just know the way of freedom is to be free. When an affliction is appearing, the way of freedom is to not do anything with that affliction at all. It's to have a holiday. So yes, that's exactly what I'm saying. But what I want to make sure I'm clear about is to give it no value at all. Not even the value of acknowledging its presence. Just don't even acknowledge it. Do you see what I mean? It's hard for me to express this, but you have to see it in your own experience. I think you will get it then.

Yes, you know it. Let's say envy appears, you know it, immediately. Then turn away, be free. You see? It's just have a holiday. Dealing with afflictions this way is completely different from the way we usually deal with the afflictions. We have been conditioned to want to do something, like witness them. Don't witness them.

> I'm glad you're saying that I don't have to do anything.
> That's good. My particular affliction is fear, that's for
> sure. It doesn't come up very often, but when it does, it's
> usually at 4:00 AM and it's very intense. Generally, it's
> this kind of hum in the background and when it gets
> intense, I do say, "Okay, have a holiday." Then absolutely
> nothing seems to happen, and I say "Shit, it's not
> working."

What do you mean, "It's not working?" This is the key right here. What's not working? What is not happening?

> I don't seem to be able to shift my attention in that
> moment to aware knowing.

Are you sure? Or do you just mean that the fear doesn't go away?

> Well, both. The fear definitely doesn't go away and I'm
> thinking, "Well, dammit, same old shit."

Fear isn't going to go away, immediately. At the same time the fear is in the body, be knowing "I am." Is it possible to know "I am" when there's fear, without giving it any juice? Do you see what I mean? Does that happen sometimes?

Yeah, I mean I know "I am."

That's a holiday. Even if fear is there, you know you are. It's the knowing that I'm talking about—the Self-knowing. I know I am. Yes, there happens to be some fear, but I know I am. You see?

I think so. So, when I have a holiday, like right now, it's very clear. I know "I am." But it's not so clear in the middle of fear or some other strong emotion.

It's just as clear. There's just a feeling of fear that's back there pulling you to attend to it.

Yeah, I think in the back of my mind (and maybe not so much in the back of my mind), I'm expecting all my attention to go to the "I am" and everything else will disappear.

Right, and it won't. It won't do that. That's not a holiday. A holiday is not about changing the feelings that are there. A holiday is, while the feeling is there, to know that you are. Even if the feeling is very strong, if there's still some knowing, that means some light is shining through. The more holidays happen, the more intense feelings can disappear.

So, are you saying it's something you get better and better at? The habit gets better ingrained, better able to turn away?

Yes, and let me be clear, we all have some afflictive tendencies that are stronger than others. To expect those to be immediately resolved is not realistic. But truth is still true, and knowing freedom, now, is the way to resolve them, more and more, and over time.

It sounds like you're saying that over time, you actually do go more into holiday.

Over time, if you are devoted to truth and remain on holiday, more and more your afflictive tendencies can resolve.

Okay, then it's a little bit like learning any skill.

It's changing a habit. The current habit is, when that fear appears, the stories start about the fear, and you go into those stories and start "poor me-ing" yourself to death or whatever else the mind does. Do you know what I mean? We all do it, not just you.

Well, often when the fear is strong at 4:00 AM, there just seems to be fear. I'm not even sure what the story is, there's just a physical sensation.

Whether there's a lot of story or not, the attention given to the fear gives the fear juice. If you fall for the fear, the fear gets juice. If you ignore the fear, even though it's there, and have some light at the same time, that light, over time, will start outshining the fear.

The light of knowing, this "I am," may seem vague at first, but it's not. The sun is always fully shining. The light may seem to be vague, but honestly, I'm not kidding, it's always shining and if you have the intention for freedom, it will outshine everything else.

Okay, that's helpful.

It has to because that fear lives on and thrives on your belief in it. Through the belief in it, you give it juice. It thrives on that food. You take the food source away by attending instead to yourself—I am free, I am. Even if it seems subtle or vague at first, if you keep doing it, that will become more dominant. Over time, that light (it's the light of you, it's the sun of truth), will outshine that fear.

One thing that's going on for me is that, even after all this time, when not much is going on emotionally, like right now, and I have a holiday, the first thing I notice after my thoughts is my body. And when nothing is going on, it feels pretty good. I mean, there's a lot of energy and juice in there, and I associate that good feeling with having a holiday. And when I'm having a holiday during fear, I'm thinking, "Well, where's that good feeling?"

Okay, and I know you've heard me say this before because we've known each other for a while, but it's a very stubborn habit we all have—a holiday has nothing to do with an experience. Any experience can be there.

In six years, I've said this a hundred thousand times, and I'll probably have to say it a hundred thousand more times—a holiday is not about feeling good. A holiday is not about feeling anything. A holiday is about knowing that you are. Knowing, Self-knowing, "I am." That's what a holiday is. That's only what a holiday is.

When a holiday happens, you know who you are, and thoughts stop for a moment. If there's a fear or any other emotion going on, it will still be there. And then you think, "I don't feel blissful, I'm not having a holiday." That's a mistake. If you think that, then of course, you're never going to get the message. That expectation is very detrimental. Why? Because then you're still valuing experience and expecting experience to make you feel whole and complete.

From the very first day that I work with people, I tell them that freedom, liberation has nothing to do with an experience, any experience—feeling good, feeling bad, etc. I say it from the very first day I work with anyone. And then, I say it a thousand more times. Still they come back and say something like this. It's a habit that you got through no fault of your own. We all think that.

Of course, we all want to feel good. So, we think, "Well, I know who I am, but I feel like shit. This is not a holiday." Well, yes, it is a holiday because you know who you are. That's it.

But another inquirer said that he was totally at peace when he had a holiday during a health scare. Something has certainly changed in his experience.

Yes, after doing this work for five years. Of course, the more you are on holiday, the more your overall experience will be peace, but peace is not a holiday, knowing is.

Well, then something does change. I mean, if there weren't any expectation of some kind of change, I'd get out of this.

As I said earlier, it will. It does become better. It does outshine everything, and it does make life better, smoother, and more peaceful. But it doesn't happen by expecting. It happens because you stop thinking that a holiday is going to make you feel differently. Because if you think that a holiday is going to make you feel good, and you don't feel good, then you're giving that feeling juice again.

Right.

You see what I'm saying? It has to be clearly understood. A holiday, knowing who you are, has nothing to do with what you're feeling like. You know who you are, period. You know who you are with a good feeling or a bad feeling.

It could be that you have a really great feeling and you're not on holiday at all. You're totally engaged in that feeling, not knowing anything about who you are, and you're feeling great, right? That doesn't mean you're on holiday, just because you're feeling good. In the midst of feeling good, have a holiday, and see, "Ah, here I am, and there's a good feeling here." Then, in the midst of feeling bad, have a holiday, "Ah, here I am, and there's a bad feeling here." See, then you shift. You have a shift of knowing, to knowing who am I. Who am I? The good feeling, the bad feeling? No, they come and go.

"I am" doesn't come and go, does it? It's always the same every time you look.

> *In fact, my cue, when I'm in the middle of a strong feeling, is "Well, what's here all the time?"*

Right.

> *My mind is not very interested in it because it's not very exciting or cool, it's just very ordinary. It's as ordinary as it can get, it's what's here all the time.*

It's the best thing in the whole world, man. I swear to you. If you were here on this retreat, you would see. After five days, people are knowing ordinary is the best. We're all sitting around like, "Wow, ordinary is the best." It's the best. Why? It's the end of all of the suffering, belief, desire, fear, wanting more, being special and expecting transcendental states. It's the end of all of that nonsense. It's peace. Ordinary consciousness is peace. And that's the best experience. I had all the other ones and the best experience is peace—ordinary consciousness. "Ahhh, thank you."

Of course, at first, it doesn't seem that ordinary consciousness is so exciting because we're used to having exciting things happening. We think that's good, but on the other end of everything exciting is a letdown. Then you get tired of that after a while and you just want "Ahhh, peace, thank you."

Look at Ramana Maharshi, do you think he was in some heightened state of excitement? He was just sitting there like, "leave me alone, don't bother me, peace." That's the ultimate, man. That is the ultimate. And it's found in ordinary consciousness.

Now, it's easy for you to recognize this beautiful light of knowing. So, let that strengthen your resolve when the fear happens again. Maybe, it feels overwhelming with the fear, but in the midst of that, you know who you are, and a crack of light starts, just a crack of "I know who I am." If you stay true to that, it's going to start outshining, over time, the fear. It becomes more dominant, more known to you.

As I've been saying the last few days, it becomes more your default condition. Now, we are conditioned to always default to whatever experience is happening. That's all we've known our whole life. We default to thoughts, we default to feelings, we default to fear, desire and experiences. We default to that because that's all we've known our whole life. It's all we have been taught. And that's a habit that's got to be shifted to defaulting to freedom. Soon that becomes your default condition. This is how it works.

If you're authentically true to "Who I am" (forget freedom, forget peace, forget bliss), if you're just authentically true to "Who I am," you can't lose. It takes time, but you can't lose. If you're authentically true to it, you can't lose.

> *I just want to make sure I'm not doing it wrong. How can you be inauthentic?*

It just means you're more interested in other things. You're still interested in the experiences, in the mind, in the story, and in supporting the fear and the desire. It's just a habit, you see. "Well, apparently I was more interested in that whole thought stream rather than freedom because I went into it." If you want freedom, here it is. If a story comes up and you go into that story and follow it along, that's what you want. Obviously, that's what you want. Just be honest. There's nothing to judge about it. If I went into a story for an hour, clearly that's what I wanted. If I want freedom, here it is. You see?

Believe it or not, it's that simple. But it's not easy because our habit is to default to the experiences and the thoughts, that's how we've been trained. It's who we think we are, it's what we think is important and valuable. Up till now in our lives, we haven't had another alternative, so that's our default condition, by habit.

I'm saying, let's make a new default condition, freedom. Who am I? Free. Who am I? Free. Who am I? Free. Until you just say, "Don't bother me, I'm free, just leave me alone." You see what I mean? Just like Ramana Maharshi. "Don't bother me, leave me alone."

Shadow Work

This brings up a thought about blind spots. I think a teacher who is well established in knowing who they are will be able to see things a person recently liberated won't catch, like shadows or aspects of the persona that aren't seen. Is this a reality?

I have heard about teachers whose sole focus is working with "shadows." I say jump—be nothing. If you admit there is a shadow, then you are right back on that carousel. What does a shadow mean? You may say something stupid or do something stupid. Is this a shadow?

I imagine it would be something like doing damage or hurting others and thinking it is fine because I feel, "I am done." I have heard of some well-known spiritual teachers who have done some really horrible things to their followers and caused a lot of damage.

That is true. This shows a person still has some need for control or power, which is clearly not freedom. Some teachers are megalomaniacs and sociopaths who are brilliant spiritual philosophers. They have many spiritual experiences that they derive their teachings from and people fall for that.

If we paint a picture of perfection that sages like Ramana or the Buddha have attained, how do we know the picture is true? If we think there are some shadows that have to be dealt with (and what is a shadow, but a psychological event), then that is back on the carousel of mind.

> *I hear what you are saying, and what I meant by shadow is more like something I don't see. I am doing some activity that I am not even aware of.*

Right, keep recognizing your essential nature, which is *nothing*, pure and untouched. Then, see how you function, which is seeing shadows as they appear. If you cause harm, you are going to know. Shadow work may be beneficial for some people, but when it is time to jump, it is time to jump.

Suffering

The Buddha Says, "Life is Suffering."

I have heard it said that one of the Buddha's teachings is that life is suffering, and I am wondering how this relates to what we are talking about?

He also said there was a way out of it—the four noble truths. Life circumstances appear that are difficult. You could label physical ailments that arise in the body, as suffering. Or you could call tough life circumstances that you are dealing with, suffering. I do not. This is just the Play of Life. Physical ailments and tough circumstances are a fact of life. Nevertheless, it is possible to know what is free from suffering and to end the suffering caused by the mental loops that we go over and over, endlessly. Going over and over in the mind why an event occurred, or what could have been done differently, is the suffering that can end. Also, the suffering of future-based fear and desire can end. In the absence of those habitual and ultimately unnecessary tendencies of suffering, peace is realized.

This body is like a resistor in a radio. When electricity hits the resistor in a radio, the radio comes to life. My view is that when life touches this body, it springs to life. When the body dies, there is no more resistance and life no longer animates the body. Even if you are fully at ease, there is going to be some resistance. Sometimes there can be experiences that create a lot of resistance, and this is felt as emotional or physical pain. This is just resistance, and this will not end. When Ramana had cancer, the people who were there said he was in a lot of pain.

That is what I was thinking. There is this body-mind that is going to experience whatever it is going to experience, and I could label it suffering, but what perpetuates the suffering is the idea that I can get out of it by doing something. This whole idea that getting enlightened will end this resistance feels really crippling.

Now, when I am having some difficult thoughts or emotions, and a holiday arises, they seem to lessen.

When you have a holiday and strong emotions are there (even though the thoughts have lessened or stopped), you see that the emotions are just included with everything else that is appearing. It is all-inclusive. When you are focusing exclusively on the emotion, it perpetuates.

The real suffering that can be resolved is the internal thought looping that keeps everything going endlessly. In the midst of a tough circumstance, when we have a holiday and recognize our essential nature is free and includes everything, it is very empowering. This is how you really resolve everything. If you get through the worst of it, by recognizing in a holiday that even the worst thing has passed, then what can touch you after that?

Suffering as Grace

I've realized that unless I make holidays a priority, it can get bad for me. And recently, it has gotten bad at times. By bad, I mean the thoughts, the old habits—taking drugs. It's like the pain is propelling me forward and making me get serious about this. I notice that I have lots of things that distract me from life. It's almost like I have a choice to have a holiday or go down that rabbit hole. It's easy for me to get caught up in the past, the sensations, and the thoughts. I feel like what you're talking about is that suffering is the grace that forces me to wake up.

That's right. That's exactly what I'm talking about, and I think most people can relate to what you are saying. If you look at most people who have become genuine inquirers, something has propelled them to do that. Quite often, it's some kind of suffering. Occasionally, someone shifts from a spontaneous spiritual experience and they are compelled to inquire. However, I think more often there's some kind of suffering that propels a person to start inquiring.

One thing you wrote was that we're not special. I've realized that my whole life I've thought my suffering was special, and I was different from everybody else. My suffering was just different than yours. And boy, that specialness is just kicking my ass.

Right. Well, everyone's suffering is unique in a way because all experiences are unique to the individual. But it's not special because everyone has suffering. Let's face it, some people have had more troubling circumstances in their life, and some people have had a fairly easy life. There is no doership, and there is no judgment. Some people have had a rougher ride because of circumstances. And, of course, it becomes more challenging.

However, the way of freedom is still the same. What you're saying is perfectly true. Although I know you're just using the word "choice," it's not a choice to have a holiday. It was not a choice for me to fall to my knees and plead for help (see Introduction, *Liberation IS*). There was no choice about it. I was just down, begging.

From one perspective, that can be seen as a calamity. For instance, my mother read the first book, and when we spoke about this, she said, "I'm so sorry you had to go through that." I told her it's the greatest thing that's ever happened to me. I don't see it as anything but incredible grace. Grace just hammered me into a complete shift. The particular things that cause you to suffer are grace because they may force you to jump. Again, you can't choose to jump or choose to surrender to the experience, as some people believe. What happens, happens.

When we take palliatives, like drugs, for example, it makes everything okay for the moment, but it doesn't allow for the crash that can lead to a shift. With palliatives, it's just status quo forever. Had I taken a Valium that night, I would have fallen asleep comfortably and nothing would have changed. I would have continued along the same road and the status quo would have continued.

You don't choose to want to have a holiday. You don't choose any of this. Anything in your mind that compels you, you didn't choose or create. If you could choose, would you choose to suffer? Of course not. Holidays just happen on their own because the seed has been planted in your mind. Now, since your intention is for freedom and you've recognized your essential being is free, and you see the value of that, when painful things happen, it's going to trigger a holiday.

Also, you can't cultivate your intention as some New Age concepts proclaim. Those ideas are unexamined ignorance. It just is or isn't. If more suffering is needed, then more suffering is needed, until it gets to be too much. When it becomes too much to handle, then it crashes. If you keep taking the soothing palliatives, it will never really become too much, and the status quo will continue.

Having a crash is one way and it doesn't have to be that way. If you're having holidays a lot, seeing the value, and staying authentic to this work, it is just as effective. But it doesn't mean a crash like that won't happen. It could.

Let's have a holiday, now.

HOLIDAY

Notice that there's no past.

There is no past!

Recognize, what do you want?

Do you want to continue to be special with that suffering?

Do you want to keep going over and over the stories and suffer?

Or, do you want freedom?

There's nothing to choose about it either,
you just see what's true.

It's not a judgment.

Obviously, if you go in the stories, that's what you want.

You're the one who knows the desire. You're not choosing it or creating it. You don't have anything to do with it. You're the knowing of what's going on, and what's going on here is that there is the interest or compulsion to go into stories. No judgment; that's just obviously what's true. Why? Because if you want freedom, here it is. And there's no choosing that either. We just see what is, what's true.

We're just being honest here. There's still the desire or the belief that there's something important going on in there, something that you have to attend to, and something you have to suffer for. Maybe there's the belief that it's your lot in life to suffer, that you deserve it, or that the suffering means something. You just have to see for yourself, without judgment, if that's what is going on. Then, see for yourself if truth is what you want.

I know truth is what you want, but there's a momentum of negative impressions, which can overpower the desire for truth, and in those moments, you want to go into that. That's why valuing truth, and being authentic, works. It takes discrimination, authentic inquiry into truth and a strong intention for freedom. This work is simple, but it is not trivial. There is a lifetime of bad habits and they need to be outshone by the light of knowing.

> *Inquirer 2: Sal, I just wanted to add something. Once I decided that I wanted to be happy, it was just over with.*

Okay, but you didn't decide it. That intention just appeared for you.

> *Yeah, that's right. Once I saw what was real, it was an instant game-changer. I was no longer willing to compromise or suck up to anything in life. I was just not willing to compromise anymore. There was a seeing. Once I saw that putting my hand over the flame of the candle burned me, there was no more choice.*

That's right; and that's what this whole conversation has been about, exactly that. That's another beautiful metaphor as well.

> *I just stopped making compromises. I became selfish according to a lot of people (laughs).*

In a way, that is very true. Yes, "Abide as the Self," says Ramana. Be very Self*ish* to truth.

Belief in Past Causes Suffering

It's hard to swallow that the past is only a memory because some things that have happened in the past are so strong that they come again and again, and they create feelings. I very often get caught up in it. Do you have any words about that?

Sometimes the brain replays thoughts from the so-called past, now. Sometimes that can cause an emotional response, either pleasant, neutral or unpleasant. If you still have some belief in their validity, or that they in some way have power over you, then they will cause you to suffer.

When we come to know what is true—there is only now, there is nothing behind the curtain—we recognize there is no past. Once that is truly reconciled, these thoughts, which seem to be referring to something that happened in the past, will no longer interest you. It may sound radical, but there is a reason to know this. It is to come to know that freedom is only now. Let's have a holiday, now.

HOLIDAY

This knowing is now, isn't it?

Jump off the carousels of time,
don't refer to mind at all, and
see that the only thing we know, in truth,
is what is, is, here and now.

In that, we see there is no past.

Just be honest.

The point of realizing this radical view (which is true), is so you can stop being a victim of past or future. What we are doing here, what we are coming to know, is the natural human condition of mental and emotional health. Health is now. The way of freedom is now. There is no true health in the psychological carousel. Ultimate health is now. I say, "Know truth and be free." Recognize that freedom is now. If you see the value in this, you will naturally lose interest in the past.

You can't control what thoughts appear in your mind; there is no doer of thoughts. But, if there is still a belief that those thoughts have some meaning, importance, or some power over you, you will still be victimized by those thoughts and suffer because of them. When you are reconciled that there is only now, those thoughts can come, but they appear more like an old dog with no teeth, sitting on a porch, completely harmless, but still barking as a cat walks by. The dog still barks because that is its habit, but it has no power, it is impotent. It is just its nature to bark. Actually, that is how it is with most thoughts.

If you don't give those thoughts the power of belief (belief being the on switch to confusion and suffering), those thoughts are just like an old, toothless dog barking on the porch. Not very scary, is it? They appear and disappear, no harm done, and you remain, untouched.

Political Beliefs

I have to admit, I was somewhat losing interest in the group calls as people were repeatedly moaning about our current president. I have no interest in that. I understand what is, is, and it is all just happening, but enough already. For me, the only use is if it leads us away from obsessing with useless mind duality (us and them) and toward living on holiday. In the last session, I think there was a shift in that direction.

I understand that sentiment, and I want to look into this issue of politics in the light of the reason we all come together, which is liberation.

Let's say a father has a son. This father is an evangelical, right-wing Christian with the appropriate self-righteous indignation about what is right and what is wrong. He knows! He fully believes, as taught to him by his religious teachings, that homosexuality is an abomination against God. A truly unacceptable crime that will send the perpetrator straight to hell. Did God come down and tell him this and ordain him as the arbiter of right and wrong, and give him the mandate to judge everyone who is on the "other side?" Of course not, they are just beliefs.

When his son grows up, it turns out he is gay, and the father suffers tremendously. He loves his son, but now he judges and condemns him. He even kicks his son out of the house. He is compelled to because he knows he is right about homosexuality being wrong. He fears his son's eternal damnation but also feels very guilty about how he is treating him. He thinks he is suffering because his son is gay.

But is he suffering because his son is gay? No, of course not. He is suffering because of his beliefs. If he did not have those beliefs, he would not suffer. The entire world of his suffering is happening solely in his own mind, nowhere else. Certainly not in reality.

Now, we liberals think we are suffering because of the current President and the Republican Party. Well, is that really why we suffer? Because of what they do? Can we not see our own self-righteous indignation about what is right and what is wrong? Has God come down and ordained us the arbiters of right and wrong and given us the mandate to judge everyone on the "other side?" No, they are just beliefs. Do we really know what is in the best interest of the world in the overall picture? What arrogance!

Do we suffer because of the President? No, of course not. We suffer because of our beliefs. If the President was aligned with our beliefs, would we suffer? Nope. Are the people suffering who agree with him and whose beliefs are aligned with his? No, they are happy.

The entire political horror show you are suffering through is only a movie in your own mind. If you need proof it is all just happening in your own mind, think about this. When you are in deep sleep, where is the world? Where is the President? Where is any of it? It is NOT. There is no world in deep sleep, is there? But YOU still exist, obviously. What is not there? Mind.

In the morning, consciousness, the mind, wakes up in the body. And it goes like this: I—AM—THE WORLD—IS. In a split second, you become aware you exist, and at the same time, the world appears. That is ALL happening in YOUR MIND. Everything you see, believe, and judge is happening nowhere else but in your own mind. There is no world OUT THERE separate from your mind. And again, the proof is, when you fall asleep, there is no mind—so there is no world.

All your suffering because of the President is really just a big cosmic joke happening in your own mind and you are falling for it. What do you want? Find out. Do you want to suffer, or do you want freedom? This is not a judgment. Simply be honest with yourself and see what is true. What do you want? Most of us want:

- To be right

- To feel justified in our suffering

- To blame others for it and be a victim

- To judge others and feel superior

- To hold on to our own sense of self/ego, which is our beliefs (i.e. I am a liberal)

- To think we know what is right or wrong as if God has granted us some secret, inside information.

These identities are deeply ingrained and habitual, and the last thing we want is to be free of any of them. The work we do is about coming to know what is free from all those ailments of suffering, which are all happening only in our own mind, and to be that freedom! Sat Chit Ananda.

Freedom is not found in correcting, judging, or blaming others. It is not found in thinking we know what the world needs, or that it is we who need to fix it. Also, it is not found in being led around like good sheep by culture (media, politicians, schools, religion, etc.).

Freedom is about seeing what is true, in and for yourself. You will never be free trying to correct anyone or anything else "out there." And what good does engaging, pondering, judging, condemning, and feeling superior about all the political information being fed to you by the media do anyway? Does it benefit you or anyone else even one iota? Or, does it do one thing only—make you suffer! Just be honest about it. It does nothing but exhaust the very life out of you.

If you want to be beneficial to yourself and to others, come to peace within yourself. And see what, if anything, the world needs from you.

Feelings - Emotions

When you have a genuine intention for freedom and continue to know yourself, in a holiday, as the free, all-inclusive knowing of whatever is appearing, instead of following the thought stream, then emotions pass in a timely, flowing way, and are harmless. That is the way of freedom.

A River Flowing, With No Dam

I was listening to an old part II audio, and you said something about emotional turmoil being really great because it can force you to end the suffering. You pointed out that, in the middle of the turmoil, you can have a holiday and see the truth of who you are. You were very specific to point out that a holiday wouldn't necessarily change anything in the way you're feeling, but that you could use the unpleasant feelings as a prod to end suffering.

Right now, I'm in the middle of quite a few unpleasant feelings, and I have been using them as prods to have holidays. When I have a holiday, it's quite clear. Then, it goes back into the same old shit, and I'm left wondering what is happening? There must be some kind of shift that occurs or there's no point to this. I can see the truth, but there's still this tidal wave of emotional crap going on.

Because I don't believe that there's a doer, or that we create anything, I don't see a someone here to get rid of what's appearing. Whatever is appearing now was not created or chosen by you. It just is as it is. There's only now, and whatever is now cannot be any different than it is now. Being reconciled with that alone is peace and freedom.

Despite that, the idea comes in, "Well, I don't like this, so let me change it and make it something better." But the truth remains—now it's unpleasant. That's the truth. When a holiday happens, it's clear that your essential being, here and now, is not limited to the painful emotional feeling. Yes, the feeling is here, you didn't create it, you didn't choose it, and it can only be as it is, now. However, you are not limited to this feeling.

In a holiday, you see that the feeling is only one aspect of the manifold experiences that are happening, here and now. All the visual, auditory and sensory experiences are included, and they are just part of the countless things going on, right now. The feeling is not the only thing.

When the unpleasant feeling is believed to be the most important thing and attention focuses on it exclusively, then suffering is greatly enhanced because that's the only thing that seems to be happening in that moment. When we start working together, we see how that feeling of exclusive focus is constricting and claustrophobic when compared to the knowing of unfocused attention, which is all-inclusive. For all of us, when something emotionally painful is appearing, it grabs the attention, and our habit is to attend to that, exclusively. Then, all there is, is that pain and nothing else. But, in a holiday, that pain becomes part of the whole environment, part of the whole milieu that's happening, not just the only thing that's happening.

That is the first aspect, to see right in the moment that it's not the only thing going on. You see that everything else that is happening is also happening now, and you are all of that. Your knowing encompasses all of it, not just that one thing. That's the first aspect that can bring a little bit of relief, now.

The other thing, of course, is the more attention focuses on that one thing, the more we believe that one thing. And the more we believe that one thing, the more power that one thing has to stick around. The power of attention is like food to that one thing. It's a vicious cycle because more thoughts come, and more thoughts come, and more thoughts come, and that makes the feeling worse, and getting into feeling worse brings more and more thoughts. Those two feed each other.

A holiday is jumping off that. The more you stay jumped off that, the more it moves to the background, not the foreground. The more it's in the background, and not fed with the energy of thought, thought, thought, thought... the more it passes on its own, in a natural timely way, like a river flowing by. When attention is focused on something and thoughts are endless, it's like putting a dam in the middle of the river; it creates resistance.

The thing is, we all live in this world, and sometimes circumstances are annoying or unpleasant, or worse, even tragic. Then, this body-mind organism, which is the experiencing mechanism, experiences that. If something unpleasant is happening, this body's response is unpleasant. We then think, "I have to get rid of it" because of course, we don't like it. However, we didn't have anything to do with creating it, and it's completely natural for the body to respond that way.

What then is there to "do" about it? The only thing one can "do" (if you want to use the word "do") is to be on holiday; recognize what is true; and see that the one experience is only part of the whole landscape. Then, it becomes less of a focus, less distracting, and it flows by.

To sum it up, freedom is not arriving at some final state of always feeling pleasant and never being distracted or bothered by something. That would be nice. Does it happen? Maybe. But, as long as we live in the world of relationships, it's normal and natural for the body to experience unpleasantness. Moreover, whether it's possible to get to that idealized state, or not, what good does it do you now? What's true is that there is something unpleasant happening, now. Thinking, "Well, I'm not there yet, and one day I'll get to the place where this doesn't bother me anymore," is ridiculous. That in itself is bondage. What place? What future? When?

The only thing that's true is this, now. The only thing to do is to recognize that it's just part of the whole environment. Don't expect it to feel good because it won't feel good. Expecting it to feel good or hoping it will feel good gives it more energy. It's more resistance and leads to more thoughts along the line of, "There's something wrong with me," or "I'm not enlightened yet because I still have this painful experience."

I'm human, I have experiences and they come, and they go. That's what is. Why argue with what is?

> *That's the part I don't get. I mean, certainly, when I first started seeking a long time ago, that's what I thought enlightenment was—being untouched by anything. Doing this work, all of that notion went away pretty quickly. But what you're talking about I still don't quite get.*
> *Everything still happens, but there's a difference.*

You have to see for yourself if what I'm saying is true. I think you can see that when there's something emotionally painful happening and the focus is only on that, then that pain is all the landscape in that moment. Whereas in a holiday, it's only part of the landscape, and you can see there is some relief from it in the moment. When you have a genuine intention for freedom and continue to know yourself, in a holiday, as the free, all-inclusive knowing of whatever is appearing, instead of following the thought stream, then emotions pass in a timely, flowing way, and you remain, unharmed. That is the way of freedom.

Inquirer 2: Thanks for bringing this up. I've been going through a lot of emotional stuff with a recent breakup, and what I find is that there have been so many years of suppressing feelings, and not wanting to feel, that it's almost like I'm actually learning how to feel my feelings again. Now, when these feelings come up, it's like I'm just noticing my feelings deeper. I'm becoming more intimate with them and just feeling the feelings without any story. Sometimes the story does pop up, but there's a depth of feeling, and it's like there are layers and layers which are quickly, and sometimes not so quickly, accessed. I feel like I'm really being with what is—really feeling the feelings. I'm just wondering what is the difference, if any, between just feeling what's here and knowing all of what's here?

What I say is that a feeling is not separate from who you are, and when you experience a feeling, you're actually experiencing yourself. Knowing is not separate from the feeling. If what's happening for you is that you are experiencing feelings without the story, that's what's happening. Without the story, there is no resistance to the feelings, which is good. Whatever feeling is now is not separate from you. It's the wave of the ocean, and feeling a feeling is being yourself in that way, in the moment.

Inquirer 1: I've heard of just letting feelings be without a story, and what I've noticed is that the intense feelings I'm having are almost always accompanied by a story about the future or the past. The feelings seem to rise and fall, and at certain times, I'll be occupied with something, and I'll have the thought, "Where did that feeling go?" They don't actually seem to be able to sustain themselves without a story.

That's why I say, "Have a holiday," because you jump off the story. Thoughts are very fast, and we can prove that to ourselves on a holiday, now.

HOLIDAY

Where'd the thoughts go? They're gone, but the feeling is not gone, is it? Because feelings are much slower, emotions are much slower. Without a story, feelings and emotions will resolve, naturally. If that story keeps going and is valued, the feeling won't ever resolve. It doesn't go anywhere, it just stays there. We can all see the mechanics of that ourselves.

A holiday is about knowing what's true, and in a holiday, we see that everything flows naturally—feelings come and go, like waves on the ocean. If there's a story, the wave stays, dammed up, in the middle, getting bigger and bigger, never resolving. Thoughts and emotions go hand in hand. One just lasts longer than the other.

You can try to get to a place where nothing is bothering you, but living in the world of form, in the world of relationships where things go "wrong" (girlfriend/boyfriend dumps you, you lose your job, etc.), you will experience emotional responses. It's completely natural.

Some people remove themselves from the world. Annamalai Swami, a disciple of Ramana Maharshi, was fully liberated after Ramana kicked him out of the ashram and told him to go live in a certain house and not talk to anyone. He lived there for fifty years, and never went more than 200 feet from that house. He didn't socialize, he didn't have a girlfriend or a wife—he just meditated and lived by himself. Obviously, he didn't have a lot of interpersonal turmoil coming up.

That's very doable. If it's one's intention to do that, it can be done. So far, it's none of our karmas. In the world, where there are a lot of conflicts and potential for things to come up, freedom is known in that context. Annamalai Swami didn't need to worry about anyone dying, he left his parents and his family when he was very young. He was by himself, alone. There was not much appearing to cause emotions to arise. We don't live like that, and freedom has to be seen within a different reference given regular daily experiences.

If something appears, you see that you didn't create it, and you didn't choose it. You had nothing to do with it, and there's only now. Since you're not the doer or the creator of what is and there's only now, what is can only be as it is. There's no other alternative than this. If this doesn't feel good, now, there's no alternative because there's nothing behind the curtain. This is it. This!

If this doesn't feel good, the mind comes in and says, "This is wrong, it has to be different. There's something wrong with me." Then, we go on the spiritual path, or we take drugs or whatever to avoid and resist what is. Well, that's one way, and it doesn't work very well. The other way is to know, to be reconciled, that what is, is. This is freedom.

Nevertheless, a breakup is painful, it elicits an emotional response, and guess what? That pain will pass. You know this without a shadow of a doubt—eventually, it will pass because everything passes. Nothing stays. Nothing. You can even see during the day, there are plenty of times when it's not there.

If you know nothing stays, then what's to sweat? Also, in a holiday, you know you're free of it because you see you're everything—all of it—not just that. This leads you to be in a condition of surrender. You don't do surrender, like surrendering as a doership, but you're reconciled with what is. You didn't create it and it can't be any different than it is. Why argue?

Inquirer 2: I bring it up because it feels like a lifetime of suppressing those feelings, especially heart feelings. What I hear you saying about holidays or surrender is that it is just knowing what's here, to all its depths.

It seems like I have to bring my attention to areas in my body that are all stuck-up from being suppressed, and then be patient with them so they can slowly open and reveal whatever's really going on. I hear you saying that a holiday is like that, but without real intention. It's just full-on.

For you, that's what's appearing. It is what it is. The thing is there's no final state that's going to be attained. There is a final reconciliation—being reconciled with the fact that what is, is. That's final. What is, is. It's finished. Then, the river flows. Some people say surrendering to what is or accepting what is. I don't use those kinds of words. It's being reconciled. Being reconciled is not a doership, you don't do reconciling, you are reconciled. And you are reconciled by knowing what is true.

It doesn't take any great spiritual revelation to realize that what is, is. It's obviously true. That's it, it can't be any other way. That's pretty simple. To me, freedom—being finished—is just being reconciled with that undeniable fact.

You say you feel like you're going into the feelings, but the question is, "Who's going into the feelings and emotions?" If that's what's happening, that's what's happening, you're not creating that, either. It's understandable, in the face of uncomfortable or painful emotions, to want to do something about it using whatever methods we have learned (drinking, avoiding, going into it, giving it space, nurturing it like a child, analyzing, accepting, etc.). Naturally, we feel we have to do something there. But what if we just know, once and for all, this moment is as it is, can be no other way, and will pass. Then, there's no doer here anymore. There's no one doing anything—avoiding, resisting, investigating or going into. No one doing anything. It's just known.

This body-mind organism with its thoughts and emotions is like a flowing river. It's not stagnant. There's not one specific long-lasting Sal here. Every moment is different and it's Sal, Sal, Sal, Sal, Sal, Sal... Like a river, it's never the same. You look at the same spot in a river, but it's not the same river. It's constantly a new river, always a new river, always a new river. It's never the same river. It's never the same person, either.

There's the idea that we are a somebody. That's what ego is, and that's natural. It's okay, that's what is, but what's really happening is the river is flowing, and it's never the same river, ever. Not one millisecond is the river the same as it was one millisecond before. Same with the human being, the thoughts, the emotions, the cells of the body, everything is in a constant flow, constant change. Any thought of doing anything at all in there is just an idea and a belief. It's adding a thing that's trying to be someone that can have some control or hold on to something. What if there is no control?

Inquirer 2: If there's no control, there's no identity there.

That's exactly what I'm saying. If there's no control, there's no controller.

Inquirer 2: And if there's suppression happening...

There's the belief that there's someone here who has control. That's just another wave going by. It's a momentary wave that comes and goes. You don't create that, and it just flows by. Unless it becomes a thing, where you believe you have to be the one in control, analyzing and investigating, and doing all those things we talked about. Then it becomes damned up and sticks around.

Personally, I think it's exciting that there's no control. It's much more fun. I get excited thinking about it. It's freedom. I think you can sense that, right?

> Inquirer 2: Yes, it's wide open. It's unknown, and it is exciting because there is no control.

So, the question is, "What would it be like to have nothing, to know nothing, and to be no one?" Look... You have nothing, and you know nothing. You don't know why anything is the way it is. You don't know where it came from or where it's going. You have no idea. You are no one. You have no control and there's no doership. This is freedom.

Of course, this is the opposite of what the entire world has been taught. We have been taught to be someone and to know as much as possible about everything, including the meaning of life and what will happen after death. We are also told to have as much as possible, not just material goods, but in the sense of a personality and a self.

> Inquirer 2: There's still believing that these thoughts are me. That's still going on.

Fine. That comes and goes, too. It's all fine. It's more and more reconciliation. You didn't create the belief that those thoughts are you. Did you make that happen? It's just another thing that's flowing by. We may think, "Well, I still believe I'm my thoughts, let me get on the path for another twenty years and meditate because I'm the doer." However, that thought is just another wave going by, isn't it?

I'm talking about nothing, no control.

I don't think there's anything wrong with anything that's appearing. What is appearing can only be as it is. There's no alternative. How then can anything be wrong? It's all true. It's all right. If you're in pain because of a breakup, that's right, it's not wrong. Thinking it's wrong is a so-called problem. The pain is right, it can only be as it is.

There's nothing to do, there's nothing to get, there's nothing to fix, and there's nothing to attain. Anyway, there's no one to do any of those things, either. That is really what enlightenment is.

Heavy Feelings of Sadness

In the last week or so, I have experienced these "heavy" feelings of sadness, meaninglessness, and tiredness. I imagine it's in my body—in the heart, stomach, and throat area. Also, in the face, almost like a cold mask. During a holiday, it doesn't matter anymore at all and everything softens somehow. Maybe, I would describe it as compassion, love, and warmth.

What I wonder about is in a holiday there is relief/love/compassion, and at the same time, a knowing of that heavy feeling. There seem to be two separate things going on at the same time. I have read or heard about "everything is one, and there is no separation" and that makes me confused. Right now, I feel I'm not clear. Are these just thoughts and feelings, and should I not engage with them? They are not there exactly during a holiday.

Yes, during a holiday, which is simply consciously knowing that you exist, all the current appearances are included. On a holiday, we see that everything is included. A holiday is not about getting rid of anything or changing any appearance. How could you anyway since you are not the creator of them in the first place?

In a holiday, you see your essential being, Sat Chit, which is peace. At the same time, there is also whatever is appearing—the computer, the birds singing outside, the heavy feeling in the body, etc. In a holiday, we see that all those appearances are equal. By that I mean two things. One, all appearances are known to me equally. Two, all appearances are ephemeral—they appear, stay awhile and vanish into the aware knowing that I am essentially. They change, I do not.

The ocean is a commonly used metaphor for aware, essential being. On the surface of ocean appear waves. These waves may be ripples, or they may be tidal waves. They may be cold or warm. But they are all equal in that they all appear, stay a while, and then vanish back into the essential nature of their source, ocean. They are never separate from ocean. They are, in fact, ocean in appearance. That is how it is with all appearances of YOU.

You abide, untouched, aware, knowing peace, and on the surface of you appears some heaviness in the body. That heaviness is not separate from who you are, it is an expression or a manifestation—a wave on the ocean of you.

The work here is very classic stuff. It is not new. I just speak it in my own way from my own experience and voice, but it's been known for thousands of years. Instead of attending to the waves, which are endless, constantly changing and insubstantial, we ignore them, turn attention around to see ourselves, the source of it all.

What is the source? It is that which is knowing all of it. The knowing is you.

When you have a holiday, look and see, are you consciously aware that you exist? Please look and see now before proceeding.

HOLIDAY

That is, you knowing yourself, not knowing the passing objects. Even if heaviness is here, have a holiday, which means stop attending to that feeling and see—I am consciously aware that I exist. That conscious existence is peace—Sat Chit Ananda.

You cannot with volition change that wave. You can only again, and again, and again... (and, oh yes, again), have a holiday and know who you are essentially, peace. Be that peace. Knowing who you are means being who you are. Just keep doing it, over and over. In this way, you come to know yourself more and more as the peace underneath it all, the ocean, instead of the constantly passing, changing and disturbing waves. See for yourself over time, if those heavy feelings subside. The more you attend to them, the longer they will linger. The more you ignore them and be your essential peace, the more they will subside.

Worry and Anxiety

The holiday is a very fleeting experience for me. It's like seconds. My experience seems to be worry or anxiety, interspersed with fleeting moments of holidays. I am still hung up on wanting to feel better all the time. When I'm feeling anxious or worried, I think I'm missing something and there's something wrong. Even in the moment of a holiday, it's all very well, but I have the thought that I will be back in contraction before I know it.

It's understandable that you want to feel good all the time. Everyone does. There are no exceptions. That's why people are seekers. There's a broad spectrum of people who come to this work. At sixteen, Ramana Maharshi had a near-death experience, and in a second, it was finished for the rest of his life. It was over. Then there's the other end of the spectrum, people who never come to work like this, and even if they did, it would do them no good because they are pathologically ill (e.g., schizophrenics). Finally, there's the rest of us who fall in the middle.

In India, they speak about vasanas, which are the habits of the mind. The momentum of habits in a person's mind has a lot do with the experiences of this life. Some people have more trying or troubling life experiences. In that case, they may have stronger vasanas that compel stronger and more persistent thoughts and emotions. For some people, they're too strong and there's no possibility of them even recognizing anything like this. On the other hand, for some people, vasanas are very light.

All of us have vasanas that compel action. That's the way humans function. For you, there are things in your body-mind, for whatever the reason, and they seem to block your view of freedom. Seemingly, they overwhelm your experience of nothing. Occasionally, for a moment or few seconds, a holiday happens and you recognize what's here in the absence of those thoughts and emotions.

Every time you come to see that in a holiday, it's the same, isn't it? Peace is your essential nature. Underneath a river of ice is water. Occasionally, you see a crack in the ice and can look into the water. A holiday is seeing into a crack of mind and recognizing your essential being, which is always present. The point of this work is to familiarize yourself with your essential nature more and more until you recognize that it is actually the most dominant aspect of you. This takes time for everyone engaged in this work.

For most people, it will never happen because there has never been an initial crack for the water to be revealed. But for everyone here, if you continue to value truth, it will happen, as you have had a shift of knowing through inquiry. It just takes a little time. And it takes the intention and discrimination to be free. It takes recognizing whether or not what is revealed in a holiday is true. If you recognize it's true, you don't need to believe in anything. You know! That knowing along with the knowledge that all the other approaches you have attempted to soothe the stress have failed will compel you to keep having holidays. The more you do it, the more dominant it will become over time.

Recognizing your essential being is the beginning! Until you recognize your essential being, you haven't even begun. To simply assume all doubt will vanish because of one recognition is unrealistic. The momentum of habits in your brain is not something trivial. It takes time for doubt to be resolved for almost everyone.

Feelings Seem Bigger Than Me

I find with thoughts I seem to be able to have a holiday, but with feelings, they almost seem like they are bigger than me. When they get really bad, I call them "shame spirals." I want to get your thoughts on that.

Are they exacerbated by thoughts?

Yes.

This is a common misunderstanding of what a holiday is. Thoughts are very fast. They come, and they go, but feelings, especially strong sensations and emotions, are slow. They don't just come and go. When you have a holiday, in that brief amount of time, there are no thoughts. You don't stop the thoughts, but they can stop immediately for a few seconds. However, if there is an accompanying strong feeling response in the body, this will remain even if there are no thoughts. People then mistakenly think they are not having a holiday because the feeling is still there.

A holiday does not mean that all of a sudden everything disappears. Feelings don't have to disappear. You can be completely aware, open and all-inclusive with whatever is appearing. Let's have a holiday.

HOLIDAY

This knowing that is here includes everything in the room, right?

It includes the sensations you are having right now,
any thoughts that come and go, and
the words you are reading on this page.

Everything is included now, in this knowing.

Even though a sensation is still here,
you are still knowing this moment of now, right?

Be clear on this.

You know this knowing that is here
knowing itself and everything is included,
even the uncomfortable feeling.

Thoughts and feelings are completely linked. If attention stays on the thought pattern, it will extend the uncomfortable feeling longer and longer. Holidays do not immediately resolve strong, emotional feelings because they do not wax and wane as quickly as thoughts do. Nevertheless, attempting to deal with thoughts by explaining, justifying, analyzing, rationalizing or doing anything with them, will only reify them, give them power and this will feed the emotion.

Having a holiday will cut the thoughts. Coming to know who you are will take the food source away from the feelings and they will starve. However, you have to get real and keep jumping, and jumping, and jumping. Through this, you will begin to see that as soon as a thought or emotion appears, the natural movement will be to have a holiday, and the whole thought/emotion process will pass quickly or immediately and go practically unnoticed.

The more you are on holiday the more you will know your essential nature as free, and you will value that instead of attending to thoughts that produce the emotions. Going into the thoughts is just a habit. You were never trained any differently. You were told you have to do something with thoughts (i.e., control them, think positively, anesthetize them, change them, understand or analyze them, etc.). But the more you do with thoughts, the more power you give them to exist and take control.

I was trained to deal with the feelings.

How do you do that?

I just say I want to get away from the feeling.

That thought right there is giving power and validity to the feeling. That just feeds it. It is giving it importance and energy. It is saying, "Feeling, you have power over me. You are in control." That feeling will keep staying around as long as you keep giving it that power. You give it power by not having a holiday.

Inquirer 2: Sometimes I just let the feelings be and they dissipate quickly, and sometimes they stay for hours. I just don't try to get away from them like I did in the past and they seem to dissipate quicker.

I don't really like the phrase "let them be" because there is nobody here to let anything be, but I understand what you mean. I just say when thoughts happen, recognize, in a holiday, that you are free. It is doing nothing with the thoughts. There is no one here "doing" the letting them be. What is, is. Who cares if I am letting them be or not?

If you have a holiday, the feelings won't last as long. If you are thinking you are letting them be, you can be in there witnessing them, which sets up a separation. Just have a holiday and see there are no thoughts for a second or two, and you are free. Keep jumping, then feelings will pass as they do and will cause no harm.

It is completely normal to attend to strong thoughts or emotions for a while. They appear and then they end. Just be reconciled that *what is, is.* If there are strong thoughts, there is no one here to argue with it. It's the same with strong feelings. Know this moment can't be any different than this moment is. It doesn't mean that it is comfortable, but there is no one else in here saying, "I want to get rid of this feeling." Just know that it is going to pass, just like you know the cloud will pass.

The waves are sometimes pleasant and warm, sometimes they are cold, sometimes they are small, and sometimes they are big. That is the way it is in the ocean. That is not going to change. Freedom does not lie in achieving a state of perfect equanimity. Freedom is when you are done arguing with the waves. Life is not flat. Life is full of all kinds of movement.

Even though this work is not about feeling good, there is a byproduct. It is that you suffer much less. It is just a fact. You are no longer arguing with what is and trying to change everything. This just naturally alleviates a lot of unnecessary suffering. In its stead, is much more ease of being.

Anger

Even on a holiday, there is a lot of anger appearing. I am reminded of the story of Jesus and the money changers. It seems like if anger is here, in the moment, then it is real. I am getting an impression there is a subtle judgment that anger is wrong.

There is no judgment. Let's have a look. Jesus walked into the church perfectly happy. For him, he was likely walking around a lot on holiday. When he saw the money changers, he got enraged and stormed around, upsetting all the tables. Then, the moment he walked out, he was likely at peace again. Do you think he carried that anger around with him month after month?

No, but I think he felt it really fully.

Of course, I feel anger fully when I get pissed off at something. In the moment, when something appears that elicits anger (there is no doer), the body-mind experiences anger. It is created that way, otherwise, it would never experience it. This is completely natural and there is nothing wrong with anger. All the emotions that appear are natural—love, sadness, shame, joy, fear, anger, etc. If they weren't natural, they would not happen.

What is not natural is continuing to engage in the story of anger for a long time after the incident is finished. Then it is affliction and suffering. This habit has been cultivated through ignorance—ignorance of our essential being and our freedom.

If something happens which elicits anger, you did not create it; it is natural. You will feel it and then it can pass. If you find you are going over it and over it, and the anger is lingering, that means that the story is lingering. Without the story, the anger won't linger. If you are saying the anger is lingering, what you are not admitting is the thoughts are also still lingering and you are going back into them.

> *What I find is that I am resisting what you are saying. I guess I am confused when you say everything is natural, but then you say to leave your body-mind behind in a holiday.*

The reason to have a holiday is to see your essential nature is free. In the moment that something is appearing, it is natural for the body-mind to have a response. You are prior to the body-mind, which can be touched by anything, positively or negatively. The body-mind will always have experiences. You are the knowing of all of it.

Don't judge what the body-mind organism does. Know who you are essentially (freedom), and let the body do whatever it does. When you believe the stories that are playing in your mind and go over and over them because they are compelling for whatever reason, it will extend the feelings. This is not natural. It is normal, but not natural.

What is natural is for the sensation to arise in the moment and then pass, like the flow of a river. Emotions may linger longer, then they pass as well. If you get into the mental orgy of story, then they won't pass.

> *It seems like being on holiday means I am not engaged. When I am on holiday, I am detached from everything.*

So, how do I engage fully with life, and with what is appearing?

If you are just going over and over a story, then that is being engaged in death, not in life because that story is not true. It sounds like you are wanting to be engaged and victimized by your stories. If you want to be engaged in life, then stop engaging in death. If you want to engage in the activities of life then, of course, do so. Freedom is not in opposition to any action or non-action.

Feelings of Guilt

I try to just do whatever I'm doing, and sometimes it upsets people. There's some guilt about that and then a holiday happens.

I try to remember that things are just as they are and to relax. When holidays happen, I remember there's nothing going on, just now. What other people didn't like yesterday is over and it's gone. I'm just me, right now, and they have to deal with it, by themselves.

It feels really strange to have that attitude, and sometimes I think, "maybe I'm fooling myself and I'm being a terrible person by not taking responsibility." I do deal with the consequences though.

It's a great question, and beneficial for everyone because culture and religion teach us that we're supposed to feel guilty. Our whole life, we're taught we're supposed to feel guilty and have regret. If we do something stupid, we should be punished. With this work, instead of feeling guilty, we realize there's no doer, and then the guilt passes.

We then think there's something wrong because we don't feel guilty. That's just conditioned belief, not truth. Guilt doesn't help anything, does it? If guilt appears, it's not wrong for it to appear, and it's not wrong for you to realize that it's just a conditioned feeling.

It doesn't mean you don't apologize if you make a mistake. Also, it doesn't mean you shouldn't feel guilty, or you shouldn't feel regret, or whatever. You will feel whatever you feel. Guilt though really doesn't help, and if it appears, it's best to have a holiday and let it pass.

> *Actually, I don't feel a lot of guilt, then I think what's wrong with me?*

Right, but why would you think that way?

> *Because of that voice, that I shouldn't feel that way.*

What voice? Let's get to the bottom of this. That's just cultural conditioned ignorance. There's no truth to that voice, is there? It's fine if there's guilt or no guilt there. It's fine that you feel bad for not having guilt. All those things are fine. Ignore them and instead have a holiday. Ignore the whole lot of it.

I totally understand. You say, "I feel bad for not feeling guilty." Isn't that also just more conditioning? It's just another idea, and what do you do? Have a holiday, and the feeling will pass. Nothing has changed, nothing bad has happened. If you did something bad, then you will apologize or make it right.

I grew up Catholic as well, and I have all the same conditioning— you're supposed to feel guilty. You're guilty for just being alive.

You're a sinner, and if you don't feel guilty, then you're a sinner for not feeling guilty. Just have a holiday and know what's true.

> *I feel this is all ocean and these are just passing waves. If I say something stupid yesterday, it's gone. It's not real and it's not coming back, but people are not going to buy that. They see the waves and they're not going to buy this, "I'm the ocean" shit.*

You don't have to convince anyone there's only ocean and you're so smart and enlightened, and they should dig where you're coming from, or something like that. You can apologize if you say something stupid, that's fine.

> *I try to apologize, but it feels insincere because I know I'm going to do it the next day. I'm not throwing bombs or anything like that, not killing anybody. I'm just being myself. I don't want to be hard on myself anymore, I want to be like, whatever happens, happens.*

Fine, you can just be like that and they just have to deal with it. If you're not doing anything harmful to anyone, then just be yourself. If they can't deal with it, that's their problem. If you do something or say something that's really stupid, you can apologize and move on. But, if you are just being yourself and someone is getting offended because of their ignorance, that's not your problem at all.

Just see that those feelings of guilt, or feelings that you should feel guilty for not feeling guilty, are all just conditioning and programming. It wasn't there when you came out of the womb, nothing like that. It's all put in by religion and culture. Just have a holiday and you'll see none of that has any benefit at all. It doesn't benefit you if you feel that way, and it doesn't benefit them if you feel that way (or don't feel that way). It's just ignorance. We just have a holiday and it will pass quickly.

Have a holiday and know that it's just ignorance and be done, quickly. Really, you can be done with it. Have a holiday, even if it's nagging you for a little while, you just say, "No, I'm having a holiday," and it will get the message. This is the point, "You can't fool me. I know you're an illusion, I know you're ignorance." The light is on, and with that light, it can't stand.

Hope and Expectation

Because of all the spiritual reading we have done and all the spiritual teachings we have heard, there are countless ideas, ideals, and concepts impressed in our minds about freedom, awakening, enlightenment, etc. Unfortunately, many of these impressions are based on misunderstandings and misinterpretations of the teachings, or on flat-out falsehoods. This creates in our mind a state of hope and expectation and a future when we will attain these cherished ideals. This is antithetical to freedom, which is and can only be *now*. As long as you want and expect *some*thing, you will never come to know the beauty and peace of *no*thing.

Wanting Liberation

> *When I first started with you, I had a shift of knowing, and I was getting it. Right now, there's a lot of things going on in my life, and I feel like I have more thoughts and more stories going on. I thought this would help me to get liberated, but it's not really working.*

You're not *going to get* liberated, I'm sorry. Are holidays happening?

> *Yes, and sometimes I don't know what liberation is, but I do know that I want it.*

That's the problem right there. You want something, and you don't even know what it is you want. If I had to define liberation, I'd say, "It's the reconciliation that, *what is, is.*" In that, there is no one here to argue. (Read that again.)

Liberation is not a new state of feeling good. Whatever state or feeling you may have, pleasant or unpleasant, will come and go. Liberation is not a final *state or experience* where you are always resting in a certain feeling or emotion. Liberation is a reconciliation that says: what is, is; it cannot possibly be any other way than it is right now; and there's no one here to do anything about it. Resistance and arguing end when this is reconciled. It's the resistance and the arguing that's ego. It's the one who believes they're the doer and there's something they can, should or need to do about *this*. That's a myth; it's not actually true. That's a wave that comes and goes.

Sounds like there are circumstances happening, and the body-mind organism is doing its job. There's nothing wrong. If thoughts and emotions are coming up because of circumstances, that's not wrong, that's right. If one of your family members is sick, and there's a lot of fear and worry, that's not wrong, that's right. That's what this body-mind organism does. If the thought comes in, "It's wrong that I have this fear and worry, and I have to get liberated," it creates a so-called problem. The idea that you're going to get liberated is causing you a lot of struggle.

> *Yes, and I keep hearing that there will be a feeling of deep peace.*

You say that because you think liberation is peace and feeling good. Like all of us, you want to feel good. It's okay, but let's just be honest about it. You say you want liberation, but see, that's not what you want. What you're saying is, "I don't give a shit about liberation, I want to feel good." Peace and feeling good are states and they come and go. Freedom is free of states. Liberation is not caring what particular state is coming or going. You have to be honest—you don't want liberation.

> *But how about the peace you're talking about?*

Peaceful feelings come and go. The peace I'm speaking about is just the reconciliation that what is, is. Sometimes it feels good and sometimes it doesn't feel good. That's life, and you are reconciled with it. In that reconciliation, is an ease of being. It is the end of arguing, and with that then yes, you are more and more at peace and less and less in the mess of mental agitation.

Everyone, not just you, has this tenacious idea that liberation is some feeling state. Everyone! The idea may sound something like: "There's some state of feeling good I'm going to attain, and when I do, I'm always going to feel good;" or "There's some state of no thoughts that I'm going to attain, and when I do, there are never going to be thoughts." Coupled with the idea of a specific state is the expectation, "When is it going to happen?" If you want freedom, have a holiday, now.

HOLIDAY

See that you are free, *now*. On a holiday, freedom is known.

You Get Nothing

I recognize that I want something. On last week's call, I had the thought, "I'm really going to get something out of being on this call." Then, after the call, it was really clear—I got nothing out of the call. Nothing! So, there was this disappointment, but something else clicked in my mind, "That's exactly what you were supposed to get out of that call—nothing." It was just beautiful; this thing that wanted something didn't get it, then the realization happened.

That's exactly true. Seekers, and not just seekers in the spiritual world, but mundane seekers as well, are seeking for something. That's the root of seeking. And, let's face it, spiritual seekers really want some great stuff. They want to merge with God, enlightenment, mystical experiences and never experiencing any disturbances ever again. These wants are even better than money. But, when you recognize that your essential being lacks nothing and you're complete and whole, you realize you get none of the concepts and desires you thought you were going to get as a seeker. You get the end of all of that. For most seekers, that's definitely not interesting. That's not interesting at all, and that's why most seekers won't come to work like this.

But, when you recognize, as you did, you see the value of truth. You see, freedom is free. Freedom is free from seeking, wanting, hoping, and longing for all those special and extraordinary states. So, it is free from desire. Also, it is free from the projections of doom and gloom, and death in the future. So, it is free from fear.

When you recognize the value of that, and it sounds like you have from what you're saying, it means that you're authentically interested in freedom, liberation, and truth. When you come to know liberation, you get nothing—none of your cherished, spiritual hopes and ideas about what you were going to get with this thing called enlightenment. You don't get what you thought you wanted. You get the end of all of that.

To me, it's great. I know nothing, I have nothing, and I am *nothing*. In liberation, you recognize that you are not what you thought you were. You are no-thing in a sense. You are no-thing, and you have nothing, as far as conceptual ideals, philosophies and the false security of the known, which is ignorance and not truth. You cannot grasp on to anything as a permanent fixed idea of self. It is called freedom, and freedom elicits ease of being.

Things come and go, everything is constantly changing and knowing stays the same. You really have nothing, and you know nothing. All you know is truth, yourself, as you appear now. You don't know why anything is, where anything is going, or the meaning of anything. You don't know any of that, no one does. We pretend to, we hope to, but we get to realize in liberation that I am no-thing, I have nothing, and I know nothing. That's freedom. For most people and seekers, that's not very interesting.

It's a tremendous relief not needing to be someone special, to know something special, or to have something special.

> *Inquirer 2: I had the thought today that I'm not even spiritual anymore. It's like normal life or something. My life before was just very confused because I was believing things that I didn't know anything about, and I thought I had to get somewhere. I noticed that I'm not interested at all in spirituality anymore. It's great, and actually so beautiful to just have nothing to do.*

That's what the first book is about, *the end of the spiritual path*. What's so spiritual about your essential being? It's you! It's just truth. It's ordinary, and it's true for everyone. Everyone's essential being is the same. What's so special or spiritual about that? The spiritual carousel that we talk about, which is primarily focused on a future self, is very compelling for most people. Most people who get on that crack pipe never get off.

Not Quite Getting It

*I keep having this feeling that liberation should feel a
certain way. When I come on these group calls, that idea
falls away a bit. However, when I am not here, there
seems to be a constant doubt that I am not quite getting it.*

Okay. Let's be on holiday.

HOLIDAY

You know what a holiday is.

It is just knowing.

Nothing more.

Whatever is appearing is of secondary importance.

A holiday is knowing, knowing itself.

It is you, knowing yourself.

You say there is a doubt. Where is that doubt, now?

It is not.

You say you are not quite getting it, or it is not clear. Look now, is it
clear to you?

It is.

Good. Now, you know this. This is true. It is not that it is not clear
to you. Knowing has nothing to do with any particular feeling that
is appearing. Regardless of how you are feeling, knowing is still
here. The proof is that you know the feeling.

What we want to recognize is knowing, knowing itself. Have a holiday.

HOLIDAY

In a holiday, there is no past and no future. A holiday is not dependent on the feeling that is here. It seems that feelings cause you to doubt. Look, now. No matter how you feel, the knowing is the same. It is not dependent on how you feel.

The important thing is to keep seeing the value of this knowing. It is untouched and free. It is you. Continue to know this. The only thing to do (and there is no doer) is to know what's true. What else can there possibly be? Can you do anything with feelings? Can you get rid of bad feelings? There is nothing you can do. The only thing to do is just know.

Knowing itself is the goal already attained. Knowing is the end already. The path and the goal are the same. This is the way of freedom.

You mentioned that it was easier on these calls. Of course, this is a meeting in truth—a satsang. Everyone is interested in the same thing, and it is easy to be here in truth. This is the value of coming here.

> *It is difficult for me to believe that liberation is always now.*

I will prove it to you. Let's have a holiday.

HOLIDAY

Knowing is here.

It isn't dependent on a feeling, good or bad.

Freedom is what is.

It is essentially true.

It is now.

Get fed up! Get fed up with the stories. Get fed up with being dependent on how things feel. Get fed up with being dependent on any particular state. Get fed up with thinking there is something more to attain and that you are not attaining it. Get fed with up thinking about spiritual matters. There is no doer who gets fed up. You will just *be* fed up, period.

Feelings are not going to stop. However, you can stop arguing with them and thinking there is something wrong. You can stop attempting to employ all the psychological methods to deal with them. Just stop completely and they have no power without a belief that they mean something.

Most people don't get fed up because they don't have an alternative. Most people go through their whole life suffering, not knowing there is a very simple way out. Once you do come to know, then there is the possibility to get fed up. Why? Because freedom is better.

See the value of freedom. Once you have a shift of knowing and see your freedom, there is a way out of the cultural ignorance and it becomes very interesting. It only takes continuing to be authentic, nothing else.

Ramana Maharshi said one thing to his mature students—"Abide as the Self." What he meant is: do nothing, just be as you are. Know the Self (knowing). He also said, "To know the Self is to be the Self." Knowing and being are not separate. Knowing is who you are. Being and knowing are synonymous. Sat Chit.

Be on holiday and know what he is speaking about.

HOLIDAY

Knowing is being.

Being is knowing.

Here it is already finished.

It is no-thing.

Pure no-thing.

Sat Chit Ananda—Being, Consciousness, Peace.

Being = Existence.

Consciousness = Knowing or Aware.

Peace = Freedom.

What more can there be?

Recognizing Truth Will Improve Personal Life

I seem to have this belief that if I am developing my recognition of truth, my personal life will get better. I am noticing that this is not true. I am going through some real upheavals in my relationship. Even though it is clear who I am, the shit is still hitting the fan.

While it may not be pleasant that there is upheaval, it is good you are aware of your essential nature when it is happening.

Like the movie The Matrix, it feels like I have been embedded in this story my whole life. However, even though I am out of the matrix, it is not all fun and games. I see there is a lot of stuff I have been tolerating that is just delusional.

Unfortunately, once you know who you are, you can't go back. You can't start believing in Santa Claus again.

I have no idea what you should or should not do. The truth is that sometimes life is challenging. It is not going to change unless you go and live in a cave. We don't live like that, we live in the world with all the events and relationships, and sometimes it sucks. This is not going to change.

Inquirer 2: The marketing of enlightenment by some spiritual teachers is that "once you wake up, you will be in bliss."

Yes, and that is a disservice. Just more silly ideas. The truth is that life flows, and sometimes it is a tsunami, not a little ripple. It still flows, and you can't change what is. The life flow is always happening whether you know it or not. When you know who you are, and you see you are not the doer, and things can only be as they are, you see that there is nothing you can do. The flow just flows whether you are arguing with it or not.

Anything can happen, and things can arise that hurt. I've had many difficult things appear in my life. Life is a long ride and there are a lot of bruises along the way. Some can be brutal, and when they occur, you are going to feel it. Nevertheless, you know that what is, is, and there is nothing you can do about it. You have no idea why it is occurring, yet you do know that it will pass.

Inquirer 3: Would you say that God is like an author who has authored all of these things to happen?

I don't believe anything like that. I honestly have no idea why what's appearing is what's appearing. Let's be on holiday, now.

HOLIDAY

Is there a past?

Is there a future?

See! There is nothing behind the curtain of this.

What seems like countless, separate things
is actually only one appearance, now.

And it is not even substantial.

It is appearing and vanishing like vapor.

Since there is no past,
it could not have come from anywhere.

This moment can only be appearing now, dissolving now.

Nothing behind the curtain.

No past, no future, no self.

Only this appearance,
which is not even actual because it is always changing.

And,
if it is always changing,
you can't grab onto anything.

Why is this like this? I have no idea.

Where did this come from? I have no idea.

The question about whether "some God made this" is looking for some explanation. This is only conditioned thought and there is no way to know any of that. People who believe in religions want to know there is a God so that they can have some comfort.

Creating Some Goal

I feel like I keep creating some goal. It's like I am supposed to be doubtless and never get wrapped up in thinking about a past or future again.

It can happen that you will lose interest in the past and future, but it is best not to make it a goal. Just keep knowing what is true, now. That is all you can know, and the only time you are going to know it is doubtless, is now. You are not going to know it is doubtless in the future.

Hope and Expectation

Let's have a holiday together.

HOLIDAY

Relax the focus of attention.

Are you familiar with this knowing that is here and now?

Knowing is now, isn't it?

Is there any doubt about that?

You know there is knowing, here and now.

Isn't this the same knowing that was here
five minutes ago?
Ten years ago?

Knowing is here, now.

If thoughts come, isn't knowing still here,
just knowing thoughts in that moment?

So then, knowing is here.

Then thoughts subside and now,
knowing knows itself,
simply knowing, with no object.

This is very natural, knowing is openly knowing itself,
everything here is included equally.

Then some thoughts come and knowing attends to thoughts,
and now it is knowing the thoughts.

Obviously, knowing is still here, but now,
it is knowing an object, instead of itself.

It's perfectly natural and that won't change.

Then after some time, thoughts subside
and knowing knows its objectless self again.

What has changed essentially through all of that? Knowing has not changed. Is that true?

Yes, that's true, but if I get wrapped up in thoughts, I don't know that.

Of course not. For example, if I am working on music for eight hours on my computer, not one moment do I know who I am in that way. I know the music and all the buttons and knobs I am dealing with. Does that mean I am not free? Of course not. Why? Because I know who I am. Have a holiday, now.

HOLIDAY

Knowing is here.

This is your essential being.

Knowing is always here,
no matter how many thoughts come and go.

Knowing is here, before, during, and after all thoughts.

No matter how many more thoughts come,
when they pass, knowing is still here, unchanged.

Hope and Expectation

Throughout your whole life,
if you had been able to recognize it,
knowing would be here.

You don't lose knowing.

Knowing is your essential being.

Do you see what I am saying?

Yes, I see that nothing essentially changes. It just feels like it when I get lost in thoughts.

Yes, and that is not going to change. However, you are not lost in thoughts. In that moment, you are completely found *as* thoughts. So, that is not a problem. There is still the desire and belief that some state is going to happen all the time, but that is not true. Freedom does not need to be in a specific state. If freedom required any particular state, it would be bondage.

I think I was confused about that because it feels very freeing when I can let go of the idea of being a person with a past and a future. It doesn't feel very free when I am stressing about something.

Just keep having holidays and the more and more you recognize your essential being in a holiday, the less and less you will care if thoughts come up. And because of that, thoughts lose their power and just flow by, like a river. Now, there is still an argument going on that "something's wrong and I am not free." Just keep coming to this knowing that knows itself, for a moment, and know this is your essential being. This hasn't changed your whole life.

Wanting Something to Change

I have a habit of thinking and feeling that this isn't it and I want to be somewhere else other than where I am. I want to get away from painful sensations by numbing them.

It is true for everyone when things don't feel good. I don't like it when things feel bad, and I have to be honest; I don't argue with it anymore. First, I did not create the feeling. I am not the doer. Second, I only know what is true now, and what is true now is that there is something uncomfortable going on. Third, I know that whatever is going on will eventually pass because everything passes. The only thing that doesn't pass is my essential nature.

Stop arguing with yourself. That is enlightenment right there—stop arguing with what is. It does not mean that what is will all of a sudden feel good. But, if you are arguing with what is, in any way (pushing it away, hiding under the cover, anesthetizing it, analyzing it or trying to understand it), it will last a lot longer. There is nothing you can do about it. So, why argue?

In the midst of the uncomfortable feeling, perhaps (most likely) a holiday will happen, then you will get to know what is not affected by anything. Let's have a holiday, now.

HOLIDAY

Here and now, aware.
Knowing is present, isn't it?

Is this the same knowing that was here five minutes ago?
Ten minutes ago? Last week?

Knowing, aware has not changed, has it?

In this last week,
how many thoughts and emotions have come and gone?

Where are they now?

They come and go, but you don't, do you?

What is more valuable?

If you want freedom, happiness, and sanity, value truth.

When something is painful, that is just the way it is. It is for me too. When the pain passes, who are you going to be? You are going to be you before, during, and after any experience. You are aware/knowing. Know what is true and value that the most. This is what Ramana means when he says, "Abide as the Self."

Karma Yoga

In the 'What about Desire' YouTube video, you mention Karma Yoga, which is "You desire what you desire, but the outcome is out of your hands." I see this, and I see I am not the doer. Nevertheless, we all have this wanting or desiring. Could we call this a "natural" progression of a life form to grow and survive?

A flowering bud naturally directs its movement towards the sun to fully bloom. If the flower is covered over by an object away from the sun's rays, it will wither and not survive. Are we not the same as flowers, animals, and birds, but with a "mind" stuck on top? Maybe some people

*naturally bloom in a certain trade, job, or art (they
desire) and other people may not find a way to bloom and
fulfill their desires. It's not bad if they don't. It just is.
There really is no good luck or bad luck. It just is.*

It's a good analogy, but the flower doesn't desire. It just moves in a totally instinctual, thoughtless way for survival. We, humans, have another aspect, which is conditioned thought. We have a sense of lack or a sense that we are not complete, even if our survival is not in jeopardy. Most of our desires are not needed for survival, and many are even frivolous. Unlike the flower, many of our desires are ego fulfilling ones. Those desires are not invalid; they are what they are, and they appear as they appear. We don't choose them.

If someone wants to make a fortune, that is just what they want. The outcome, however, is not guaranteed. If someone is naturally drawn to a particular trade, it is the same. Either way, Karma is true. Good luck and bad luck are personal viewpoints. Often, so-called bad luck can lead to something good, and vice versa.

In Indian Vedanta, Karma Yoga is one of the three paths to enlightenment. The other two are Jnana and Bhakti. Jnana Yoga, is wisdom or Self-knowledge (recognizing your essential being); Bhakti Yoga, is devotion or worship (valuing your essential being, not valuing God or anything like that); and Karma Yoga, is wanting whatever you want, but giving up the fruits of your actions (you have no idea what's going to happen). We do all of the three Yogas of Vedanta here. It's all one, and it's all the same.

In truth, Karma is the result of knowing your essential being is free, you lack nothing, and you are already complete and whole. Therefore, you are not fearfully concerned with the future outcome and are not overly bothered when things you desire don't materialize, or you lose things you have gained. That is just how you are when you know you are free, you lack nothing, and you are complete already.

Be a Karma Yogi with this work—intend for freedom, and have holidays because of that intention, and that's it, you are finished. Don't worry about the fruits of that action in the future. Be a Jnani, know who you are and what's true. Be a Bhakta, worship truth, your essential being.

Free Will - Doership - Choice

From working with many people over the years, it is clear that the topic of free will and doership elicits some of the greatest confusion and misunderstanding. It is a topic that has vast implications because the belief in free will is the cause of enormous trouble for each person individually and for the world at large. There is a lot to look into and I hope that much of the confusion can be clarified here.

Doing Holidays

You have mentioned that you can't really do a holiday. I know there's no doer, but could you clarify that?

I don't say, "take or do holidays." I usually say, "have holidays," but the more accurate saying is, "holidays happen" because there's no doer. This is important. When I say, "have holidays," I don't mean you're going to start doing holidays. I put that seed, "have holidays," into your head so it sprouts, spontaneously.

I'll give you an example that will make it clear.

Let's say thoughts are happening and you're "lost in thoughts," so to speak, for an hour or a day—attention is completely on thoughts. In this case, attention is exclusively focused and limited, isn't it? We all know that experience. Then, all of a sudden, out of the blue, the thought appears, "have a holiday." Did you *do* that? No. It just appeared. Why? Because the seed is in there, and it just sprouts, spontaneously. In fact, all thoughts just sprout, spontaneously. You don't create any thoughts, do you?

No.

Do you create the thought, "have a holiday?" Do you have the thought, "now, I'm going to create (or have) the thought, 'have a holiday'?" No, of course not. There's no one in there who can do that. Actually, the thought usually doesn't even happen, the holiday just happens, spontaneously. Attention is solely focused on thoughts, then a holiday happens.

There are two things to look at. First, maybe the thought does come, "have a holiday." That means the holiday already happened. If the thought comes, "have a holiday," that means you *recognize* you're "lost in thoughts," which means you're already on a holiday. The thought, "have a holiday," comes afterward. If you didn't recognize that, why would the thought come? Second, that thought really doesn't have to come at all. The intention, which I put in your head a lot, is to have holidays. And I keep saying it, "have holidays, have holidays..." So, when exclusive attention to thoughts happens, you just jump, spontaneously.

Just keep having holidays. You don't have to think about it. You don't have to do anything. That's why I speak about intention a lot. When I speak about intention, it has nothing to do with willpower. It has nothing to do with doership. The intention for freedom is either there or it isn't. There is no choice in the matter.

I didn't choose to go for enlightenment, whenever that happened many years ago. It just happened. The thought crossed my mind, "Liberation, what is it? I want to find out." I didn't choose with willpower to go for that. I didn't choose to quit drugs, and I didn't choose to be a seeker. These things just happened. There was no doer. There's no doer now, and there's no doer ever.

You can even have the thought, "I'm doing something," no problem. You can call yourself a doer all you want, until the cows come home, no problem. It doesn't change the fact that there's no doer. Even if

I say, "I'm creating a great song here," it doesn't change the fact that there is no me here to create anything and that the song is appearing in this mind without any control or choice. So even if you say you're the doer, it doesn't matter; you're not.

You are here because you are here, not because you chose to be here. You could say, I chose to read *Liberation IS*. Really? Well, let's just do this experiment. Did you see my interview on Buddha at the Gas Pump (BATGAP)?

> *Yes.*

And you have seen many videos on BATGAP because you are interested in spirituality or enlightenment?

> *Yes.*

Do you know why you are interested in those things?

> *No.*

Right, you are just interested, and you have no idea where that interest came from. So, you happened to watch my interview on BATGAP and it resonated with you?

> *Right.*

Did you choose to have it resonate or did it just resonate?

> *It just resonated.*

Then you hear I wrote a book, and you think, "Maybe I'll buy the book." Did you choose that thought or did it just appear?

> *It just appeared.*

Right, you did not think, "Now, I am going to create the thought, 'maybe I'll buy the book.'" No, the thought, "maybe I'll buy the book," just appeared because you resonated with the interview.

From this thought, which you did not create, the intention arose to go on Amazon (or wherever) and buy the book. The action follows intention. None of which you are creating. You didn't even create the action to buy the book. That is just a reaction/response from the original intention, which again, you did not create.

Then you bought and read the book. Perhaps there was some recognition you had from reading the book. Did you do any of that?

No. Again, it just resonated with me.

Right, then you saw on my website that I give sessions and you sent an email. That just happened. You did nothing to be here. You get no credit whatsoever.

True, and I come from years of New Age thought that says I'm creating all of this, everything. It's ridiculous.

It's good you see that. Is this true what I'm saying or am I making it up? You have to see for yourself.

No, it's true.

That's important. The New Agers tell you you're creating this and that, but there's no real investigation into whether it's true or not. The reason they do not realize there is no doer is because they have not yet recognized who they are, prior to thought, and they are only investigating at the level *of* thought. At the level of thought, it can appear that there is a doer here who has free will. You need to see prior to that (have a shift of knowing) to know what is actually happening.

When we are seekers, we just take their word for it and believe—I am the creator. However, it doesn't take much investigation to find out that it's not true at all. It takes very little, but we don't know how to do it because no one is showing us. They're only showing you how to have free will, how to create your own life, and how to have your own intention. It's exhausting. I'm too lazy for all of that.

I'm lazy too.

That's good. Enlightenment is for lazy people. Not for doers.

Free Will in Relationship

I told you guys last week that my girlfriend cheated on me and I went through a breakup. This no free will thing is hard. When I am feeling these tough feelings, I just want to say, "Fuck you!" I don't feel like there's anything wrong with expressing it a little bit, but I'm trying to not continuously belabor the point.

This is perfect. This is where the rubber meets the road, this kind of situation. First of all, that's a challenging thing you went through. It would be for anyone. But we have to see, first of all, truth is still true, whether it's pleasant or unpleasant. Whatever the experience, truth is still true. The truth is, for whatever reason, your ex-girlfriend did what she did. Maybe there were some reasons, and again, we'd have to go back to the Big Bang to find out why, but we're not going to do that. Whatever it was, it was. It happened.

Let's go through an experiment. Let's say you were born in the slums, in the inner city of Detroit or something like that. You're a ghetto kid, and your father is gone. You don't even know your father. Your mother is a crackhead and that's how you grow up. This is actually how it is for many people, isn't it? It's not some fictional story I am making up. It happens a lot. So, those are the

255

circumstances you are born into. Did you choose to be born into those circumstances?

No.

Right. You grow up with no father, a crackhead mother, on the slum streets of an inner city. What are you surrounded with? Gangs, drugs and violence, and that's what you grow up with, right? By the time you're a teenager, you probably have a gun, like everybody else. Did you choose that lifestyle?

No.

Right. And by the time you're eighteen, you get into some trouble, and you shoot someone. Then our compassionate justice system says you're going to prison for the rest of your life because you're evil. You're evil, or as one of our recent Presidential candidates said, "You're a super predator." And because you are an evil super predator, you're going to prison for the rest of your life. The system says, "It's your fault and you're hopeless." Really? It's their fault? Seriously! Did that happen to you? No, it didn't happen to you because you grew up in a much saner environment.

However, we want to blame. We blame, and we want to get revenge and impose punishment. I don't believe in punishment, but society wants to punish the "evildoer." The "evildoer" was also a victim, right? Jesus said, "Father, forgive them for they know not what they do." So, that person's not to blame. As liberals, we can understand this situation. It's easy to see and we have compassion.

What about if you grow up in Mississippi and your father is in the Ku Klux Klan, and all your parents' friends are white supremacists. They are burning black people at the stake and hanging them from trees. That's what you grow up in, and by the time you're eighteen, that's who you are—a skinhead Nazi. Is that your fault? Of course not. Liberals, however, don't have sympathy for those people. We have sympathy for the inner-city youth because that's a pet cause, but we don't have sympathy for the Nazi skinheads because they're conservative Christians and they're "evil." However, are either of them at fault for how they are?

If it's true, it's true, isn't it? Truth is true either way you look at it, right? You see what I'm saying? No one created themselves. You didn't create yourself. I didn't create myself. I didn't create the fact that I like playing guitar, I just like playing guitar. You see?

For whatever reason, your ex-girlfriend cheated on you. Of course, it sucks, it's painful, and maybe you're going to lash out, get mad at her and say, "Fuck you." That's fine too. You're not to blame for that either.

Jesus knew when he was hanging on the cross that he wasn't the doer. He knew he didn't have free will. He knew he did not create himself. Why did he want to find God and get enlightened? He didn't know. It's just what happened. How do we know he felt that way? Because as he was hanging on the cross with nails in his hands, he said, "Forgive them, they know not what they do." He knew they didn't create themselves because he knew he didn't create himself.

If you know you didn't create yourself, you, first of all, give yourself a break. Then, you give other people a break as well. Nevertheless, we're human and if your girlfriend cheats on you, of course, you get mad. Naturally, you feel hurt. Of course, you do. But, over time, the benefits of knowing there's no doer are compassion, empathy, and understanding.

Knowing there is no doer is not so you can be a philosopher or something. There needs to be some type of an effect, and compassion, empathy, and understanding are the effects. Even if it's difficult and you act out in anger or hurt, that's natural, of course. Even then, truth is still true. If you didn't create yourself, then the other person didn't create herself either.

Right. It's a difficult thing to navigate.

You don't have to navigate it because then you're judging yourself and you're acting like the doer again. Who's navigating? You don't have to navigate anything. Just know what's true. Whatever is, is. If in this moment, there's anger because your ex-girlfriend cheated on you, then that's what is. Nothing to navigate. I don't really go for this navigating thing.

> *What I mean is, this understanding makes me act differently than I normally would. Cheating is a thing that happens. You're allowed to do that, but emotionally it's upsetting. Initially, there may be a "fuck you," but I'm trying to not belabor the point and let go to the best of my ability.*

Well again, I hate to be a naysayer, but I don't ever say, "let anything go" either. You can't let anything go. Who's to let anything go? The doer? There's no doer. If you think "I'm going to let something go," then you're saying there's someone in here who has free will to let something go. I say that's not true. You'll be mad as long as you're mad, and you'll say, "fuck you" as many times as you say, "fuck you." That's just the way it is.

There's no one to let go of anything. Just know what's true, and truth shall set you free. The more you really know yourself as free, and the more you know yourself as not the doer, the more you naturally become more compassionate and understanding, simply because you know it is true for others as well. Then, that kind of blame and acrimony doesn't happen as much, that's all. There's no one doing or not doing. You see the point I'm making here?

Yeah, that's actually very clear.

Good. I never say, "let everything be as it is," or "let everything go," or "let go of this and that." I never say those things. I say, "whatever is, is," and "know what's true, and knowing what's true is what sets you free." There is no letting things go, being unattached, doing understanding, or doing compassion intentionally. Compassion and empathy happen because you know what's true. They don't happen because you're trying to be compassionate or empathetic; that doesn't work.

Still, my mind is thinking, there's no harm in not lashing out, do your best.

Yes, exactly, and in that case, that thought just appears too. You didn't create that thought either. You're not the doer of that thought. You can even think you're the doer as much as you want, but the truth is, there is no doer. Even if you think you're the doer, it still doesn't change the fact that there is no doer. Once you really see that, then the thought, "I'm the doer," doesn't really come up anymore.

If the intention appears for you to be more chilled out, you didn't create that intention. That intention is there because you know what's true, and because the intention for goodness and compassion is there, without you doing or creating it. It simply is what is.

Free Will is Paradoxical

It is hard to talk about free will. It seems paradoxical to me because who is the "one" that is saying there is no free will.

No one is saying there is no free will. You, knowing, recognize there is no free will, now. "No free will" is a concept in the mind. Although it is a concept, it points to something true. The seeing of it is not conceptual. It is a recognition. When we speak, it becomes conceptual because we are using words. When we speak, it is just programming in the brain that is coming out.

Inquirer 2: The thing is that "free will" needs a person to be free, but there is no person. So, there is no one here that can have free will. Also, with freely aware, there is no someone here to be freely aware. There is just aware.

Right. There is no one here as a separate self. The self is non-existent, it is just a waxing and waning of experience and movement, moment by moment. But you are aware of all of it. Some people think they have free will because there is a feeling of having free will. However, you are aware of that feeling which is not always there. It comes and goes. When it appears, you are aware of it. Then the natural question is, who is this you?

This person, who we think is a separate self, is just appearing moment to moment. It is not long-standing. What is long-standing is aware, you. You (being, knowing, peace) are aware of so-called choices and that the so-called choices are being made by a so-called person. Whatever thoughts appear in the brain, no one is creating them. They are just appearing. If there is free will, we would see a someone creating the thoughts, but when we look, we see that is not the case. Whatever appears, just appears. There is nothing behind the curtain of any appearance, and if there is nothing behind the curtain then there is no one backstage controlling the play.

Even though there is no free will, it does not mean you don't act.

Action happens. For instance, let's say you have a question about the concept of free will and you desire to get clearer about it. One day, you are looking on social media and you see a book advertisement that claims to explain "no free will." Based on your desire, the intention may appear to purchase the book. If the intention is there, the action may follow to purchase the book. It is all based on events which you did not create—a question and a desire for an answer, then an accidental appearance of a book with the answer, then the intention to buy the book, and finally the action of buying the book. The action of buying the book is just the logical, uncreated response to the previous spontaneous happenings. So yes, there is action, but there is no creator of the action. See, in your own experience, if this is true or I am just making it up.

No Doer and Responsibility

Can you speak a little bit about no doer and responsibility, and the fact that we are very responsible?

That's a good question because it is very easy to come up with a misconception. By hearing that there is no doer, many people assume that what is being said is that there is no responsibility. It is a logical conclusion to think, "If there is no doer, I am not responsible for anything, and I can run amok and go crazy." But having no free will is not an excuse for that. There are other aspects to look at.

First, recognizing there is no free will for yourself means it is also true for everyone else. To me, the only reason to recognize there is no free will is because what emerges is compassion because you know that no one creates themselves—the good, the bad or the ugly. This is not something philosophical, and what is born from that knowing is natural compassion for yourself and others.

Second, from doing this work, we realize that as mature people, we want freedom. One aspect of freedom is freedom from being a victim of anything—your thoughts, your "past," your "future," your parents, other people, culture, society, government... everything. You are free from being a victim of anything, which means you are fully responsible for yourself, now. You can't blame anyone or anything else. For a mature person who wants freedom, there is no one to blame. It's obvious, a free person cannot be a victim.

Someone who is a victim is obviously not free. Someone who recognizes their essential nature of freedom and who wants freedom can no longer be a victim. In that way, you can say you are fully responsible for yourself. However, even being fully responsible for yourself, there is no doership.

You don't "do freedom," you don't "do coming to know freedom." You didn't choose to become a seeker. Something happens, and you become a seeker. For whatever reason, you hear a message like this, it resonates, and you go for it. But there is no chooser of any of it. It is just what is. Even taking full responsibility for yourself because you know you are not a victim does not mean there is free will. That is just what happens in a mind that is free. You are free to be responsible. You know there is no one else to blame.

When you recognize your essential nature and you realize you are complete and lack nothing, you become mostly benign in this world. Where is the seed for greed when you know you lack nothing? Where is the seed for envy, for comparison, for power and for all the other human malignancies in the world? When you know you are not higher or lower than anyone and you can only be yourself, then those malignancies really have no soil to appear. Therefore, you don't need this moralistic idea of "being responsible" because those things mostly don't appear.

Responsibility, as we normally think about it, is a very doership type of thing. But, as I see it, you really can't assign blame to anyone else for your actions because you are free, now. You are in this alone! You are not a victim of anything else in the so-called past. In this way, you can say you are being responsible for yourself. If you want to be free, you can't blame anyone else.

> *Out of compassion, does action result, or can doing the right thing appear?*

First of all, I have no idea how anything is going to play out, or how anyone, including myself, is going to act or respond in any situation until it happens. But, clearly, an action that comes from compassion is going to look different from an action that comes from judgment, blame, acrimony, etc. That's a pretty safe bet, but I never make absolutes about behavior, or right action, or moralistic things. I leave that to the religions and philosophers.

> *What about someone who is not awake and has not had these realizations, like a Hitler. He is also not responsible. He is incapable of changing, isn't he?*

Yes, that is why there is compassion, even for someone like that. You can't let someone like that run around killing people. Society has to do something about it, but we see that they are not the creator of themselves. In that realization (that no one is the creator of themselves), we see that someone "bad" like Hitler or someone "great" like Ramana Maharshi did not create themselves. No one creates what they are. This is where compassion comes in. The actions of certain politicians are horribly malignant and there is no question about that. Something needs to be done to prevent people from doing terrible things, but then again, these people did not create themselves.

Once you realize there is no doer and you come from compassion, there is a natural desire to stand up against "evil" like that, am I right?

Perhaps. I see what these "leaders" are doing, and it saddens me greatly. I am not immune from criticizing malignant behavior, but I stop short of condemning the human being because they didn't create themselves. I understand why there is the lust for power and greed. It is because people pathologically believe in self/ego and self-importance. This leads to the sense of lack and causes people to take as much for themselves as they can. They fully buy into their story, their beliefs, their fears and all of that. It is not their fault they believe that. Until something happens spontaneously, for whatever reason, to wake them up from their slumber of self, they will never change.

For me, what appears is sharing this work. For someone else, it may be political activism, or animal activism, or ecological activism, etc. Or it may be simply being a healthy benign expression with friends and family and in that way, you are shining a true light.

Being More Disciplined

I think I should have more holidays and I should be more disciplined or dedicated to truth.

Discipline has nothing to do with this work at all. The thought comes, "I should be more disciplined or dedicated." This appears because there were some impressions in your mind that it is important to be dedicated and disciplined, all based on the belief that there is free will. This applies to everything, not just this work. When you came out of the womb, did you have those thoughts? With the birth of self, culture imparts the ideas that we should be dedicated and disciplined to succeed at something. You did not have anything to do with those ideas. They are just cultural impressions, and they are based on a belief in free will.

So, when you come to work like this, that same belief is still active. It's completely natural.

> *I seem to get hijacked by angry thoughts and it hurts.*

Right. Then the thought appears, "I need to be more disciplined." This is fine, but this work is not about that. Let's investigate this. If the thought comes that you should be more disciplined, you had nothing to do with it appearing, right?

> *Right.*

Holidays happen spontaneously, like everything else. You are not the doer of a holiday. If the thought, intention or desire comes to be free and be on holiday more, you don't create that thought, intention or desire, right? It is just what is.

> *Right.*

If that leads to more holidays happening, then you are not doing that either are you?

> *Right.*

You are not doing anything. Even having more holidays, does not mean that you are being more disciplined. It does mean that there is an intention within you for freedom. Why? Because the alternative to freedom is to suffer with the thoughts of anger. Until you heard this message, you did not know there was a way out.

You create none of the thoughts you have, and you don't create the suffering that arises when certain thoughts appear. Also, you did not create the thought that there was a way out of the suffering. The saying is, "know what is true and truth shall set you free." In this case, you know that freedom is now. Knowing this is what will free you from suffering, by itself. You don't do anything. There is no discipline, dedication or trying harder. Nothing. You just know freedom, and this is what you want because you see how valuable it is.

This is the end of suffering. You know the value of what a holiday reveals, and when there is suffering, you see that you don't want it. And, in that moment, a holiday may happen all by itself. Knowing the value of a holiday will liberate the mind from suffering.

> *The key thing I heard you say is that I don't create the feeling either. I thought I was responsible for feelings and I should get rid of them.*

I don't equate feelings with being the doer. I have nothing to do with them. We may be confused because there is a feeling here, which we equate with a doer. This does not change what is true. We attribute a lot of things to a particular feeling or we think that a feeling means something. What if we don't do that?

Feel whatever you feel and think whatever you think. It does not matter. Just know what is true. You can review any particular situation and see there is no one doing anything. When I am being irritated with the Internet company, the irritation is there and of course, there is action occurring. From the outside, someone may say that he is doing something, but if I look, I see there isn't anyone doing anything. What is true is that everything appears by itself.

There is a lot of relief in this. You don't do holidays, they just happen. You know what freedom is and you know the value of freedom. When the mind is in a state of suffering, you know there is an alternative and a holiday appears.

This is why I stress the value of your essential nature because once you know the value, then you will value it, and it is what you want because it is better than suffering. Knowing the value of freedom is the end of suffering, basically. Suffering can appear for you and when it does, you won't want it and a holiday happens.

> *Inquirer 2: In another talk, you mentioned that you had one rule regarding actions people should take and it was, "try not to hurt anyone." I am wondering how this fits in with this discussion.*

I may have said something like that and it is hard to use words sometimes to convey a particular point. It is very hard to not speak in terms of doership when talking about no doer. For instance, I say that I went to the movies or I went to dinner. I have to use language.

My main point is that I have no idea how anyone should live their life or what they should do. There are many teachings that are very caught up in right action and how you should live. This leads to a lot of trouble. Essentially, what I am saying is that as long as you are not harming anyone, then do whatever you want. Who cares. And, of course, it is good if you don't harm anyone.

You can't "try not to harm anyone." There is no doer. The best way not to harm is to know that your essential nature is free, you lack nothing, you are complete and whole, and you don't need to be superior or inferior to anyone or get anything from anyone else. This is the value of knowing truth, and so, morality and right behavior are moot. If you don't have the soil for greed, envy, comparison, and the need to be right, for the most part, you are benign.

At the same time, I say we are human and we are not perfect. Know that you are free and know that if you harm out of ignorance, it is just something to notice. See why the harm occurred and be free.

In my view, if you are not harming anyone, there are absolutely no rules. Do whatever you want. I am clear in pointing this out because I see the problems caused by other teachings that espouse right behavior and right action. This leads to judgment and revenge and they fail. They think they know how you should live. I don't even know how I am supposed to live. How am I or anyone else going to know how you should live?

Being a Couch Potato

You said that there is no one thinking, there are just thoughts. If I am using my mind to solve a problem on an exam in front of me, who is doing that? Who is the doer?

There is no one doing it. It is just happening, spontaneously. Let's have a look.

You are at the university and as part of the curriculum, there is an exam. You didn't create that, right? Of course, this exam needs to be completed because it is part of the process, and you didn't create that either.

Input comes in and I am just responding to it?

You could say you are responding, but in truth, there is no one responding. There is just a unitary movement—

thought/intention/action. Nowhere is there a "you" who creates or responds to anything.

> *The thought just came, "This is what needs to be done,"*
> *then I just write it down?*

Yes, the thought comes, "this needs to be done," and because of that thought, there is an action that follows, which is the movement of arriving at the solution to the question. If the thought, "this needs to be done," didn't appear, then there would be no action. If you read that again you will see that there was no *you* mentioned.

From whatever the dominant thought or intention is, which you do not choose or create, comes an action that follows that intention. This all happens by itself. You are not creating any of it. In this case, the intention is to read the exam questions and answer them, then the ensuing action happens.

> *You said you create "couch potatoes." What does that*
> *mean? Is this the outcome of this, that you just lie on your*
> *couch?*

I am saying that metaphorically. As it turns out, I seem to do a hell of a lot—making albums, film scores, writing books, working with many people on inquiries, etc. But none of it is based on a desire to be anything; an ambition or need to be someone; or a feeling that I have to accomplish something. It's not based on any desire to succeed, or on any motivation to get anywhere or become anything. If in any moment there is no intention to do something, then nothing will be done, and there is no one here to judge that as wrong. So, lying on the couch all day is perfectly fine.

I am not the doer. For example, several years ago, someone asked me to do this work and I finally agreed, after saying no several times. Then, one thing just leads to another. When I say I am lazy, it does not mean I don't work. I can work a lot actually, but I am very lazy about getting somewhere or being anything. I just do what appears to be done, or not.

The action follows the intention to work. For example, I am just being lazy, and then maybe a thought and intention appears, "Edit some talks for the book." I didn't create that thought or intention. Reading, typing, editing—all happen as a result of that thought/intention, which I did not create. It is not, however, based on some ideas of becoming, like, "I have to be successful, I have to be something, or I have to be special." There is no desire or becoming in it at all.

If it all ends, which of course it will someday, it will be okay with me. I could just lie on my couch forever, but often that does not seem to be what is happening. If I look at all of the things I have "done" in recent years, I can't imagine how it all happened. It is all just flowing by, like a river. If action happens, then action happens. If no action happens, then no action happens.

Whatever I am doing, I can be very focused. For example, when I am making music, I can be very focused, but there is still a laziness about it and I am just doing what is in front of me at the time. There is an ease about it, and the reason for that is I am not invested in the outcome. I do what is needed to be done, and I have no control over the outcome. I just do it because that is what is happening now. That is the way of freedom as well.

Now, you may say, "but who is doing?" It's difficult to speak without using words that sound like a doer, but in truth, the doing itself is just happening as well. Action follows intention. An intention appears, spontaneously and the action follows, spontaneously, based on that intention. It is all a unitary movement that is not created by a "me," but we speak language, which is duality. So, I say, "I do what is needed to be done."

What I am describing is what Vedanta describes as Karma Yoga—you are entitled to want whatever you want and do whatever you do, but the outcome is not in your control. It is one of the spiritual practices in Vedanta. For me, and for those who really recognize their essential being and are finished, it is not a practice, it is just how you are. That is freedom. Freedom from becoming.

> *From an outside perspective, people could conclude that there is a lack of care. As you say, it can all end and that will be fine with you.*

Yes, someone could surmise that, but that would be wrong. There is all the care in the world. I care about this work and the people I work with. If I am making music, I care to make it as good as I am able. But again, if, in the next moment, it is gone, I am fine. That's what is and there is a reconciliation—what is, is. If it is work, then that is what is, and if there is no work, then that is what is. Nevertheless, there is all the care when I am doing something, and that care is also just what is here. Caring is just what is. It's spontaneously appearing, the same as thoughts and actions.

Thinking You Should Be Doing Something

One of the big things I notice is there is this belief that I should be doing something.

In Western cultures, this is very true. In warmer climates where there is more leisure, it is less so.

In America, it feels like a plague. It is like being enslaved. I see how damaging it can be.

I agree. It is a cultural vasana. I saw this early in my spiritual seeking by going to India and experiencing the absence of that drive to achieve. I was not attached to their culture and in that way was free of it. The Indians had to work, and I could just be there and do nothing. After years of being there, I saw the vasana clearly. When I come back to America, I feel that cultural vasana—everybody thinking they have to do something all the time. It's intense.

By being in a different culture, as well as coming to know liberation from culture through inquiry, the vasana faded for me. Now, I just do what is in front of me. A while ago, I was talking to my girlfriend about a friend of hers who paints. This friend told my girlfriend that she did not "identify as being an artist." To me, identifying is just a concept. I don't identify myself as a musician because right now, I am not making music. Right now, I am speaking about this. So now, I am a speaker. Later, I may be cutting the lawn. At that moment, I will be a person pushing a lawnmower.

Culture programs you to want to know who you are (i.e. I am an artist, banker, dentist, accountant, etc.). This friend mentioned that since she did not identify as an artist, she did not take it very seriously. That is a very Western view. I used to look at it that way as well. Now, I don't know what I am. I am nothing. I am whatever

I am doing in the moment. If I am making music, then, in that moment, I seem to be a musician.

When I was on the bus early in my spiritual seeking, I saw that I never changed my whole life. That is still the same. I am not going anywhere. Different actions show up and I engage them when they appear: speaking, making music, eating, etc. Most people can't live like this. They have to keep knowing who they are as an identity and keep becoming, more and more. They end up pushing life around, struggling, striving, and arguing with what is.

It Feels Like There is a Doer

> *What I noticed just now is, every time we talk about there being no doer, I sort of tense up because I've got it wired in my brain that I don't get that bit. The thought that comes up is, "It sort of feels like it's me doing the knowing." However, I think I may be just making a story out of it. I'd like to blow that away somehow.*

Okay, alright. Let's say you're wrapped up in thinking for an hour, then the thought, "have a holiday" appears. Did you do that thought?

> *No.*

It just appeared, didn't it?

> *Yes.*

Okay, did you have anything to do with it?

No. That says it pretty well.

This work is always about you seeing for yourself, not me explaining something. When you are "wrapped up in thoughts" and the thought, "have a holiday" happens, that just appeared for some reason, didn't it? Then you're on a holiday. There may even be the thought, "let's stay on a holiday," but did you do that thought either?

No. That wraps it up.

Okay, good.

I don't have much else to say about that one. That's great.

Just keep seeing for yourself if you create any thoughts. What's the next thought that you're going to come up with?

It kind of fits in with what other people have spoken about on this call. I keep thinking it's going to feel a certain way or I'm going to have an "oh, wow" moment where I really get it and there's no "me," and it's going to be amazing.

There are feelings here in this body-mind organism, and it can feel like there's a self here, but it isn't true. Just because there is a feeling, doesn't mean there is actually a self. What is, is. There's the knowing, and the feeling is included with all the other objects. Then, along with that, there's the belief these feelings mean there's a doer. Just see that. Have a holiday, and see you have nothing to do with any of that stuff.

One of the exercises in Liberation IS is to look back at different times in my life and see that the knowing is the same. Actually, if I just look back five minutes ago, and ask, "Did I decide," I see that thoughts just appear. For example, where did the thought to have a cup of tea come from?

Right, it's just like the thought, "have a holiday." That thought just appears, right? Where did it come from? It just appears. You didn't create it, right?

Right, good stuff.

This is what inquiry is. Inquiry is not understanding, figuring out or describing. Inquiry is looking in your own laboratory, here and now. The body-mind is the laboratory that you investigate—you see how things are working and how you function.

Questions About Choice and Doership

If I am "all that is," both "seen and unseen," can it be said that "I am the chooser?" I mean, who else, or from where else would choices come from? Of course, I'm keenly aware that thoughts "just arise," but "technically," it must be from I! I'm curious to hear your insights!

If you are, as you say, "all that is," then in this moment, whatever is, is you. Is there a "you" separate from the so-called choice that's making the choice? If you are all there is, is there a "where else" for a choice to come from?

If, for example, the idea appears to watch a movie, is there a you separate from that idea who created that idea, or are *you in fact, in that moment, the idea itself*? Who created whatever is in this moment? Who chose to make it appear? How can you create yourself? There would have to be another you to do that. A chooser or creator implies something "else" that the chooser or creator is choosing or creating.

Truly, in a non-separate reality, who is there to do any of that? There only is what is. No reason, no rhyme.

> *Amazing, how you always dispel ignorance! If I get you right, saying, "I am the chooser," is using four words too many... It's going into philosophy.*

Yes, it is philosophy. To say, "I am the chooser," implies there is something other than you that is choosing. What I am saying is that you are whatever is appearing in this moment. This thought is you, in this moment. This emotion is you, in this moment. This feeling or sensation is you, in this moment. You are not something "else" choosing this, you are this. So then, where is the choice at all?

Here is another way to look at it. Not only is there no chooser, there are no choices. Whatever is, is choicelessly so. It simply is with no reason why. Only a philosopher will come up with a "why." If it is true that there are no choices, and there is only what is, then where is the chooser? Is it you, God, the universe or anything else? If there are no choices, clearly, there is no chooser.

Then the question becomes: What would it be like to no longer indulge or engage in questions about free will? What is the need to have those questions? Is it amusement or entertainment? Possibly fear of knowing nothing, having nothing and being no one? How about having something to "do," a purpose, or some meaning?

Life can get pretty stark, spacious and "empty" without the need or desire to figure out and understand. To be ordinary, here and now, not knowing why anything is as it is. Just life, as it is, now. That is freedom.

Thoughts - Beliefs

Wrapped Up in Thoughts

I seem to be wrapped up in thoughts a lot lately.

I have thoughts too. I don't consider it being wrapped up. There are just thoughts going on. The idea that there will be no thoughts from doing this work is not realistic. The affliction happens when you believe the thoughts.

How do you not believe them?

You know what is true—the thoughts were not created by you. They are just the result of impressions programmed in the mind. The mind's job is to record impressions of its day and of its life, and to replay those impressions as thoughts. If something so-called negative is recorded, then it will replay that so-called negative impression.

For example, if we believe thoughts about our parents doing certain things to us and then believe that is why we are the way we are, we are going to suffer now because of those thoughts. However, we now know this is just a story and there is no past. There is only now. If there is only now, then it is time to stop believing the story of anybody doing anything to you in the past. Just see now that freedom is your essential nature. Look now, there are no parents. Where are they? Do you see them? If you want to get real, you need to be reconciled with the fact that the belief about them doing something to you is just myth.

I realize that many people have had traumatic childhoods and they do need assistance. I have nothing but compassion for people who grew up in tough environments. Many parents, through no fault of their own, are not great parents. If someone needs to engage in therapeutic methods, then that is what they need to do. But, for someone who is ready and willing to be free, it is time to move beyond that.

Are you living without memories?

No, I did not say that. I have memories. I rarely, however, engage in thoughts about the past and I don't replay so-called problems from the past. Nothing is less interesting to me. Occasionally, there is a memory of something that happened, which is completely normal for the mind to do. It is an impression programmed in the brain, a samskara. When a memory pops up, I see very little value in it. I just don't believe in the past, and I am not sentimental or nostalgic. I don't care to engage in it.

If there are tough situations that people have lived through, those memories can be replayed, now, and if people believe them and give them importance, now, it will cause suffering, now. Also, if you go into the psychological model and start investigating the memories, you are just giving them credence and value; making them appear to be actual, now, which is clearly not truth.

A free person is no longer a victim. This work is not for everyone. How many people are ready to no longer place importance and value on their stories? I am compassionate and I recognize that for many people, it has been a rough life, with many traumatic experiences that are not easily resolved. That is why therapists are needed.

I have a job that I hate, and I have been thinking about going back to school. I have been going back and forth on

*what to do for the past seven years, and it is ridiculous. I
need to figure it out.*

There is no figuring it out because there is no doer. What will
happen will happen. There is only now. All your attempts to figure
it out have caused you a lot of stress. So then, what is the point? The
problem is, there is a "should" in there. I "should" know what to do.
Society and family have programmed this into us. It is not yours.
You don't have an "I should do this, or I should do that."

I understand it is scary not knowing what to do, but to keep doing
something that adds stress for you is not the wisest thing. I never
offer suggestions on what to do. Just notice that attempting to
figure it out is not helping. I know that things just unfold as they do
even though I may have ideas on how they should go. So, I just don't
bother.

Intentions will appear, and there is nothing you can do about it.
What is, is. Right now, you have a job that you don't like and you
have been attempting to change your circumstances through your
so-called "will power." It is not working. This is causing you stress,
and you still have a job that you don't like. So, it serves no purpose.
It does not make anything happen.

> *Inquirer 2: I once had a teacher who said that only
> awakened individuals have free will.*

I disagree. Awakened or not, there is no free will.

Need to Be More Aware

What I noticed this week is that I just showed up here at this work, yet there is still a sense I did something to get here. Also, I have this notion I need to be more aware. I am seeing how insidious these thoughts are.

Okay, let's take a look and see what that is. When you say, "I need to be more aware," the core belief is there is *someone* here who needs to be more aware. What has to be recognized is that this is just a thought appearing in empty mind. "I have to be more aware" is just a thought. That is not you. It is a habitual thought. It is a bad habit that keeps replaying.

We see that thought and believe, "Oh, there is an 'I' here that needs to be more aware in the future, and this 'I' that is going to be fully liberated in the future is who I am." What we have to see is that this is just a thought that is appearing. It means nothing. It does not mean there is a self here. It is simple.

If this is true, then just stop and see again, here and now, there is nothing. This *now* is the ocean of Sat Chit Ananda, and on the surface of the ocean appears a thought, now, and then it is gone. The ocean of Sat Chit Ananda remains. The thought comes, "I need to be more aware," but this is just a thought, and it passes like a wave.

How can you be "more aware?" Let's see the ultimate joke of this. Have a holiday.

HOLIDAY

How can you be more aware? You are aware. You are it. How can you be more of you? You are aware. You can't be more or less aware.

Even if you are only aware of thoughts for a day, you are still aware. You are just as aware as if you were aware of yourself as the knowing. There is no more or less aware. You may be aware of objects and the belief in a self, but there is full awareness of those objects. When that object passes, then there is full awareness of yourself. Aware does not change.

Two things are happening. One is the idea that you need to be more aware, which creates the belief that there is a self which needs to be more aware. That is obviously not true. The other thing is that the idea is wrong anyway—you can't be more aware, you are aware. There is no more or less aware. See for yourself.

I love these questions. They are great. Whenever a question appears, I have no idea what the answer is. I am not pedantic. I don't go into my mind and find the answer. A question like that comes and I say, "Let's look." Then, the answer appears by seeing right now. Everyone can do that. The answer is not in the encyclopedia. The answer is now. My words come now, not from a book. Whenever a question appears for you, look and see what is true.

No Connection with Past Events

I had an incident with a co-worker where they brought up something from five years ago. I saw that I could not connect with a "me" in the past and yet, there was some emotion that came up about what I did and a sense of feeling guilty.

That is normal. It arises, but what do you want? If you want freedom, then right away, you are going to ignore that. If some residual memory appears in my mind about the past where I did something "stupid" and an emotion of guilt is triggered, I am going to ignore that right away because truth is here, now.

> *I think what shocks me is how much memories and*
> *feelings about the past used to run my life prior to*
> *working with you.*

Of course, because it was the only thing you knew.

> *It feels like I am losing my conscience because guilt is my*
> *moral compass.*

You are not losing your conscience at all. Those memories and triggers about the "past" used to run your life because you did not know any other way. It is all we know until we have this shift of knowing. The only thing we have been told to value is the past, the future, the "self," and the morality of right and wrong. It is what we have been taught. We have been told to put a lot of importance on our past (i.e. what we have done and what has been done to us). We have been told that our life stories are very precious and important. This view then rules our life—it IS our life. That is a joke because none of it is true.

With this work, we see it is a complete myth. There is no truth to it at all. You have the shift of knowing and value something different— freedom, truth. You will be amazed at how the myth used to rule your life. This amazement is a good sign.

It is fine that stories come up and you go into them for a moment (or a period of time) and that emotions appear. And it is also good to learn from those "mistakes." But learning from mistakes and continuing to suffer are two different things.

You know you are free. It doesn't matter what comes up because what you want and what you value is freedom. So, do as Annamalai Swami says, "Ignore, and just be the consciousness." I say, just know who you are, be this knowing.

Nothing is lost if you "go into stories." By continuing to have holidays, you will not go into the stories as much because you will lose interest.

The thought of guilt just builds itself up more.

The thought "I am guilty" is self. That is what self is. When that thought goes away and you are just here, now, there is no self here. Then the next silly thought arises, and if you believe it is you, that is self again. There are hundreds or thousands of births of self each day. They start with, "I was, I am, or I will be..." For example, "I was stupid in the past." Then, a holiday appears and there is no "I" (self) to be stupid. There is no past; there is no self.

The thought does not add on to a self. The thought *is* the so-called self, then it is gone. It is just a glitch to believe that—since the thought begins with "I," there is a self in here. Every thought arises and then passes. With each new thought, a potential new "self" arises.

For instance, the thought "I was so great in the past" arises, stays for a moment and then is gone. Then another thought comes, "I am going to get so enlightened in the future." This "self" appears for a moment and then is gone. Each thought is a different "self." They are all just residual thoughts that we believe means there is an "I." They don't. The residual thoughts always start with "I am this...", or "I am that..." There is always the "I" attached to the thought, whether the "I" is said or not.

On a holiday, there is no self, no past, and no future. There is now, freedom. You are unborn. Then there is a thought and you take another birth of self. Your attention goes to it and then there is a thought, "have a holiday," and you recognize, there is no self.

I Might Be Hooked Somewhere

I am thinking that if everything is fine and nothing bad is happening, I still might be hooked somewhere. This seems to happen quite frequently with me. I feel really unsettled and unstable.

Why do you think that those uncertainties appear? What is the root of those uncertainties?

I don't know.

It must have come from some impression that was put in your mind such as, "There must be something wrong with me." This is what our culture teaches us. Even if things are good, now, there must be something that is going to go wrong. This is just cultural programming and it was not here when you came out of the womb. These impressions, which you did not create, are not here now in empty mind (your essential being). They lead you to think you have to improve and you have to be better. These are just based on ignorance. These false assumptions have been placed in our mind over the years.

The purpose of a holiday is to see our essential mind is not touched by anything and there is nothing wrong with us. Also, there is nothing more to achieve or attain. In this no-thing, which is empty mind, there is nothing to fix or change. If we know our freedom, now, what could be added to this? What fixing or improving is needed?

The point is that all these assumptions are just impressions that have been imprinted upon us by cultural ignorance. We are taught in our Western culture that we are sinners and there is something wrong with us. This is done through ignorance and there is no fault here. Even if something is good, our mind is impressed with this belief that something is wrong, and we have to find it and fix it.

It is possible over time that these assumptions won't appear anymore. It takes being authentic to truth. If I could flip a switch in your head and say, "You are done and not to worry," I would. Actually, that is what I am saying; don't worry about anything that appears in the mind. There is nothing wrong and it is all fine. Whatever goes on in the mind has nothing to do with you. You did not create any of the stuff in your head.

Feels like there is a process going on.

Many say that and have a look, now. What process? Wake up, now. Truth is here. Keep knowing what is true, now. There is nothing to get rid of. There is no doer to get rid of anything. Know what's true and truth shall set you free. Knowing is what sets you free. There is nothing to do.

Thoughts About No Time and No Doer

You talk about there being no past, no future, and no self. When I have holidays, I recognize that. However, when I'm not on a holiday, the whole concept of no past, no future, and no self only comes in as an intellectual thing. I think about it and I say, "Oh yeah, there's no self, no past, and no future." So, it doesn't carry with me outside of the holiday.

Also, a lot of the forum posts deal with the fact that there is no doer. To me, it's an intellectual thing. When I see there is no doer, it takes the charge off of something I did or something someone else did, but it doesn't follow me in everyday living.

I still sense a future; I still sense a past and I don't know if that's something that eventually resolves with more holidays or if it needs to be resolved. When I'm on a holiday, I get it, but it's just when I'm not on a holiday, I don't get it.

There are two questions, one is about time and one is about no doer. Of course, both can be conceptual, but for you, they are not conceptual. Let's have a holiday right now.

HOLIDAY

I want you to look now and tell me honestly, now. In your own knowing, look now, is there a past?

No.

Do you know that?

Yes. I know it when I'm on a holiday.

I knew you were going to say that. Be simple. You know that, right? You know there's no Santa Claus? Is it conceptual that you know there is no Santa Claus or is it finished, you know there's no Santa Claus?

It's already finished.

Okay, with this it's the same. It's only different in that knowing there is no Santa Claus is easy, but knowing you're free, there's no past or future, and no self, seems to be more challenging because there is the habitual momentum of mental impressions—conditioned thought—telling you differently. Nevertheless, does it change the fact that there is no past?

No, there's no past, but when I think about it outside of the holiday, I think about it. Maybe, thinking isn't such a bad thing...

Let's keep going a little bit. It's not like there's no past when you are having a holiday, but when you're not having a holiday, there is a past. That's not what I'm saying. It's very simple. *There is no past.* Is that true or not? Where is the past? Is there a past because you have a thought occurring now? Does that mean there's a past?

It's just a thought.

When is the thought occurring, in the past? It's occurring now. So, is there a past or isn't there?

There isn't.

If you're lost in thoughts, is there a past, or isn't there?

No, there isn't because it's just thoughts coming up.

Whether you're lost in thoughts or on a holiday, I want you to tell me, is there a past?

No, there's no past.

Okay, stop there. Even if you think there's a past, does it mean there is a past?

No.

If I think, "Santa's alive, Santa's alive," does that mean he's alive? No, because I know there's no Santa. You know there's no past. You can think there's a past all you want, but it doesn't change the *fact* that there is no past. It becomes a conviction, and it takes time because it's a momentum of habit. The more you recognize on a holiday that there is no past, eventually you will just simply know there's no past. Think about the past all you want, it doesn't mean there is one.

Yes.

The same with the doer. You can tell me you're the doer until the cows come home, I don't care. Take all the credit you want. It doesn't change the fact that there's no doer, does it?

No.

Do you create the thoughts in your head, or don't you?

No, they just come on their own.

Well, what if you start thinking, "I do actually create them," does that change the fact that you don't create them? No! The *fact* is you don't create them. Know what's true and truth shall set you free. Is there a past? No. Is there a future? No. Is there a doer? No. So, go ahead and think all you want about those things, it doesn't change the fact that they don't exist.

Gotcha.

The point of you knowing that you're not the doer is that it brings about compassion for yourself and others. That compassion unfolds more and more, maybe endlessly.

When it comes up with other people and I realize there's no doer, I see myself thinking about it. It's a thought process that goes, "Oh, you know that person is not responsible because there's no doer," but it comes up as part of a thinking process.

Fine. The reason it comes up as thought is because you know it's true.

Yeah, okay. I guess my idea was that knowing required no thought, it was just something that is there.

Yes, when it is known, it is known. I never think there's a doer. I know there is no doer and it doesn't mean that thoughts like that don't arise. It's fine if they arise or don't arise. Again, it doesn't change the fact that you know.

Alright.

That's the job of the mind, to take input from experience, record it, play it back, and subsequently, take credit or blame as the doer (which is a lie). It doesn't matter if thoughts come up about something like that or not. Actually, they likely will. Fine, no problem.

Self-Blame and Self-judgment

I see that I'm not in control of any of it—negative feelings, guilt, shame, physical pain, ups, downs. I have beat myself up over things for years. So, this is a big relief that there's no blame. However, how do I stop judging myself? Just by seeing that I don't have control over anything?

I wonder where all these negative thoughts come from and why so many people have them. I know that for years I was concerned that I was not positive. I tried positive affirmations and I saw that they don't work AT ALL. So, I gave them up. However, I had no substitute or way to handle the negativity. Now, with you, I see that the thoughts just flow through this vessel.

I would like to get to the point of not caring what I think. Unfortunately, I take thoughts personally and seriously. I don't know how to stop. This is a very big lesson for me.

The only way to stop taking them seriously is to see that they are unreal, ephemeral appearances in spacious knowing-aware, who you are; to know that you did not create any of it; and to stay true to that knowing until the habitual pattern of believing those stories no longer holds sway. That means to know who you are, prior to all that judgment, and to *be that*. The more you are knowing that, the more you will see the value in it, and the less you will be interested in falling for all the ignorance of culturally created thought. It is living the way of freedom, instead of the way of ignorance and bondage.

Also, you don't stop judging yourself. You are not judging yourself in the first place. There are only thoughts, which are highly habitual, created from impressions in your mind from years of input. There's the belief that those thoughts mean something about you and you need to value and attend to them. What if you do not value them? Will something bad happen?

Does it really matter where the thoughts come from? I know you were being rhetorical, but it is still a good observation. It doesn't matter. You could go the psychological route and trace the events that may have created them in your mind (negative experiences, etc.), but that is an endless and ultimately fruitless exercise.

Also, notice, are the thoughts true? Here and now, stop and recognize what is—know that you exist, here and now, in no time. The stories that play in your mind *are not actual now, they are non-existent.* But *you* are—you exist! Do the stories have any actual truth or value? Do they serve any purpose, other than to cause suffering?

Truth is true. See the value of truth and continue to value it. Hoping to get to the point of not caring is looking towards a future when things will, presumably, be better. What about now? Freedom is now. The only thing you can concern yourself with is now. Freedom is not in the future.

Having said that, and although it sounds paradoxical, this work takes time. After a lifetime of these habitual beliefs, there is no reason to expect the momentum of belief to stop immediately. However, it does stop immediately in a holiday, when you are recognizing that here and now, none of the beliefs are true. By being authentic to truth, you are free, now; and the unresolved beliefs resolve of their own accord, without you having to do anything about them.

Yes, this is a new habit that will, with authenticity and valuing, become your default habit... just as the opposite became the default habit because of knowing no other alternative.

Negative self-Talk

I get into real negative self-talk and I know I have to stop believing my thoughts. A lot of them are about the past. I say to myself, "I didn't pick these thoughts, I didn't put them here, and I don't have to believe them." It seems like this is a holiday. I'd like to get some feedback from you.

Is it true that you didn't create your thoughts?

Yes.

Okay, good. You know that. Is it true that those thoughts (which you didn't create and just come spontaneously) don't actually mean anything, and have no power, in and of themselves?

In and of themselves, no.

What has to happen for them to have power?

I have to believe them.

That's right. You know they're the result of a lifetime of circumstances and impressions recorded in your mind, mostly negative in this case, which you had nothing to do with. You didn't create them. It's just what happened. Now you know that.

Let's take it one step at a time. It's very good to know that—know what's true and truth will set you free. Just by knowing, the stranglehold of beliefs can ease.

Telling yourself, "I don't have to believe these thoughts" is like an affirmation. It is just a thought that appears because you have come to know that thoughts are not reality, they are based on impressions in your mind from previous experiences, and those experiences are not true, now. Since that is true and truth is what you want, then you will not believe them. Whether that thought/affirmation appears or not is unimportant, simply knowing that there is no truth in there will end the belief.

The thought appears because I've suffered so badly.

Yes, the suffering can elicit that thought, but that thought wouldn't appear if you didn't know it was true. You know you didn't create those negative thoughts; and you know that if you don't believe them, they don't actually have any power, and they dissipate.

Belief is like electricity going to a fan, it keeps the fan going. When that belief switch turns off, all that thinking and emoting has to subside because there's no power going to it.

I want to go a little further. You know those things. It's fine that the affirmation, "I don't have to believe these thoughts" comes up. You don't create that either. It just happens because you *know*. Ultimately, that affirmation doesn't have to happen either, because you already know that's true. The thought is not needed. What is needed is to *be free*. That is a holiday. Freedom is here and now and is known to you whenever a holiday happens. It happens spontaneously because you already know what is true.

I put a lot of story around that by saying, "I'm the one who's supposed to suffer." That's me! It's a story.

Yes, it's a lifetime of training for all of us. Let's face it, due to life circumstances, some people's negative input and influence are more challenging. For some, there's more and for some there's less. There's no fault. For you, there have been seventy-three years of challenging, negative samskaras, or impressions. Give yourself a break. It takes time and being dedicated to truth.

What does being dedicated to truth mean? It doesn't mean I'm going to find truth in the future and I'm going to keep seeking until I find truth. That's not being dedicated to truth, that's being dedicated to seeking. Being dedicated to truth means stopping now and seeing the freedom that's here, now. Truth is only now. Dedication to truth is only now.

After seventy-three years of negative impressions, it's unrealistic to think that all those impressions are going to end after doing this work for only a few months. It takes time. It's just the way it works. Truth is true and the way it works is to know that in a holiday. Just be free, NOW, only now. Maybe in five minutes, you will be right back in the story. You can't deal with five minutes from now, you can only deal with now. So, just know freedom in a holiday, now.

That's the key, that's the key.

Yes. Truth is true, and truth is only NOW. Freedom is freedom and freedom is only NOW. Freedom is not attained in the future. You're not going to be dedicated to being free from your suffering in the future; that's seeking forever. Freedom is NOW only. Dedication to truth happens, NOW.

The suffering, or to use another word, the *grace* you have will force you to have a holiday. Once you know what's true and then stay authentic, you can't lose. You can't fail. Why? Because freedom is true, now. Be free, now. Being free now doesn't mean be free now and then worry that tomorrow you're not going to be free. You can't deal with tomorrow, just be free now. Have a holiday.

HOLIDAY

Be nothing—in truth, you get nothing. Whereas with the stories we tell ourselves, we get a lot, don't we? We get the belief in separation and self-importance. We get me, me, me... the poor me, the great me, the self-important me, the suffering me, etc. You see? But you don't get that in truth. You get nothing.

I've experienced that self-importance of being the sufferer. Yeah, I get that.

It's very common, isn't it? There are even whole societies that are based on self-victimization and they make the whole world feel like they're victims. There's that self-importance.

You just have to stay authentic, which you clearly are. Let's have a holiday, now.

HOLIDAY

Where are those stories, now?

There is an emptiness to it. There is a nothingness to it.

Okay. I don't use those words. Emptiness is a thing. Emptiness and nothingness are objects of perception. I just say there is no-thing. What there is in a holiday is—no story, no past, and no self. No-thing. You don't get anything else in return, except freedom. You only get the end of the self story, now.

Does this resonate with you? You see that it's actually true?

Well, I've experienced it.

No! What about NOW? Forget what you have experienced in the past. What past? Freedom is now, and now, in holiday, without referring to anything, is there a story?

No.

Know that and just keep being authentic. There's no other way. I don't care that some teachers say they're going to give you some shakti, then your whole history is going to disappear, or all vasanas are going to go away, or some other nonsense. See that whole history is not existent, now!

This takes being authentic, which is the truth. There's only now. There's no magic bullet for this. The only magic bullet is this: have a holiday. Recognize, it's already over.

Nothing Matters

I found myself revisiting the bleakness this past week that we talked about during my individual sessions. I found myself thinking a lot about how everything is preordained and nothing really matters. I realized this was just a thought, but I seem to keep revisiting this bleakness.

What do you mean by "nothing matters?"

There is no one here. There is no chooser and no doer. So, things just happen and none of it really matters.

None of it really matters to whom? Let's look. Does it matter if someone you love is sick? Does it matter if someone is abusing a child? Does it matter if our crazy politicians start these wars in foreign countries and slaughter millions of innocent people? I think it matters.

In freedom, you have all the care in the world. You can care and feel deeply people's pain and the insanity of the lunatic mind. "Nothing matters" is just a concept. Because there is no doer does not mean regular emotions like compassion, sadness or empathy won't arise. No doer just means there's no one creating those emotions, they are just arising. Of course, the care for your children and the care for your family matters.

The most valuable thing is to know your essential nature is free. That is the most important thing. Everything else comes and goes without exception. I think when you recognize your essential nature, you care more deeply.

If you look at the opposite of a free person, someone who is schizophrenic, they don't care about anything. They are too wrapped up in their own pathologies to care. Someone who is open and healthy, and not so focused on self, can care for others. I often say that enlightenment is not for you, it is for everyone else. As Douglas Harding said, "Can't you see, I'm space for you to be." What he is saying is that there is no one here, there's only freedom. What we are usually saying is, "Can't you see, I am a psychological mess that you have to deal with?"

The pathological mind is a burden not just to oneself, but to the whole world. Look at the shape the world is in. I look at the news and it breaks my heart. I think it matters and I am disgusted by what is going on. Why is this going on? Because there are pathologies in the human mind. The mind is filled with them. The personal pathologies create the pathologies in the world.

Usually, the people with the most power have the most pathologies. The most destructive pathologies are greed, the lust for power and control. People in power achieve these positions because of these pathologies.

"Nothing matters" is a halfway around the circle concept like the Neo-Advaita view—I am only awareness. The Neo-Advaitists say, "I am awareness and the body does not matter because all of this is an illusion." Under this philosophy, people believe it does not matter if they lose a child. What a ridiculous philosophy of conceptualism.

Full circle means you see that you are human, and you can care because you are healthy. You can care more. You feel more.

"Nothing matters" is a bit philosophical as well. It needs to go full circle. You are not just awareness. You are the Absolute appearing as you. You are the Absolute. You are it. You are IT. The body is the appearance of IT. The body is not something appearing separate from the Absolute, God. It is the appearance of God. This is full circle and is what non-duality really means.

A healthy, free person, who knows their essential nature and who values truth, knows all this form is ephemeral. It all comes and goes. It all changes, and to be fully pathologically attached to something that causes suffering is not healthy. This does not mean that in the time of an appearance of your family, friends, or the world, that nothing matters. It is called the Play of Leela. Enjoy, as it is a play! It is not called the "The illusion that does not matter."

Of course, we want to care, but we have these concepts of what enlightenment is and we think we should not care about anything. This is not true. What good is enlightenment if there is no caring. It is pointless. My favorite saying is from the Zen master Dogen, "Next to kindness, enlightenment is the most important thing." I think wanting to be free is all about caring. The more you recognize your essential freedom and see the value in it, the more you recognize it is not about you. With this work, you are removing one more malignancy from the world, and you are caring.

We hear all these spiritual concepts that if you are enlightened, then nothing will touch you, and you won't be attached. In a way it is true, but it is not the way we think. We are still human.

> *Inquirer 2: Meaninglessness and purposelessness are concepts that I have heard and misunderstood. I can see why because when I am living through concepts, things*

can appear meaningless. But, when there are no concepts, there can be no meaning.

It is good that you brought this up because when we are on a holiday, we see this moment can only be as it is. The question, "What is the meaning of this moment?" becomes irrelevant. There is no meaning for this moment. It just is. The word *meaningless* brings with it a connotation of cynicism and negativity. People think it is very depressing. However, no meaning does not equate to meaninglessness. No meaning simply means *what is, is.*

In truth, there is no meaning for this moment. Any meaning we could find for this moment has to be some idea generated by the mind. You can ascribe a meaning to this moment if you want. It is fine. I don't particularly see a reason to do it. Some people like to feel they have a purpose. If they feel the need to have a purpose, that is okay, but know it is just a self-ascribed purpose. It does not mean it is the actual purpose.

What is the meaning of my life? What is my purpose? These are very philosophical questions and they never get answered because there are no answers. Let's be on holiday.

HOLIDAY

This moment just is.

What is the meaning of this moment?

No one knows.

It does not have a meaning, and it is not meaningless.

Those are just concepts.

It just is.

What is, is.

Who knows why?

It is nice to not care about why anything is the way that it is. I don't care to attempt to know why this moment is. I do care about the people in my life, humanity and the world. Those I care about. I just don't care to know why this moment is the way that it is. There is no answer. It just is.

Synchronicity or Random Chaos

It seems like there must be some reason why things happen. For example, when I meet someone who seems so familiar, there seems to be some kind of connection or something. So, is life just random chaos or is there predestination?

The funny thing is, when something like that happens, we immediately filter it through the belief we hold the most, such as, "I met this person and she seemed so familiar, I must have known her in a past life." That is a big leap, isn't it? It's just an assumption based on a belief, which is not known to be true at all.

But there does seem to be some kind of causality, Jung calls it synchronicity. I am just trying to figure out how things happen. It's just too much like things are connected for it to be random chaos. Is this philosophical?

Yes. If there was a real answer to those questions, it would be in all the books already. Then you could have an intellectual understanding and the question would be solved. The reason it is not in the books is because there's really no answer. Or, if there is, we have no way of knowing. I say, the answer to that question, as with all philosophical questions, is when that question no longer appears. Let's have a holiday together.

HOLIDAY

Here and now, this knowing is present, right?

This knowing that is aware is not separate from you, is it?

It is essential to who you are.

There is only now,
and now, whatever is, is.

Without going into your mind of questions,
just looking, here and now,
does this, now, have some meaning?

Here and now, look.

This knowing, what is, is.

There is nothing behind the curtain.

If you see this, then you see that what is, only is. You see there is no past and no future. This now didn't come from somewhere. It only is, here and now. If there is no past, then what is now, is appearing now, only. Whatever happens (like a meeting with someone), if you don't go into the mind to try to understand why, it simply is what is. Freedom is in this. It is the end of looking for the meaning because it is a moot point; the reason has never been found before.

You can go into why I met this person or why this happened, and the synchronicity, but really you are just going back into the philosophical carousel. What I share—freedom—is radical. It is nothing. You don't get answers to those questions. That is why it is for people who are mature and just happy to be, and for people who do not need answers to unanswerable questions.

In the absence of beliefs, we become very comfortable in knowing nothing. When we want only what we can actually know (which is very little), we see philosophical questions such as, "Where did I come from? Where am I going? What is the meaning of life? What will happen after I die? Why did I meet that person?", are unanswerable. If we are reconciled with that fact, we are at ease in not knowing and no longer needing to know. Then these questions don't arise. This is freedom from beliefs.

Prayer and Belief

> *I went through a really painful experience of letting go of my concepts of prayer, meditation, and connecting to the divine. It was really painful. I felt like I was letting go of a huge part of my life. This must be such a normal part of the process. We have all these ideas and concepts. For me, they have been comforting and have given me a sense of being taken care of or having some comprehension that there is a reason.*

I agree. Look at how many people believe in God. They do for exactly those reasons you explained. It gives comfort, hope, meaning, and a purpose, as well as the feeling of being taken care of. When seekers raised in a Western culture and religious beliefs start to doubt, they move over to more Eastern beliefs and start to derive hope from enlightenment in the future, or nirvana, or other dearly held beliefs about spirituality (Advaita, non-duality or whatever). So, in that way, nothing has changed essentially for them; they have just switched to a new set of beliefs. These new beliefs feel exciting and offer new hopes and comforts of becoming in the future. But they are the same false security.

How many people are willing to be free and to stand alone? How many are ready to be fully reconciled with the fact that what is, is, and there is no escape? How many are willing to be fully human, with all its joys and pains? Suffering comes from not being reconciled with what is and instead, arguing with what is. It's understandable to want to avoid painful or unpleasant experiences, but if we are honest, we must see that these are facts of life. This body-mind organism not only experiences pleasure; it also experiences pain—physical, mental and emotional.

That's why what you are doing is not for everyone. It's very mature to want to actually know what is true. We can only know for ourselves, now. Now, is where freedom is. Most people are too afraid to lose that sense of security of the known that their beliefs offer. They are not ready to stop believing in a perfected future, which includes enlightenment, Heaven, Nirvana, etc. These beliefs almost always have to do with an escape of some sort. I understand that, of course. No one wants to feel bad. So, those beliefs may offer comfort in the midst of unpleasant experiences.

For whatever reason, and we have no idea why, the intention to find out what is true appeared for you. Because of that, these things I mentioned can be reconciled. Then the suffering that comes from arguing with what is, in the form of avoidance, escape, hope, and becoming, can end. It can definitely be painful to have those beliefs fall away, or even be challenged. But it is not something you even need to think about. Just keep knowing what is true and those beliefs will just be gone, and you won't miss them.

But you can still have fun with it, right?

Just be honest. Is it fun or is there a belief there? You have to see for yourself. You can say it is just fun, but still be secretly harboring some hope that it is true or seeking comfort there. Only you know that and there is nothing for you to do. Just by having holidays, a shift of knowing has happened for you. And you are coming to know something that is essentially true, here and now. By knowing this, those beliefs have been put into question and can be finished. You didn't do that. You didn't even let go of it. Knowing truth started it and knowing truth will end it. Just keep knowing what is true and whatever is not true will go, without you needing to let go, or do anything at all.

I Am Just a Follower

Sometimes I think, "I used to follow a bunch of other teachers and now I am just following you."

Don't follow me. You are a master. See for yourself if anything I say is true. Then, you know for yourself and you kill me along the way. I just keep telling everybody each week to look for themselves.

What I meant is that the search is not over yet.

The search is over. It is over. You know who you are. What is not over is the resolution of habitual beliefs. Is there anything more for you to attain in terms of knowing who you are?

No.

Are you sure?

Yes.

This means your search is over. You found what is true. Now, just stay true, even when it is tough. If the momentum of thoughts and beliefs in any moment is stronger than your intention for freedom, then they will win. However, if your intention for freedom is stronger, that will win out over the thoughts and beliefs. If you stay authentic and keep valuing truth, truth will become dominant.

> *Sometimes I feel like I get lost in the thoughts and emotions.*

Yes, and you are aware of the thoughts and emotions. You are the thoughts and emotions like the wave is the ocean. It is the appearance of you, the Absolute. So, you are found. You are not lost, you are the thoughts and emotions. You are found.

Suffering is caused because there is a belief there that you should do something to not get lost in thoughts. There is nothing you can do except have the intention for freedom (which you don't do) and value that. Keep knowing what is true naturally. If it is overwhelming, you can throw on an audio of a group talk.

> *If I am the thoughts appearing, this means that all the monsters (Hitler, pedophiles, etc.) are also included in aware?*

Yes, they are all waves appearing in the ocean. However, we can only look within ourselves. The most malignant people on the planet are very obvious; and if we look at ourselves, we also see malignancies. We work in our own laboratory and when we come to see that we are free and lack nothing, we become mostly benign.

Let's say that something appears in the mind to do something bad. That appearance of a thought to do something bad is harmless. It only becomes harmful if there is some action taken to further the thought. On the other hand, it can be harmful to you if you suffer from it. You are not going to change the whole world, so the only thing you can do (there's no doer) is to be concerned with your own peace and freedom.

> *I feel like I am stubbornly believing all the thoughts, and on the other side, I am being stubborn in following the truth.*

There is no one here to be stubborn. There is a belief, which you did not create (there is no you to create the belief), and this belief causes you to suffer when thoughts appear. It causes you to think there's still meaning in there. You keep going over and over the thoughts, and they overpower you.

The intention for truth is not stubborn. It is genuine, and it is based on recognizing the value of truth. The more you value truth, the less thoughts will be able to overpower you. Of course, for our whole life, we have been overpowered by thoughts and believed there was no answer except through drugs and shock therapy, etc. See now, there is another way and it is to know what is true. This will stop the momentum of the belief that thoughts mean something. When that momentum slows down, there is more and more peace.

Becoming

Becoming implies future. And it implies a self that is going to be improved in that future. Knowing your essential being means you have seen who you are, free of self, and what is true and complete already. There is no becoming for you, essentially. If you feel the need to improve in the future, then clearly you are referring to self/ego. Freedom is knowing who you are, prior to that self/ego and knowing there is no becoming for *you*.

This Work as a Means to an End

> *I have really done a lot of trying to figure out liberation through the mind, and lately, the word "jump" keeps coming up over and over again. I had a belief that if I did something like this teaching, my life was going to change, and I was going to know I was complete because my life circumstances were different. This teaching was sort of a means to an end. Now, I realize that it's not about the life circumstances changing. It's about having holidays no matter what's coming up. So, I'm no longer seeking certain life circumstances.*

Right, in one way or another, I think that's true for all of us. We all want something to change. Something is unsatisfactory and the reason it's unsatisfactory is we're looking for satisfaction and value in objects and in mind. Those things are not stable, there's no ultimate satisfaction there. The ultimate satisfaction is you, your essential being, which is free and unchanging.

The thing that's also been playing in my head is the idea that "you can't get there from here." You can't use thoughts, you can't use techniques, and you can't use books to get wherever. It's just jumping every time I'm in the middle of something.

Right, exactly. Actually, going somewhere is heading in the opposite direction. There is no path to here and now, to your essential being. To be where you already are, and always have been, is the end of getting somewhere. We are always wanting to get somewhere, but what we actually want is to get nowhere—now here. What we really want is to be who we are, as we are—Sat Chit Ananda. That's what we're looking for, ultimately.

It's all about stopping. Stop trying to get someplace and become something. Stop going outward into understanding and experience. Come back home to what is, which is already here and free. The way of freedom is to be free, here and now.

Becoming Childlike

When I was a kid, I was always playing and there were no thoughts about past or future. Is this what Jesus meant when he said, "unless you change and become like little children, you will never enter the Kingdom of Heaven?"

A holiday is becoming as a child because a holiday is the recognition that there is no self. As an infant, you have not taken the first birth of self and separateness. You are in the Garden of Eden, and then the 'mistake' of taking the first birth of self occurs. Now, you are doing this work and you come to see you have not changed, you are free, and there is no self. This is what Jesus was talking about—to be as you are before the birth of self happens.

You are now, and you can see there is no self and there is no history. Everything is included here, now, in this moment. This body and all the objects are appearing now. This is the way it was when you came out of the womb. Recognize that, and that is what Jesus meant.

Intention for Clarity

If I have the intention to make things clearer, is that an attempt to become something?

First of all, the intention in you to "become clearer" appears without you doing anything. You have been around for a while on these group calls being authentic, and you have this intention, which you did not create. Seeing that you did not create it shows there is no self. There is only the intention to see this more clearly. It does not mean there is a self/ego involved.

Until it is finished, there is going to be the intention or desire to get resolution. Once it is finished, the intention for it to be clearer will not arise anymore. I would not call this intention "becoming" because you already see your essential nature is free, and there is nothing more for you to become. You just want doubts to be resolved.

Sometimes I am not sure though because I still try to figure something out or I keep trying to see something. Is this a self?

There is no self. If there is a desire or intention to see something, then that is just what is. That intention is in the mind. The existence of the intention does not mean there is a self here. There is no self, period. We believe that because there is a desire, it must mean there is a self "in here" desiring. Actually, there is just the desire to see something. You don't have to be concerned with the idea that there is a self because there isn't one.

Trying to be a "Better Person"

> *I saw this week that part of my suffering is related to me always trying to be a better human being. I am always working on aspects of myself to be better. I never saw this in the past as being a form of fixing or becoming.*

Wanting goodness is very natural for a sane and healthy person. I am not, however, of the belief that you can work on yourself. Instead, I say, "Know what is true and value that." Know and value your essential being, which is goodness itself. Then, unhealthy "aspects," as you called them, are exposed to *you*, and they can naturally resolve or fall away, on their own. This is not becoming, it is not a doership. It is simply knowing and valuing truth and being authentic to what is valuable.

You know your essential nature is only goodness, and when you come to rest in this goodness, you then learn from "mistakes." You are always learning in the course of living, but the goal of being a good person drops, and you just become essentially benign, which is the goodness.

I see that sometimes I think I am just an asshole. For instance, the other day, I noticed I wasn't listening to someone, and I thought, "I have to listen better." Then, I realized I just wasn't interested in what they were saying.

I can relate. Where did you get the idea that you always have to be interested in what someone else is saying? It is just an ideal, which no one can ever live up to. The fact is, you are not always interested. Some spiritual people say if you are not paying attention to what is being said, you are unaware. Actually, you are always aware. In that particular moment, you are just aware of something else.

The State of the World

World Events

World events seem to rattle me. There is just so much suffering going on that when I focus on it, my attention gets stuck. I don't seem to be able to keep a balance, and I don't see how I will ever be able to.

I am not agreeing or disagreeing with what you say. If that is the way it is for you now, that is the way it is. If it is this black and white for you, you have to see what you want, suffering or freedom.

This brings up something else for me. It seems like there is good and evil in the world. For me, it seems like a lot of evil is coming to the forefront.

You are anthropomorphizing and personifying something; evil and good are very Biblical. There are things that are harmful and things that are not harmful. There are things that are beneficial and things that are not beneficial. There are many different perspectives you can take on any particular event. For example, the right to reproductive freedom. Liberals think women should have the right to choose. Christians think it is murder. Both are opinions. Who is right? Both sides think they are right. Is there an empirical truth to either side?

Our current President seems to be a very bad guy in many people's opinion. They say he is evil and yet, approximately three million women came out to march against him after he was sworn in. So, the alleged *evil* may be bringing out the best in people, and he can be seen as *good* in that way. It is not so easy to decide from a limited personal perspective what's good and what's evil.

I don't like the word evil. I see the things that America does around the world, and it disgusts me. I don't see anything beneficial about some of our foreign policy decisions (e.g., drone-bombing other countries). However, broadening the perspective is what is required. We have to go way beyond our egocentric viewpoint. Who knows what comes out of specific events? No one knows. The only thing you can know is you, yourself as free. The only thing you can really do is to be free. Be a light in the world.

Yes, you can be involved in activities you feel are beneficial, and yet you can't change the fact that the former President authorized bombing seven countries and was at war every single day of his presidency. And all everyone saw was this smooth, funny, polite guy talking. Nevertheless, we can paint a much different picture when we look at how many people were killed from this perpetual war. You are not going to change that. Getting pissed off is not going to change it.

What can change is my own expression. I can be a light myself and maybe shine a little on others close to me. I am not going to change three hundred million Americans' viewpoints or the politicians who are imbued with greed and lust for power. My question is what are you doing within yourself to be that light?

If your "karma" is to be engaged in political activities, the first thing to do is to be free yourself. When you do, you will be able to see the best way to contribute. Ranting and raving are very reactionary and not beneficial. Your suffering is not helping anything. So, what is the point in it?

You came here to this work, and the only thing I can say to you is, "Be free." Get real and jump! Take being free seriously for your own benefit and for the benefit of others. By being at peace, you benefit other people in ways you can't imagine.

Why all the Meanness in the World?

Over the last few weeks, I have been looking into "alternative media," and what I found was rather sickening, to say the least. It seems that those in power are insatiably driven for more power. Also, they have some very dark pathologies which lead them to purposefully create wars and use people as puppets. All that really matters to them seems to be money and power.

Some call it "satanic." I don't know anything about that, but it sure looks "very evil, extremely evil."

I remembered someone on a recent group call mentioning how her Latin/Catholic upbringing and relationships are "challenging her new way of seeing" (paraphrasing). Your response to her was something like, "It's all your mind." This really had me thinking a lot lately, in the face of all the alternative news.

You wrote in "What Is the World?":

> *The world I perceive is only my consciousness, my mind.*
>
> *It appears in and as consciousness.*

And my consciousness is only the knowing aspect of me.

I know of no world other than my conscious knowing of it.

The world I perceive is the ephemeral,

evanescent appearance of who I am.

When looking at it this way, I see that it has to be so! But that means that all this meanness and sickness would COME FROM ME! No one else to blame!

I could, of course, just stop looking at the alternative news, and, at least for me, it would not exist anymore. But just because I'm not paying attention to something or ignoring it, doesn't make it go away. Governments wouldn't become suddenly benign, just because I was ignoring them.

I know that I, for sure, have become more benign thanks to this work, and compared to the maniacs that are running the world, my perceived malignancy is nothing.

Also, I know that there are no answers to "why" questions, but I still ask it: "WHY would I have the appearance of all this meanness?" In a way, I feel responsible for all of it, and to have a holiday seems like sticking my head into the sand and ignoring everything, while the shitstorm is blowing over me.

Sorry for this negative post, but I'm really struggling with this.

All of that crazy insanity you mentioned comes from ignorance. It comes from believing oneself to be separate. That is the root cause.

In all of us, that root cause creates suffering. The more one believes in and worships self/ego, the more one suffers and creates suffering. It is narcissism. You are right that your malignancy has never been that malignant compared to many others, but the root cause is the same: ignorance. Therefore, one who knows about the root cause in themselves has to understand that it is the same root cause for everyone.

Stemming from the root cause is the sense of lack: "I need more, I am inadequate, I need to be someone special, I need to be in control, I need to be right, etc." All of it is based on a sense of insufficiency or lack. If there was no sense of insufficiency or lack, why would any of that be needed?

We all have a sense of lack (until it no longer appears). For many people, the harm caused by it is marginal. For many others, the harm caused is much greater, far-reaching and impactful. The lust for satisfaction, based on acquiring more and more—wealth, power, control—is unquenchable and causes great harm.

I suspect that the more one acquires because of that lust, the more malignant and uglier one gets. It feeds on itself. All those things you describe seem to point to that. But, as far out there into insanity as you can see, you can always look inward and see the same root within yourself. And then, wisdom says, "Forgive them, they know not what they do."

You say that all this meanness comes from you. If you want to think about it that way and see it from a universal perspective, meaning that everything is you, then I would say take it even one step further. In the macro/universal scheme of things, all this so-called insanity on this infinitesimally small rock, called Earth, is just some cells and atoms re-organizing themselves. Who says it is negative? Does the Universe say that? No, your mind says it.

Now, to get really radical: don't be so arrogant. How do you know that any of it is negative? Maybe like a strong storm, it is all needed to clear the shit out. Maybe me taking too many drugs was not bad, but wonderful. Maybe Donald Trump is the catalyst that is required to mobilize the overall movement of good (the 2017 Women's March is an example). How do you know any of it? You don't. And, even more than that, how do you know that all the stuff you watch on YouTube or TV, or even the alternative news, has even one shred of truth to it. You don't.

What do you know? Really, tell the truth and stop pretending. What do you actually know? Scarce little, I say. The only thing you know for sure, that no one can convince you of otherwise, that you neither need to prove nor can deny, is that you exist. As what? It doesn't matter. All the rest of that mental understanding is dogma, right behavior, right action, morality, and religion. It is hubris.

Now, let's just take it way down to the very human level. Of course, all of what you describe is cruel and harmful to other humans. In the realm of the micro, the human aspect, that kind of action is bad and raises some questions. Why is it so? Well, we know that it is caused by ignorance, but why is there ignorance? Who knows? It just is. Is there something you can do about all of that? What would that be? Has religion, politics, or culture ever solved those problems? Clearly not, since they themselves are the expressions of the root cause, ego. Then, what is there to do?

Well, that ties in with what do you actually know for yourself? You can investigate only here, within yourself. Any change that happens (not that you do it at all), happens here, within yourself. It's perfectly natural to get pissed off at the insanity of those people, of course. I do too!

> Would it be fair to state, "All that is, is the will of source
> (Shiva)," since there really isn't any free will in the

manifest (Shakti)? I think there is a similar saying in the Bible, "Not a single leaf moves without the Lord's will..."

Following the same line, would it be fair to say that source is content with the way matters are right now, and so, any change could only come from source, if at all? I note that this goes into philosophy, but I ask the question anyway since it has lingered in my mind for a long time now.

Let me answer these one at a time.

Would it be fair to state, "All that is, is the will of source (Shiva)?"

Shiva is a concept. In my view, that concept simply points to the changeless, knowing aspect of you. Ascribing will to Shiva or Source is yet another concept and is based on the fact that you are not in control. It is true that there is no free will, but to then state you are not in control because Shiva, Source or God is, takes it one step too far, in my opinion. That concept is a religious-based idea that most people seem to believe because they want, or feel the need, to have a big daddy or someone who is taking care of things. A nice teddy bear for security.

What if there is none of that? What if there is no one in charge? What if there is no meaning? I'm not saying there is or isn't. But, if there isn't, how would that leave you? It would leave you completely alone. Can you stand alone?

You have no free will, but that does not mean there is some higher power that has free will and is in charge. I simply say, what is, is.

All these ideas, like the Arabic saying, "Inshallah" ("If God wills it"); or the Leonard Cohen song, "If It Be Thy Will," are all well and good as far as beautiful poetic imagery. They also have some benefit as far as relaxing the idea that humans have about free will and control. However, they are not factual, and they are certainly, in no way, provable or even truly knowable. For one who wants to be real and honest, those concepts are not needed or even wanted. You stand alone, blowing like a leaf in the wind. Things are simply as they are now. There is no other possibility, now.

> *"Apparently, source is content with the way matters are right now, and so, any change could only come from Source, if at all?"*

This sentence turns Source into an anthropomorphic being that wants to see things in a certain way, or that is at peace with what is. But is Source some THING, or a BEING, that has these qualities of wanting or being content? No. Source simply is. It is being (not "a" Being). It is Existence. There are no characteristics or human qualities. And again, the way I see it is—what is, is. No reason. No meaning. Otherwise, we start praying to Source to give us what we want. This need and desire for *something*—security or whatever—is the birth of religion, myth, belief, and ignorance.

The question is, "Can you stand alone, knowing that what is, is, as it is, and can only *be* as it is now?"

> *Inquirer 2: I like it. This clears away a few cobwebs of deeper belief. So, if I (whatever that points to) react to animal abuse, which is an ancient story, there is no real will or choice here. Even if Source (whatever that is) isn't fine with what is, this would at least allow a little relaxation into it being okay and seeing that "it just is." This, however, leads me to ask, "Can I allow what is to be, on one hand, and then do something to stop it?" Maybe, the bigger question is, "Can I allow/accept it (realizing there is no real choice), but also allow the reaction that seems sure to follow, as just what is happening?"*

Those are good queries. Yes, there is no choice—reaction to the ancient story happens. If that story emerges as a thought, it is perfectly right that the body will react with feelings and emotions as well. This can also work in reverse. When some feelings and emotions related to past abuse arise, they can trigger thoughts to appear. It is all perfectly spontaneous and natural. There is nothing to "do" about it.

Source is neither fine nor not fine. In my usage, Source is just You— the knowing of what appears. As knowing, you are not a doer, chooser, judge or critic. You simply know what is appearing. All the rest of that happens in mind, and all of that is not a decider or chooser either. It just happens automatically based on things like conditioned thought, and other natural, genetic, biological movements.

I don't say to allow anything, accept anything or let everything be as it is. All of those presuppose a doer of those actions. We ascribe doership to ego, the "I" that we believe ourselves to be. But that ego/I is spontaneously arising, uncreated by any "you."

Yes, if a reaction appears, or an intention to do something appears, it is appearing spontaneously without a "you" there as a doer, chooser, etc. Then, if from that intention, some action appears to "do" something, that is also spontaneous, and there is no one here that is a doer of that action.

If you get what I am saying (and that is what real inquiry is about), you will see that this is the end of ego. Ego, in this conversation, means: I am a doer.

I simply say, "What is, is." Whatever thought, feeling or intention is appearing simply is. Instead of all the doership language like, I accept, I allow, I let everything be, etc., how about really knowing this moment is as it is, now, and being fully reconciled with it. This will bring ease of being and peace. To be clear, you don't do the reconciling. Reconciliation either is (because of coming to know yourself and what is true), or it isn't. There's no doer there either.

As you may sense, there is no place for you as an ego in any of this.

> *Inquirer 3: I have struggled with this as well. I feel the quote, "What you see in others is a reflection of yourself," applies just to personal relationships and cannot apply to world events. Otherwise, justice would never be served. Truth is a difficult burden to shoulder. That is why most run from it.*
>
> *I can say from experience, as one who researches and reports on events, it takes a toll. I need regular breaks to cleanse and detox from it all.*
>
> *Having said all that, I wasn't made to look away. Could that be ego or having a sense of purpose? I do not know, but I continue to try to serve others by telling truth.*

Although we can project onto others what we feel within ourselves, that quote is not exactly what I was speaking about. What I am saying is that many of the pathological actions we see in others come from the same root cause we experience within ourselves—the separate sense of self or ego. The self/ego means: I am separate, I am lacking something, and I need something to feel complete. This is true for everyone. It is deeply ingrained from when we are very young.

For most of us, that root cause does not turn into pathologically greedy and lustful behavior. Nevertheless, it is still there in a latent form as "I am separate." We can see it in ourselves in our daily interactions, our dissatisfactions, our need to be in control or to be right, and in many other small and large ways. It could just be a feeling that we lack something. That sense of lacking something is why we seek.

People who seem to be the worst and most malignant of society (and there are many examples), at their root, are no different than you and me. It is only that their fear, greed, need for power and control, etc., have grown to malignant and pathological proportions.

That is why wisdom equals compassion. To know thyself, which is the only true knowing, is to know others as well. In knowing thyself, we come to know that we did not create who we are. This needs to be recognized, through sincere inquiry. Most people haven't really done this investigation, and they believe they have created themselves. All cultures, especially American culture, certainly support that fallacy.

If we did not create who we are, then neither did anyone else. In my opinion, that is what Jesus meant when he said, "Forgive them, they know not what they do." He knew he did not create himself and neither did the guys condemning and torturing him.

As far as justice, who is to decide what is justice? It is arbitrary.

It's great that you weren't made to look away. To serve others by telling the truth, it is best to look for truth within yourself—to "know thyself." If you know yourself, you will understand everyone, and compassion, and real justice will be born.

> *Inquirer 4: How long do you think it will take the so-called ego shell to be dismantled? I, and at least some of your Facebook followers, still probably operate as if the ego exists. Examples of its existence are defensiveness, aggression, anger, pride and many other behaviors.*
>
> *Also, I see that the awareness is present at times during moments of sadness, anger, etc., and the emotions become less and last only a fraction of the "time."*

I don't think about it as dismantling the ego, or anything else. That's, of course, a common idea in spiritual teachings. This work is about seeing what is actually happening and how I am actually functioning. See, there is a belief in something called an ego, and it is negative and may even be thought of as the enemy. Ego simply means I am separate. What I was saying previously was don't get rid of ego, but rather know what is true. What is true is that all those things you mentioned come from the core belief—I am separate. Is there anything to "do" about that?

Know how you are functioning—know thyself. Don't get rid of ego or dismantle it. We all (me included) act as if ego exists. That is part of the Play of Life. I see no problem with that, in and of itself. You act your part in the play, and it looks like ego. When the belief in ego causes the emergence of suffering, based on a sense of lack (which creates things like pride, greed, defensiveness, etc.), then "self-awareness" or "self-knowing" can be a powerful means of resolution.

The question, "How long until the ego is dismantled," is not a correct understanding. There is no endgame, as far as some kind of human perfection where none of those things will ever appear again. Continuing to know what is true, or to recognize "awareness," as you called it, and to be that, is the end. That end is always and only NOW.

When you come to know yourself, then you come to know others as well, and naturally, there will be more compassion.

The Nature of Questions

Questions and Their Nature

Sometimes I feel like I need to come prepared to these meetings with questions. I have been trying to figure things out and they are just not clear.

The problem is you are trying to figure things out. This just means you are looking for something to grasp on to that is not actually here. People can go that route and become a philosopher and attempt to understand everything. Of course, there are things that can be understood, but what I am sharing is not understandable, it is known. It is just about being knowing. Free, now, without knowing anything in particular. Let's be on holiday. This is important.

HOLIDAY

There is only now, right?

This aware knowing is here.

This aware knowing is your essential being.

You are aware knowing.

Be the knowing for a moment and tell me something.

What's the meaning of this moment?

If there is no meaning, this moment simply is, isn't it?

What aspect of you would want a meaning?

It has to be the mind, right?

Yes. The aspect of me that thinks I need to have a question.

This is simply programming. This is just thought, and that thought is not you. *You* don't actually have a question about anything. Let's look at this a little more closely.

You, aware knowing, don't have any questions. Questions are formulated in the mind based on ideas that have been conditioned therein. And, if there are no questions, there may be the idea you should have questions. This is just another conditioned idea, which is: that for you to be serious here, you should have questions. It is not even you who has that question. You don't have that question. That question is just something that appears in the mind. You are the knowing of that question.

There are no questions in this now, who you are. Questions are just habitual, mental data, programming that's floating around and takes the form of a question. Then there is the belief, "I have a question," but actually, you don't have a question. There is just a question, that is all.

> *Questions come all the time for me, then they disappear. I debate whether I should write them down.*

What I want to do is answer all questions in one fell swoop, now. The answer is—all questions are not yours. They are all based on mental impressions recorded from input, like experiences, reading, etc. Even though they appear to be genuine, they are not. Even if they feel very necessary and needed, they are not. Questions are just born out of data that has been impressed in your mind.

This is a perfect example. The thought appears that you should come up with a question. All questions are like this. For example, many people have the belief there must be something more than this ordinary aware knowing, then the question appears, "What more is there?" Why would this question appear? You read or heard something somewhere that there must be something more, something special. Then, the question about "What more is there?" shows up. But in truth, you are already complete and whole, and you don't have a question. You are already finished.

It's good to ask questions. They have to be asked. Nevertheless, I want to chop it right now. Any question that appears is just some residue from something heard or experienced. It is just appearing in the mind, then there is the belief, "I have a problem and I have to solve it." The reality is—no, you don't have a problem.

> *Questions seem to come when I think of the past and future as something real. When I drop that thinking, the questions disappear.*

Right, and that is why I say the answer to all of the questions is when the questions stop appearing. The end of the question is the answer. When there is no question, the answer is you, you are it. The question is not truth. You are truth, and you don't have a question. So, the answer to any question does not matter. They can be very interesting questions, but ultimately, they don't matter. When the question is gone, you remain empty, now and free. That is the answer to the question.

> *When I see a question appear, it is really no different than seeing a car passing by on the road.*

It is just like that. Why put any credence on questions? Annamalai Swami says, "ignore anything that appears in the mind." If you want to know freedom and be finished, just ignore. Don't do anything. Don't answer the questions. Don't figure out the questions. Don't resolve the questions. Just ignore and be the knowing. Annamalai also says, "be the consciousness." I say, "knowing is being, being is knowing." The only answer to all questions is to not get an answer. It is just to be finished with the questions. Be the knowing that is present, here and now. This is the way of freedom.

Not Knowing What to Ask

Sometimes I don't know what to ask. So, I guess that is sort of like a question.

You have asked a lot of questions in the past. It seems like you are looking for questions to ask even when there aren't any there because you feel the need to ask questions. If there aren't any questions, that is good. If there is a question, then ask it.

What is the difference between not asking questions and being finished? I know I am not finished and I don't know what to ask either.

If you don't know what to ask, it means there are no specific questions. That is okay. You don't have to ask questions. Believing the thought, "I know I am not finished," is keeping you from being finished. Just keep doing what you are doing, keep having holidays.

If you think there should be a question when there isn't one, then it means you are not yet willing to be *nothing*, to live the starkness of the unknown, which is freedom. It means your mind still feels the need to understand and feel secure in that understanding. It is the maintenance of a separate self. You just have to keep "abiding as the Self" as Ramana said. Keep having holidays because a holiday shows you that you are already finished. Let's have a holiday.

HOLIDAY

There is only now, right?

Ego/self needs time to exist—
past, personal stories and
future longings and plans.

Right now, there is none of that.

There is only this aware knowing.

This is true knowledge.

It's called attaining Self-knowledge.

Knowing your essential nature, here and now.

This is the way and the goal.

They are the same.

The goal is already attained now, have a look.

It is very obvious. The more you recognize it, the more you can be overwhelmed at how simple it is. All that needs to be done is to keep recognizing this. Keep knowing yourself as Sat Chit Ananda, the being knowing that is peace. It does not mean you have to force yourself like there is some effort required. That is not what it means. It just means to keep recognizing whenever it naturally occurs, and it occurs by itself. It is always occurring. It is never not occurring. You just don't notice it all the time. When you do notice it, just sit and be this knowing that is peace.

The way and the goal are one. The way of having a holiday is the goal. You recognize you are free. This is the highest teaching of all the great masters. The thing is until you recognize your essential being, it can't happen. You can't abide as Self until you know what Self is. Many people never get to this point even after studying Ramana and other great teachers for years and years. They are still looking for "the Self." The Self Ramana speaks about is simply *you*, knowing, here and now.

What we do together first is discover what this is. It is the first thing. It is not something to be discovered after twenty years of self-inquiry. It is what we do first. In our inquiry sessions, we stop everything, have a holiday and see that we are free. From then on, you know your essential nature, what Ramana called *the Self*. It is nothing more than this. This is the ultimate—knowing being peace.

Be finished, now. Right now, for a moment, see that it is finished. See it is finished already. Doubts that you are not finished may appear. It is just a belief that you are not finished. Recognize again that it is already attained. It is always already perfectly attained. See it, again. Then, one day, it will be over, and you may not even notice right away. You will just stop doubting that you are finished. The only thing not finished is the belief that you are not finished. In truth, look now, have a holiday.

HOLIDAY

We are all the same. There is no one who is more or less aware. There is no one who is finished or not finished. There is just a thought that you are not finished. That is it. It doesn't mean anything.

> *Inquirer 2: I see that I think I should be something. If I am at peace or ease, then I equate that with having a holiday. When I feel turmoil, I think I am not seeing it, I lost it, or I am not there yet.*

You are aware of the turmoil, aren't you?

Yes.

You are still aware. You are aware when you feel good and when you feel turmoil. I also feel relief when a turmoil ceases. We all do. However, in the midst of that turmoil, you can have a holiday and see that you are aware. Within aware, you see everything is appearing (the room and all the contents) along with the turmoil. Aware is here regardless of whether it feels good or whether it feels bad. So, you can say aware is prior to anything that appears.

Even prior to any story that I am not there yet?

Yes, because you are aware of that story. Aware is always here. You are aware that you feel good and you are aware that you feel bad. You are always aware. When you have a holiday, you notice aware is—not of any particular objects, just aware itself. Aware is before anything, then aware focuses on objects like, "I feel turmoil." When aware focuses on that, then a self seems to be created that says, "I feel bad, I am so unenlightened, etc." All of these are just thoughts. Have a holiday and see that aware is here prior to all the thoughts. This is your essential nature.

You appear as the feeling of turmoil, and you appear as the feeling of peace. These appearances are like waves appearing in the ocean. Below that, you are always aware of it all. Aware has to be here for anything else to appear. When we have a holiday, we are aware of aware—aware is aware of itself. We can have doubts sometimes because we are looking for something else, but it is really quite ordinary, obvious and simple.

In the experiments we do together, you realize you need to use memory to say there are two eyes and a head here. In your direct experience, you can't say there are two eyes and a head, but can you deny you are aware? It is obvious. This aware is self-evident. Notice this again and again. Keep coming to recognize your essential nature.

There is nothing higher than this. This is already the end. You don't do anything. You just recognize it is already finished again, and again, and again, and again... If something like confusion appears in the mind, that is just its nature. It is just the way it is. This body-mind organism was created to do that. Otherwise, it wouldn't. It doesn't mean a damn thing. In the midst of turmoil, if your intention for freedom is strong, a holiday will happen and you will see that nothing is wrong and that truth is here.

Doubts that you are not finished and that you are not liberated resolve over time. You come to know they are not true.

Looking for More Understanding

A few times this week, I had questions. I thought, "This is the question I want to ask on the call." They're all kind of varied, but in general, there's some kind of question or looking for more understanding.

It seems to be that when a question appears, the answer is to have a holiday. Even when I do, the question is still kind of dancing around in the corner of my mind. I'm not sure how to say it and I remember you saying to not make a personality out of certain habits. But it's a recurring thing, so I'm not sure if I'm being more honest by recognizing.

What's a recurring thing, the desire to ask questions, you mean?

Yeah. It doesn't matter what the question is. Most of the time my life is peaceful, whether I am on holiday or not. It's just fine. It's not that terrible, but I'm not very satisfied with it.

If questions come up, it's good to ask them, and one day you won't feel the need or interest to ask questions.

I guess my question is more about questions because I had a bunch of questions. They didn't seem to matter because one hour it was one question, and another hour it was another question.

It's a good point you bring up. Let me ask you a question, "What aspect of you has these questions?"

Some thought.

Right, the mind. There's this "I am separate" belief and this creates questions. Without that belief, there are no questions. When that thought appears, immediately there is the sense of separation and there are questions. The aspect of you that is interested in all those questions is ego. I don't mean ego in a negative way. I just mean the ego that your essential being is misidentified with. You, Self (Atman, in Ramana's words), essential being, or the true *I*, makes a mistake and thinks, "I am the body." *I exist* is truth, "I am the body" is only partial truth; it's limited. When the "I am the body" belief springs to life, all the ego ideas of separation, limitation, and questions appear. Without that first "I am separate" idea, there are no questions, are there?

No.

Right. What we're doing with this work is chopping off the head. That's why my answer to the questions always comes back to the same thing, which is chopping the head off. If you want to get real and do the real work, which you do, then the answer to all the questions is to chop the head off the ego. When you take out that first card ("I am separate, I am the body"), the whole house of cards collapses. That one card is holding up the entire house of cards.

All the other methods (psychology, philosophy, and spirituality) are trying to remove certain cards and rearrange others. If you really want to end it all, just take out the first card and it all comes tumbling down. In my opinion, this work is the highest teaching— take out the first card and chop off the head. Then, there's no one there to have any questions, and if there's no one there to have questions, there are no questions. How do we do that? We jump. We just be on a holiday, here and now.

We can all say, "I exist," but then we add on to that. We add attributes, like, "I exist as this body, I exist as a man/woman, I exist as an American, I exist as a Democrat, etc." Let's forget all those attributes because that's very limiting, isn't it? Original sin means we limit ourselves to this body. But a holiday is *I exist,* without any attributes. This is the only actual I, this is who you are.

We make a mistake when we say, "I am this…" No, leave the "I am this" out and just say I, then you know the true and only Self. Some teachers talk about the capital "S" Self and the small "s" self. The Self is I—I = Self. People think "I am this little self/ego," and that's where they are mistaken. There is no little self or false self, there is only I, Self.

If we jump and just know what's true—I, with no attributes, no past and no future—there's no ego/self. That card is removed and there are no questions.

> *You've said all this stuff wonderfully in a bunch of different ways, and I've asked similar questions on different audios. I listen to one or two audios a day and the strange thing is, it doesn't seem to matter if I know the answer is to "get real, have a holiday in the midst of*

everything, and see that the questions are not there now."
That doesn't seem to matter. It's almost like I want
something new and fresh. I think, "I'll talk to Sal live and
it's going to somehow be better."

Even though it's all here and I already know the value of
it, I don't seem to want that because I'm thinking of
getting something else. So clearly, that's the thing I want.
It reminds me of the marijuana thing. I could say I don't
want some marijuana, then at some point, I do it anyway.

Okay. You're speaking wisdom here because when you recognize that about yourself, that's wisdom. Smoking marijuana is clearly some kind of avoidance, right? What about all these questions? That's also some kind of avoidance, no?

I'm not saying you're wrong, I just don't see it in my
experience.

Well, actually, when you get down to business, they are. It's just the excuse to keep the mind, the separate self, going for a while longer, isn't it? It's like, "Well I know truth, but I'm not quite so sure, so let me hold on to some things here, otherwise I have to really be nothing." It's the same for me. If something comes into the mind and I go along with it, then obviously, that's what I want.

Truth is so obvious. What do you want? What are you doing it for? You know the answer to all those questions. The answer is—there is no answer. The answer does not matter. What matters is the end to the questions, which is also the end of the questioner. All the questions only have to do with ego. All the questions.

It's good to keep asking the questions until one day they stop coming. Realize every single question is mind, ego. That's all they can be. You, essential being, have no questions, do you? Does Self have any questions? No, the ego mind has questions, it *is* the questions. Just realize that every question is ego mind and recognize what we are doing here. We're chopping off the head. If we chop off the head, and we say, "Wait a minute, let me keep a few questions in my pocket, let me stay alive a bit longer," then we're not really chopping off the head, are we?

There's no judgment. It's just habit. You're young; you haven't been doing this for very long. These habits come until they don't come anymore, so that's why the answer to all the questions is always the same. The answer to the questions is not an answer to the questions. The answer to the questions is the end of the questions because the end of the questions is the end of the one who has the questions, ego. What's important is chopping off the head. One chop. Take this head and remove it, then where are all the questions? There's nothing but space, is there?

Definitely, yeah.

When you come here, you don't come for a little trim, you know? You don't even come for a full haircut. You come to have the head removed, and not replaced with anything else. That head is where all the questions are. No head, no questions.

Importance of Questions

It seems like all the questions end up being the same.

They are, and they eventually go. All the questions about what enlightenment is and what is aware just go; then it is just over and there is no great state of awareness all the time. It is just over.

When questions come up, it is still important to ask them even though they appear to be similar.

Inquirer 2: I notice that questions come up, but I don't even care.

That is the answer. Soon, because you don't even care, those questions won't even appear for you anymore. The answer to all questions is just, "I don't care" because there is nothing. Let's be on holiday.

HOLIDAY

Here now, this knowing is nothing, right?

What questions?

What answers?

No questioner, no answerer.

What description or meaning is there for this?

What a relief.

What does this moment mean?

Isn't that a ridiculous question?

Nevertheless, keep asking questions because that is just the way that it goes and that is how they get resolved. The questions are tenacious. They come from the many beliefs that have been put in our brain. When you have a holiday, there are no questions in this knowing.

No Questions, Is This Enough?

A lot of the time when I read questions in the online forum, I don't understand them. Then, I start asking myself more questions. Is that something I should just ignore?

If you don't understand the questions, then don't bother. Why create problems? Not everyone has the same questions. Maybe you read a question and it doesn't make sense to you because you don't have the same question. Why bother creating a problem that's not there? Just be nothing. Be nothing, and there are no questions.

Let's have a holiday together right now.

HOLIDAY

Here and now, I exist.

This is the answer to every single question.

Nothing.

Be nothing.

The Nature of Questions

Know nothing.

Have nothing.

Here I am.

Those questions from the forum,
where are they now?

Just be free.

That's what I want.

If that's what you want, look how simple it is.

It feels like there's a lot more to this liberation that I don't understand.

There isn't. See, that thought is the problem right there. By believing that thought, you just created a huge problem for yourself. There's a lot less to understand about liberation, not a lot more. Let's be on holiday together.

HOLIDAY

I know I exist.

Stop there.

Just stop.

Is this enough?

Nothing?

You don't need all that mentation, all those thoughts, and all those questions about freedom. That's the habit of the mind, habitually coming up with things. Have a holiday.

HOLIDAY

I know I exist, here.

Nothing.

Don't add something onto nothing and be free.

It's very stark.

Is it enough?

No Separation - Knowing Permeates Form

There is no big ocean and little ocean, there is only ocean appearing as waves. Similarly, there is no big I and little I, there is only I appearing as forms. Knowing and the appearance of thoughts, emotions, sensations or sense objects are not separate. Within any appearance, is imbued the knowing of it. The knowing aspect of you never changes regardless of what's appearing, just as the water of ocean doesn't change when waves appear. Only the appearance, or form, aspect of you changes, just like the wave aspect of ocean changes. This is the meaning of non-separation. And since that is so, what is there to transcend and what is to merge with what?

Transparency of Experiences

Let's be on holiday together.

We tend to think that any experience—
thought, feeling, emotion or sense experience—
is something that I am aware of.

This is true.

But that can give the impression that I—
the one aware of the experience—
is somehow separate from the experience.

That is not actually the way it is.
It is more intimate than that.

The Way of Freedom

Let's look.

Whatever feeling or emotion is here now in the body-mind,
whether it be positive, neutral, or negative,
be cognizant of it for a moment.

The knowing of this, whatever experience is happening now,
is not separate from the experience.

Knowing permeates the experience itself.

Whatever experience is here
now is imbued with the knowing of it.

There is no separation.

Have a look.

The experience itself is transparent, insubstantial.
There is no solidity to it.

Even intense feelings or emotional states.

Using a visual metaphor, if we had a microscope
that could see down to the smallest particles (quarks),
what we would see imbued within that particle field is space.

The space is within and throughout all the quarks.
Space is not separate from the quarks.

It is imbued within and encompasses the quarks.
It is the very fabric of that particle field.

What is most apparent is the transparent field
and the space in between the quarks.

This is a metaphor that applies to whatever feeling,
emotion or state that is appearing right now.

Knowing is like the space.

Knowing is imbued in the experience itself—it is not separate.

The experience is insubstantial.

Knowing is the substance.
Knowing is what is essential.

Seen this way, there is nothing to escape.
You are here in the midst of all of it—whatever is appearing.

The substantial aspect of it is always You—the knowing.

Again, metaphorically, whatever is appearing is just
particles, lacking any solidity.

Seen this way, experience is less formidable and intimidating.

It is all transparent particles, imbued with the light of You.

Always.

Absolute and Form are not Separate

*I've been listening to the audios, and I've heard you say a
few times, the knowing is not separate from the objects
that are known. I'm finding it a little hard to differentiate*

*between the knowing and what's known. I'm making a
little bit of a thing out of it, so it would be helpful to air it.*

What I say is, absolute and form are not separate. Wave is ocean.
Your essential being is the knowing. What separates the knowing
from objects is a belief. For instance, there's a belief that wave is
separate from ocean. But, in truth, wave is ocean. This knowing,
which you can call the absolute, and the changeful aspects, which
are the form, are not separate. Therefore, there's nothing to
transcend. This is it.

There's no transcendence elsewhere. There's no heaven, nirvana, or
absolute that your consciousness is going to transcend to and be
separate from everything. It's not going to become just "awareness"
or something. I say, what you're looking at is you, it's it. The belief,
"I am separate," causes the apparent separation between you and
the objects.

*I see. I suppose this knowing is all there is and there is
nothing else. In this case, what's known is all just the same
thing.*

As we've all seen through the inquiry work, knowing doesn't change.
Have a holiday, now.

HOLIDAY

Knowing/aware is here, now.

If we have a holiday five minutes from now,
knowing hasn't changed, it's the same knowing.

Twenty years ago, it's the same.

Throughout your whole life,
knowing hasn't changed.

It's not a thing, it's not an object, and it doesn't change.

Within this knowing,
every single object is in constant change.

It's in constant change, now.
It's not in constant change over time.

There's only now and everything's changing, now.

This is the changeful aspect of who you are.

You are the knowing of yourself as the objects,
just like the ocean knows itself as the wave.

There's not two, the wave IS you.

There's just the knowing.

Right, there's just the knowing which appears as objects. None of the objects (and you have to see if it's true, for yourself) are in any way substantial because they are constantly changing. There's no stagnation in any of the objects.

If you look at a photo of a wave, it looks like a fixed object. However, during the life of a wave, there is not one billionth of a second that it is stagnant or the same. Its whole appearance is in constant change and movement. Although it is not a solid, fixed object, and it is in constant change, it is always, never-changing, water. And although your body-mind experience is in constant change, not one billionth of a second fixed or stagnant, you are always knowing.

> *There are different objects appearing all the time. I look over there and different thoughts come up, which have no relation to the previous thoughts.*

That's right. Even this felt sense of "I am here" is constantly changing. It's not the same feeling all the time. The feeling is a living movement that changes.

> *Inquirer 2: Sal has sometimes used the phrase, "I am that in which all things appear, and I am that as which all things appear." Early on, I had some questions and I recall him saying, "You're never going to experience yourself as a tree, so get rid of that notion."*

Yes, this knowing we're speaking about, it's not an experience like that. As I always say, "Know what's true and truth shall set you free." I don't say, "Experience something and experiencing will set you free." Know what's true! And the way you know there's no separation is by seeing that separation is only an idea, and that idea is not appearing, now. The way that happens is by just being here, now. Be this knowing without attending to anything (ideas, philosophies, etc.). In this knowing, there is no *idea* of separation. If there's no *idea* of separation, there is no separation.

> *In a way, it's sort of a non-issue, the whole separation thing.*

Yes, but it's an issue because we have a lot of ideas in our mind that we're going to experience ourselves as the tree or something. But that's not the way I see it. The way I see it is, there's an idea, "I'm separate." It's a belief. When we have a holiday, that idea isn't here. In the absence of that idea, there's only the knowing of this, here, now. It takes an idea for you to think you're separate, doesn't it?

> *Yes. I need to think about it.*

Yes, and you have to believe it. When we came out of the womb (and we don't remember, but we can see anyway), we didn't believe we were separate. We got the idea at some point, "Oh, that's right, I'm separate" (original sin). We got that idea and have taken it as gospel this whole time.

There was just the knowing.

Yes, and it's still true, now. Let's be on holiday together and see what's true.

HOLIDAY

Within this knowing, all these appearances are equal, including any personal feelings, aren't they?

They're all equal and they're all constantly changing.

All of them.

They're coming and they're going.

So, they're equal.

They're insubstantial.

Absolute and Form Are One Seems Conceptual

In your book, you talk about the absolute and the form being one and that still feels like a concept to me.

Ok, let's look into it. The question comes because there is the idea that there is something called the absolute and form, and that form has to be transcended to get to the absolute. These are ideas. Were these ideas here when you came out of the womb?

No.

So, obviously, this is something that was put in your head. You may have heard from religion that there was a heaven. Then, after some spiritual seeking, you heard that there was an absolute and that the idea of heaven was not true. Actually, you just changed one idea for another.

Be on holiday and just ignore all those ideas.

HOLIDAY

There is only now, and obviously, this knowing is present.

Is this clear?

Don't refer to the mind at all.
Don't refer to concepts at all.

Don't refer to the idea that there is something called the absolute and something called form.

In your own knowing, right now, is there anything other than this, what is?

There is nothing other than this knowing, right now, which includes all these objects.

You have to go into your mind to come up with some concept called the absolute.

If that concept never existed, what you would know is this.

No Separation - Knowing Permeates Form

Everything that is here, is here, now.

There is no absolute separate from this.

There is just a concept of the absolute that is
separate from this.

It is simply a concept.

The only thing you know is this, here and now.

This work is about what you know, not about what you conceive. What you know, which is undeniable and does not take thought, is this, in which everything is appearing. So then, this must be it.

Knowing that the absolute and form are one is not a new concept. It is the end of all concepts, and in the absence of concepts, it is seen that *what is, is*. It is not some new experience you are going to have. It is just the absence of the concept that there is the absolute and form.

There is nothing dual about this. There is just this. This knowing, with everything included, is one. There is only now, and there is nothing behind the curtain.

In the absence of the concept to the contrary, which is simply mind dividing experience, this knowing, which includes everything, is one. What else could there be?

How is the Non-separation of Absolute and Form Realized?

If a wave believes it is separate from ocean,
it will not know itself as ocean.

If this belief vanishes,
the concept of being separate from ocean does not appear.

In the non-appearance of this concept,
there is no longer a cause of ignorance.

In this lack of ignorance, truth is.

When the idea—
absolute and form are two—is realized to be a concept only,
the concept vanishes.

In its vanishing,
it is not replaced by the concept absolute and form are one.

What is simply is, no conceptual separation occurs.

The non-arising of conceptual separation is the knowing.

It is not known by concept,
but known by the absence of a concept to the contrary.

Experiences

A River Flowing, Appearing to You

You are free to have happiness, sadness, anxiousness, and anything else that might appear. There is no need to be in any particular state. All states are appearing to you. Life as it is. With this work, you no longer have the idea that enlightenment means some kind of particular "blissful" state—it's good to lose that idea.

It's like unlearning everything I thought I knew.

Yes. And recognizing the utter simplicity of here and now as it is. Nothing more or less. Very simple.

It's simple, yet we miss the point entirely sometimes.

Yes, we can because of the spiritual stories and philosophies we have heard. There is a phenomenon I call halfway around the circle. People get caught in this idea of "being" as opposed to "doing" and thinking enlightenment is a state of non-doing. It is a non-doing, but that just means there is no one here as the doer. Action still happens, but people assume if you are doing something, like living an ordinary life, then you are not just "being." Freedom is life as it is, ordinary. No need to hide in meditation or just "be."

Full circle is when you are back to where you began. You have just come to know and value your essential being. This knowing is free, and in that, everything can appear. The good news is many of the things that appeared before don't appear as much, or at all. And the things that do appear that previously would have made you spin out, just flow on by freely. You know you are fine, safe, and free.

Those unpleasant states don't indicate anything at all about your freedom, they do not impact it one iota. They cannot. It all just flows on by, the good and the bad. Life as it is, a river flowing, appearing to you.

Here, Before, During, and After all Experiences

I know there is something like an unwinding going on, but I still find myself getting into ideas about the future and the past. I seem to just be bouncing back and forth. Am I supposed to notice it and let it go?

Don't let it go. Who's here to let it go? Just know what's true—before, during, and after those thoughts, you are here, free. Before the thought of the future came, you are here—aware, knowing, now. While the thought is appearing, you are here—aware, knowing, now. After it is gone, you are here—aware, knowing, now. So, you know there is no problem. I don't like the term "letting go" because it creates the idea of a self here doing something. Just know what's true. Everything is fine. So, what if some thoughts about the past, or the future, or any other thoughts are appearing, no problem.

Something will happen that will be very hard to deal with emotionally. It is true for all of us. This is life after all, and sometimes life is very challenging. When something troubling happens, there will be many thoughts and emotions, but it doesn't mean you are not free. I don't say, "Let it be as it is." I just say, "Know what's true." It is completely natural for thoughts and emotions to appear, and it is completely natural for them to disappear as well. Who is to argue with it? It doesn't mean anything at all about whether one is enlightened or not, or getting there or not, or something like that. Let's have a holiday together, now.

HOLIDAY

This knowing is here, right?

This knowing is essential, isn't it?

It is before, during, and after all appearances.

The same knowing has been here your whole life, hasn't it?

Even before you were aware of this knowing as your essential being, it was still true, wasn't it?

Your whole life has been a series of so-called misidentifications, but as soon as you "woke up" you were fine, weren't you?

And, at any point of your life,
if you had been able to have a holiday and recognize this,
you would have known you were fine,
wouldn't you have?

I'm free, here and now, right? Is that clear for you?

At the moment, yes.

What? At the moment? Are you saying it's not going to be clear for you tomorrow at 3:00 PM?

I feel like I get caught up in things, and I lose it.

Lose it? You lose yourself? Have a holiday.

HOLIDAY

Look now. You know this knowing that is here, aware, all-inclusive, now?

Yes.

Can you lose this?

No.

It's been you your whole life, hasn't it?

Yes.

The only thing you lose is the nonsense coming and going. You don't lose you, do you?

Right.

Okay, good. Because of what we have heard and taken for granted, we believe if there is something going on in the mind, there is something wrong with a me (self). We believe this self is who I am. Then we believe we need to correct ourselves with therapy, philosophy, spirituality, or by purifying the mind and getting rid of this and that and transcending the self, etc. Have a holiday, now.

HOLIDAY

Recognize this knowing that's here.

See that self, fear, and hope comes and goes, doesn't it?

Do you come and go?

No.

Good. How are you going to lose this? And isn't it doubtless already, now?

Yes.

It is good to ask these questions to allay these doubts and be finished. It is the same for everyone. See, here and now—I am free. I can't lose this. It is impossible. If you fantasize about the future for an hour, six hours, a day, who cares? You are present during that "future" aren't you? As soon as that thought ends—here I am, free. Nothing has changed. Is there any difference in this aware/knowing between now and six hours ago?

No. But maybe I have this idea that I am going to get into this knowingness and it is going to be there all the time.

Yes, exactly. That is why I always stress that we are not looking for some state, such as a state of awareness where you have to walk around like some kind of zombie always being aware that you are aware. Some teachings are like that. That is not freedom, that is bondage.

This is a really great question because we all have these same ideas.

When I talk to you, I start seeing it more clearly.

That is why we come together like this, so you will be doubtless. Then, you won't need me anymore. You know there is no self. You know there is no Santa Claus. You don't have to keep your head in the chimney for rest of your life making sure there is no Santa Claus. Imagine telling people: "Don't talk to me! I'm making sure there is no Santa Claus." or "I'm sorry, I can't work today. I have to make sure there is no Santa Claus." or "I have to keep checking, otherwise I am going to forget there is no Santa Claus. I'm going to lose the *fact* there is no Santa Claus."

Know what's true. Is there a self?

No.

Good. Thoughts come and go, no problem. When a holiday happens, know what is true. You are here and now, free, before, during, and after all experiences.

Bondage with Velvet Ropes

In one of your talks, you mentioned that bliss was "bondage with velvet ropes." This seems to point to something, and I am not quite sure what you mean.

As far as bondage goes, bliss is a pretty good one. A lot of people think enlightenment is about being in bliss all the time. If you think this, you will keep looking for it. On the other hand, sometimes bliss just happens, and it feels very good. You may think when bliss occurs, you are getting enlightened. However, bliss is just a state that comes and goes. People can get attached to wanting that state, and when it is gone, they think they are not enlightened. They, then keep seeking bliss. It is a very tempting state to long for because it feels good.

Seeking bliss, or wanting to hold on to the bliss, or believing bliss is enlightenment is bondage because bliss is something you are aware of. You are not the bliss. You are not any experience. Even the *great silence,* which is subtler than bliss, can be very compelling. When I was meditating a lot, I had an experience of silence in my whole being. The experience faded, and for a time, I thought I had to cultivate this silence because that's what I was told to do—cultivate desired states such as love, bliss, silence, etc. I tried to cultivate this silence, so it would always be present. Of course, this never happened. Why? Because all experiences come and go.

Wanting any particular state, no matter how peaceful and beautiful it is, is bondage because that state is not always going to be here. Any thought that you need to be in any particular state is bondage, not freedom. Freedom is not dependent on any particular state. Freedom is now, with whatever state is appearing.

> In another talk, you mentioned that your teacher told you
> during a retreat that she did not want any of the
> participants experiencing any bliss because they would
> not wake up if they did.

My teacher did say this on the intensive retreats. She said if people were having spiritual experiences or bliss, they would not wake up. She would say she wanted challenging events to happen to the people because then they would wake up. What she meant was if you have bliss, you are going to get lost in that experience and think it means something. You will then disregard your essential being which is not the bliss, but rather the one who knows bliss.

I say the same thing to make the point that liberation is not an experience. No experience you have is going to be essential truth, because all experiences come and go.

> I think I had some belief that experiencing bliss would
> then lead to some opposite negative experience
> afterwards. The reason why I ask is because I did some
> drugs this weekend and I noticed that it caused some
> confusion afterwards.

In my experience, whenever I used drugs, I always had some gross or subtle negative experiences afterwards. There was always a low after the high. For all my spiritual experiences, I did not have any negative physical or mental downsides afterwards. The only downside was that the experiences left me longing for more extraordinary states, and I was disappointed with the current ordinary state. Experiencing bliss is not like taking drugs where there will be a low afterwards. There can, however, be the desire to get back to that state, which is why I call it bondage.

One thing to remember, when you are taking drugs, especially psychedelics, you are seeking an experience. I don't have a judgement, and I never tell anyone how to live. Just see that you are looking for some extraordinary experience. Don't try to change anything. Just keep doing whatever you are doing and see for yourself if you are looking for some special experience. Maybe one day, you will get sick of it and you won't need it anymore. Of course, there is nothing wrong or bad with it.

The drug experience comes, and it goes, and you remain untouched. In fact, if in the middle of a drug experience, a holiday happens, see that you are aware of the drug experience. See that you are prior to it—the knowing of it. See, the experience means nothing.

Wanting Doubtlessness, Now

I am still trying to shake the idea that this recognition I have had about my true nature should allow me to remain relatively calm and prevent me from getting stressed at work. It was not a great week. I pretty much forgot about having holidays because I was exhausted and stressed at work.

Also, there is this belief that even though I recognize something, other people recognize it more than me and they are having a better experience than me.

I don't recognize it more than you. You either recognize it or you don't. I just have no doubt about it, and I don't care what comes and goes. You just have to stick with it.

I guess I want the doubtlessness now.

Okay. I will "give it" to you, now. Let's have a holiday.

HOLIDAY

Be here open, aware.

If thoughts come and you are focused on them,
relax the focus of attention.

Be here, now, for a moment.

You recognize this aware/knowing that is here, now?

Is there a past or a future?

Has this aware always been true for you?

Is it here every time you look, without exception?

It must be true because every time you look it is here.

Every time it is here and every time it is the same.

Any doubt about that?

No.

The purpose of a holiday is to know what is true and to be doubtless for a moment. If a doubt comes up in a holiday, just jump again. Ignore the doubt, get real and see what is true. You can't fail if you stay authentic because your essential nature is you. Every time you see truth, it is doubtless.

Of course, things at work can be stressful. It is natural.

> *I guess I can put down the notion that life always has to be nice.*

Yes, you can stop arguing with what is.

> *Inquirer 2: I had this notion when I first started this work that when I woke up, things would not bother me. Now, I see things still bother me, but I am not bothered by the fact they bother me.*

And in this, you will see you are not bothered. Do I get bothered? I don't know. I don't pay attention. I see it as things just flowing by.

> *Inquirer 3: Could you say you would not have a doubt if you went through the experience of being crucified, like Jesus?*

I know who I am. It is over. If someone is nailing spikes into my hands, I will be in extreme pain. At that point, I won't give a shit who I am. However, I will still not forget what is true.

> *Inquirer 3: Do you have no questions at all about your true nature, or is it just that you don't have certain questions anymore?*

I have no questions about it. All questions can be finished in one fell swoop. You will ask questions until you just know so clearly that it is doubtless, then no more questions will arise. Until you are doubtless, the potential for questions can still arise about your nature. Even after it is doubtless, questions about practical matters still arise, like how to make a recipe or how to fix a problem with your car, house, etc.

I am no-thing and I don't know what anything means or why anything is. I just know that I am. To me that is enough. The ultimate answer to all questions is when no more questions appear. When no more questions appear, then there is no need for any answers.

For example, the answer is, "There is a God," then the question appears, "How do I merge with God?" If you never heard there was a God, how could that question appear? The answers have been programmed into our brains by culture: "There is enlightenment." "You have to purify your mind." etc. This is why people have questions.

Let's answer all questions, now—forever.

HOLIDAY

Just be here, now.

Any past?

Any future?

Nothing—here and now.

Are any questions needed to know this?

See how simple this is? It is ultimate simplicity. You get nothing. Nothing. You don't get your questions answered. Questions just go away.

Let's do it again.

HOLIDAY

Is any philosophy needed to explain this moment?

Could it?

If you don't refer to mind, is there anything to understand?

Or anyone who needs to understand?

Is there anything you need to know about the meaning of life
to live, here and now?

Questions are just a tenacious habit of the mind. That is why these meetings are so important. If we don't keep knowing our true nature, we can get wrapped up in some nonsense in the mind. Then in six months, we are all of a sudden thinking we need to get a spiritual teacher.

I only know one thing—I am now!

Headless Perspective

I had a moment where I saw myself with no head, and the whole world was on top of my shoulders. I had this shift where I was aware.

That is good. I also had a similar experience years ago. It lasted about a week and then, like all experiences, it went. Since then, I no longer experience myself trapped in this body. What we have perceived and believed our whole life is that we are inside this body looking out these two eyes. In a way, this is true because this is where consciousness is housed and where the objective world is known through the senses. There is a vantage point from this location because of the senses, the thoughts and the feelings. Because of that, we think we are located at this vantage point only.

In a holiday, we can see something different. No longer is it true that we are only at this vantage point. This vantage point is not separate from what we previously thought was outside of us. Now, there no longer seems to be a line demarcating an inside from an outside. My personal experience is that there is an experiential vantage point here and yet, it is not separate from the omnipresent knowing. Let's have a holiday and see if that is clear.

HOLIDAY

This knowing is not just inside this head somewhere.

You see, it is ubiquitous.

It just seems like it is in the head
because there is a conscious,
sense-based perspective here.

When you see that you have no head,
all of a sudden there is no border here,
there is no body.

There is just knowing... (pause).

It is good to keep on seeing that you have no head,
because now there is no "inside" any longer.

There is only openness.

*When I first recognized this, my internal dialog kept
showing up and taking me away. Then, the dialog just
blended in as one thing. It was no longer occurring for me
as internal, and it was not distracting me. It was just
there with everything else.*

This occurred because you know yourself as unlimited, rather than limited to this perspective inside here. You know yourself in a much vaster way, and the dialog becomes much less significant and overwhelming. *You* are the most obvious thing. You are much more obvious than anything that is happening inside the brain.

How Can I Get Back Spiritual Experiences?

*I don't practice spiritual experiences very much and I
would like to know what sudden spiritual experiences
are? Also, once these experiences are had by a sadhaka
(spiritual aspirant), why does it become difficult to realize
them again?*

These kinds of experiences can happen whether a person is on the spiritual path or not. But, like every other experience—without exception—they appear, last for some time, and then vanish. Once any experience happens, it cannot be regained. Perhaps something similar may happen, mostly not, but there is no way for you to create that exact experience again.

More importantly, these experiences are not liberation, and they will not liberate you. Liberation is something else. I had many such experiences when I was seeking, but none of them liberated me.

Liberation is about coming to know the truth of who you are and allowing that *knowing* to liberate the mind from the beliefs that seem to keep you in bondage and suffering.

If you over value experiences, you are believing in a past and trying to relive it. Past is self. If you value self this way, you won't come to know liberation. These experiences will most likely never happen again for you. The good news is that it does not matter. Here and now, you are already free. Come to know this for yourself and be done with these experiences. This is freedom.

Just This

> *I want to describe an experience I had the other night. I was walking down a street that has a lot of tall trees. I was looking at these trees, and there was JUST THIS. I mean there was JUST THIS. It was unmixed with anything. There wasn't anything else and that's the best way to describe it. I've read "just this" in other places, but I've never known "just this," where there was nothing else, no duality, nothing. There was no "I" that was saying "just this." It was "just this," and it was like a holiday on steroids. Really amazing.*

I understand. I've had those experiences too. That's great and that's wonderful, and it came, and it went, right?

> *Yes.*

That's all good. That experience came and went, but what didn't come and go is the knowing of truth. Now, you know something.

That experience itself is not necessary, and you don't always have be in that state. You now know, there's just this. Just know that. Know what's true. That was revealed to you for whatever reason and it is fine.

> *It sort of carried on the next day when I was in the garden, and it was "just this" again. So really, it's just pretty amazing to watch all of this happening, spontaneously. The value for me is these freedom experiences that arise spontaneously and continuously.*

They may never come again though, so don't value the experience so much. Value this, you see? If you value that experience as a memory, you're not valuing what I'm talking about.

> *Right, which I do because I think about that experience and then give it some value. I think, "Wow, that was cool!"*

What a horrible thing for that to happen to you. I wouldn't wish that on my worst enemy. It's like being addicted to a drug. Now, you want that drug again and you're not valuing truth because that is a lie. That experience is a lie because where is it now? Where is it?

> *Right. Well, there is a sense of wanting it to be repeated. However, I think, "Well, how much am I going to invest in it?" I realized I couldn't repeat it because it was just a spontaneous event. So, all of this is just being witnessed as well.*

You see that, that's good.

> *When I say I value it, I'm just witnessing that it's a memory. So, I'm knowing the memory.*

It's good you say that you realize you're valuing it because you come to know what's true—I'm valuing a memory. The memory of that experience is complete horseshit (I'm a bit radical). It has no value because there's only now.

I had so many experiences in the past and I don't care about them at all. Why? Because they're not true. There's only *just this,* now. There's only *just this.* There wasn't only *just this* during that experience, there's only *just this,* now.

> *Right, that's what I was trying to say. I also had an experience later that...*

What about now though? What about now? Now, there's only *just this,* isn't there?

> *Right.*

Don't give me the correct answer. Is it true or not?

> *Absolutely. I'm looking at your screen, there's only this.*

There's only this, there's only this, there's only this, there's only this... I have no respect for that experience. I'm sorry to tell you. I have no respect for any of my experiences either; they mean nothing to me. If I gained some wisdom or knowledge from them that I have now, then that's good, but the experience itself is meaningless to me. There's no past. There's nothing behind the curtain. There's nothing, you see?

> *Right. The experience gave me nothing, except the sense of euphoria. This is a really interesting conversation. I agree with you being radical. I'm not insulted by you saying that it's just horseshit.*

I know. I'm being a little tough and I don't mean to be.

> *No, that's okay. You're on point, you're right.*

I have too much respect for everyone on this call. I'm not going to mess around and lie. I have to tell it like it is. There's nothing! This is it, this is it, this is it... And it doesn't matter what's appearing now, either. It doesn't matter. You are free.

Let's not value what appears too much, including those experiences, and let's not value the past at all. Also, let's not consider the current experience, like a negative experience, to be an indication there's something wrong with you either. None of that matters. What matters is you are here, now, before, during, and after all those experiences. There's only this. So, value only this. Your essential being is free.

It's very easy to say you don't want to value the negative experiences that come up. It's like, "Okay good! Thank God, I don't have to value the negative experiences because I just have to value truth." Well, guess what? You don't get to value the blissful experiences either because those are equally horseshit. I'm an equal opportunity horse-shitter. Where is any of it now? Come on, let's get real. I respect all of you too much to lie. Let's just be honest, is there anything other than this?

No.

Good. That experience may never happen again, and it doesn't matter. It doesn't matter at all. You know there's only this. Know it now, know it now... There's only this.

In a sense, that experience is always happening because...

The knowing of it is known. There's no Santa Claus, right? Do you have to look up the chimney anymore to see there's no Santa Claus, or is it already known?

Yes, already known.

Good, so do you need to have that blissful experience to know there's only this, or do you already know?

I don't need the experience. I know.

Okay good, same thing. Once you know, you know. That's it, you know. There's only this. You never think, "Oh no, I forgot there's no Santa Claus! Hold on, I have to look up the chimney to make sure there's no Santa Claus." That would be silly, wouldn't it?

Yes, and that experience had a certain euphoria, and other present "just this-es," may not have the same euphoria.

Right. Even if there is no euphoria going on, the *just this* is *just this* anyways.

These subtle things we still believe are extremely important to recognize because who you are is obvious. However, there are many levels of beliefs in the mind. There are very gross level beliefs, of course, like there's a God and I'm going to heaven. There are also very subtle beliefs that we are talking about, which we all have. They definitely need to be seen.

The recognition takes no time. You don't get a bigger recognition or more recognition. The recognition *is* the recognition and it's obvious. It never gets bigger or better, but continuing to recognize it just resolves doubt over time. You just become at ease with what is. You stop arguing, and that's the peace that passes understanding.

Strong Movements of Energy

*I have strong energy flows in the body, like kriyas
(spontaneous body movements). What are these and are
they related to spiritual inquiry? What should I do with
them, and can they be used to go deeper or help open up
the inquiry even more?*

It depends on what you are interested in. Many spiritual practices
can elicit different types of experiences. In and of themselves, there
is nothing wrong with them, but we have been given the impression
that they have something to do with awakening. That is not so. They
are not at all related to the inquiry into who you are. Coming to
know who you are, and having that knowing lead to liberation, has
nothing to do with those types of experiences. In fact, believing
them to be a way to awaken is a mistake, and depending on them or
trying to develop them for that purpose will deter you from
inquiring into your essential being and coming to know freedom.

Why? Because when you are focusing on what's appearing in this
body-mind (whether mundane or transcendent), and when you are
trying to improve it, get somewhere, or go deeper, you are ignoring
what is always present, before, during, and after each experience—
your essential nature. Also, you strengthen the belief in an
individual self that is having these experiences because it is all in
the realm of the mind or ego. All authentic teachers, and I have met
a few, want you to wake up. Their message is to ignore these
experiences, to put zero value on them, and to see that they come
and go.

Come to know who you are beyond these experiences and anything
else happening in this body-mind. Do not make yourself special
because these things appear. Look closely to see if this is the case
and be honest with yourself about it. I had many experiences on the
path, and there was a belief, "I am getting somewhere because I am

having experiences." I didn't even consciously notice that was going on, but it was true, nonetheless.

Another belief is that you need to go deeper. Awakening is not deep. It is here, it is obvious, and it is simple. Depth refers to form, an inside and outside, and it refers to mind. Liberation is free of mental concepts and experiences. It is that in and as which mind appears. It is not deep and it is not subtle. It is here and it is obvious.

First, find out who you are, then see that all these kriyas are happening only to the body-mind, and you are the knowing of them. If you come to know this and are committed to liberation in a real sense, these experiences will most likely stop.

I have not had a single spiritual experience since awakening. Good riddance! They came when I was on the path, intensely seeking and believing experiences had something to do with liberation. If you are interested in awakening, you are willing for those experiences to never happen again. See if that is true for you.

The only way these things can help your inquiry is if you see they are appearances in and as you, and that you, knowing, are here before, during, and after their appearance. Then, there is a value, but no more value than any other "good" or "bad" experience. All appearances appear in and as you. In that way, all appearances are equal, and they can all be used to point to you, the knowing.

Find out what you really want. Truth? Liberation? Experiences? To be special? Find out, because that is what you will get.

The Carousels of Mind

Prayer and Meditation

You said we don't need to pray or meditate anymore. I have been praying almost my whole life and meditating for eight years. It's hard to stop. I am still doing both, but a lot less these days. I think I can stop praying, but meditating is a lot harder because it helps me sleep. Will these practices slow me down?

A holiday is what I call true meditation. It is knowing that you are, here and now. By "you," I do not mean the feeling of I am in the body, this separate sense of self, limited and localized. I mean knowing, knowing itself, not locatable, not limited, and prior to the *sense* or *feeling* of I am. Almost always our attention, or knowing, is fixed on an object, which includes the felt sense of I am separate. For a moment, stop attending to any object in particular, and know that you are, know that you exist, here and now, not as a body-mind, not as a conscious center in a body, not as a feeling in a body, but simply—knowing. This knowing is not dual, not subject/object, it is self-luminous, or self-aware. There is not a separate "you" knowing this. It is "you," knowing yourself.

If you meditate on an object, like breath, visualization, mantra, or any other object, including the sense or *feeling* of I am, you are not knowing yourself, essentially. You are knowing an object. If you meditate for the purpose of stilling the mind and getting some peace, then there is a goal, a trying to get somewhere. Who is trying to get somewhere? It's the self/ego that thinks it is lacking. If it helps you to fall asleep, then why not? If, however, you are doing it for other reasons (to attain, achieve, change or get rid of something) then it is not the way of freedom, which is "know thyself," here and now.

If you are praying, to whom are you praying? You are believing in someone other than you. Someone, of course, far superior to you who is going to help you in some way. This is completely a mental projection and a concept given to you by religion/ignorance. I say, "Be still and know, 'I am God.'" There is no god other than you.

I do not recommend praying. Also, I do not recommend worship or bhakti in the usual way it is used, which is to worship the guru, god or deity. I do highly recommend true bhakti, which is devotion to Self—the one, the knowing, which is your essential being, here and now. Be devoted to that at all times. Then, you are a genuine Bhakta, a worshiper of truth, freedom and the true God. In fact, be extremely intentional about that, do that always, day and night, while eating, talking, walking, watching TV, etc. Know thyself, have holidays.

The thought, "Will these slow me down?" is just an idea in your mind. Slow you down from what? Here and now, you are free. See this again, and again, and again... and oh yes, again, and again. Freedom has no past and no future. Freedom is only NOW.

Reading Spiritual Books

I have been reading other books by Ramana and Nisargadatta and I have some questions how they relate to your book.

That is why you are confused. You can do what you want, but I don't recommend reading anything, even my book. You are wasting your time reading these books.

By continuing to read spiritual books, you are not allowing the mind to come to rest in its natural condition of open knowing, which is devoid of concepts and other thoughts *about* liberation. This natural condition is free from the comparisons your mind creates between what is now and the great, wonderful, exalted condition you have come to believe and expect from reading those books. All expectations come from those books and spiritual teachings. When you come to this work, I say be finished. You will never be finished if you keep reading that stuff. But you may have to do it for a while until you see the futility in it and get fed up.

I can't make you do anything. My suggestion is that you stop and be finished. You can't do that either, as there is no doer. I am just planting a seed in your head. Just be reconciled with the fact that you know one thing only—this, here and now. This knowing, which is aware, is the only true knowing. Not knowing anything about philosophies or meanings or whys is the true security.

The value of life is living. It's not about attempting to figure everything out and understand everything. That is neurotic because it is futile, although it is what we have been taught to do.

Anyway, me telling you there is nothing more is useless. Let's have a look. Have a holiday.

HOLIDAY

Know, now.

What is the meaning of this, here and now?

The only possible meaning would have to be one appearing in
mind, mostly based on desire or fear.

Without that thought structure, how can *this* have a meaning?

And why would there even need to be a meaning for this?

That need only appears in a mind conditioned by concepts and
fueled by fear.

Who are you free of conditioned mind?

The desire for meaning is only happening because of the fear of not
knowing what will happen. By attaching meaning to this, we think
we are going to get some comfort. However, this comfort is both
false and fickle because *this* is in constant change, birth and death.
This, here and now, has no inherent meaning. Have a look for
yourself.

HOLIDAY

Aware, free, all-inclusive.

There is only now.

What more is there than this?

If there is only now,
how can there be more?

More implies that there is a desire,

based on dissatisfaction and expectation.

Don't judge it.
Just know it.

If there is anything more,
it will just be something in the mind, in thought,
which is appearing within aware.

Even the greatest spiritual experience on Earth
is an appearance in the mind;
it is appearing to and in you.

I say be finished. Be reconciled. See that you are not as smart as you think. It's easier. I am not a guru that is going to help keep you on the path. I am the guy you talk to when you want your head chopped off and you want to be finished.

I don't know anything, and I don't want to know anything. There are a million teachers out there that will keep you searching forever. I went to many and we all have. The value in those teachings is that eventually, you will see that it is all rubbish. When you see this, you want to be finished.

Effort to Be in the Now

It seems like in the beginning, there is an effort to hold myself in the "now," and then there is a flip where I know I am the "now." For me, the longer it goes on, the more I relax and see that "now" is the effortless part and everything else is the effort. Is this effort of trying to hold myself in the "now" just a habitual pattern?

With this work you are not trying to "hold yourself in the now." That is a different teaching. This work is about recognizing, in a holiday, that your essential being is free, briefly or for however long it naturally happens. This work is not about intentionally trying to maintain anything. With this, when a holiday happens naturally, you see you are free and completely finished. Holidays happen for as long as they happen, and when they occur, you know who you are. Continually recognizing who you are in a holiday, resolves doubts and tendencies that cause suffering. And of course, the more holidays happen and the more you see the value in that, then being on holiday becomes your default condition. It does happen to be that the more you know who you are and the more you see the value in it, the more you come to rest there. This occurs naturally without doership involved trying to maintain something.

To me, when Nisargadatta says to "hold on to the sense of I Am," it sounds effortful. It seems hard to jump from this sense of self.

This work is not Nisargadatta's work. It is not holding on to the felt sense of I Am. By the way, that is great work, but it is not what this work is. That is holding on to the felt sense of I Am to the exclusion of all else until you transcend the felt sense of I Am.

This work is about recognizing that now you are free. As I was saying, with this work, you come to see right away that you are the *knowing* of the felt sense of I Am. You are not holding on to the sense of I Am. The sense of I Am is ego. Nisargadatta says hold on to the ego until finally, after a long time, the ego dissolves. Or, if you are lucky like him, after three years.

However, this is not what I am saying. I am saying, don't hold on to the ego—go beyond it immediately. See, for a moment, you are the knowing of the ego. In that, you see there is no past, no future, no self and *you are free*. Do you see what I mean?

> *I do, and it seems like it is hard for me to even notice when I am free. This sense of I Am is more intense than all the other objects.*

You know the feeling I Am?

> *Yes.*

How do you know the feeling I Am? You must be the knowing of the feeling I Am.

> *Right.*

To paraphrase Nisargadatta's words, prior to this felt sense of I Am, you are the knowing. Prior to this feeling of I Am, you know it, like all the other objects in the room. You know all objects in the room, and you know the feeling of I Am. That is why I say everything is equal and included in this knowing. All objects are equal, including this object labeled I Am. Do you see what I am saying?

> *I do.*

Let's be on holiday together.

HOLIDAY

Know that you consciously exist.

I want you to know the knowing,
not knowing any of the objects.

I and knowing are not separate.

Knowing is not an object.

I am knowing.

Be that.

Now, know the sense/feeling of I Am as an object.

This is already "prior to" and going beyond what Nisargadatta told people to do. This is the end, basically. You know there is no past and there is no future, so there is no truth to the story of self. That story is a myth. It doesn't actually exist. The afflictions and pathologies that are in there don't exist either. You are free of all of that because they are a myth. You might as well believe you are Harry Potter.

Let's get real, here and now. Where is the past you have been telling yourself exists? It is not here, is it? It is all a story based on the first feeling of I Am. The story "I am my name, nationality, sex, ethnicity, etc." It all comes back to this first touch of ego (the felt sense of I Am). However, you are the knowing of that.

> I get from Nisargadatta that you can end psychological suffering, and it seems like work. However, I see what you are talking about.

It takes no time to see that you are free. Let's have a holiday.

HOLIDAY

See, it takes no time to know you are free. What takes time for everyone to resolve is the habit of belief in the story. This belief keeps you continuing to suffer in bondage. The momentum of the habit of believing that story takes time to resolve for everyone. How do you resolve that? By having a holiday, because when you have a holiday, you see you are free and you are the knowing of the felt sense of I Am.

You know there is no past. You know the story is a myth and is not true. Just know this for a moment (or for however long it lasts) in a holiday. Then, keep having holidays until you no longer doubt. It does not mean things stop appearing. Stories and thoughts come, but you no longer doubt. You no longer think you have to find some other work (meditation, therapy, etc.) to fix yourself. Now, on a holiday, you recognize it is already doubtless in this moment. You are this knowing that knows itself and the felt sense of I Am. You know you exist, right? Is this clear?

> *It is.*

You don't sound positive. Is it clear?

> *Feels like I am looking for some event, some "aha." If that "aha" is not happening, I don't know how to say it is clear.*

Let's just be on holiday.

HOLIDAY

Relax the focus of attention.

See, I know I exist.

It's the knowing itself, which is not an object.

I know.

Is that clear?

> *It is, but you say that it takes time for everyone.*

No. I say it takes no time to recognize your essential nature. The more you see it, the more you will recognize the profundity of it. It is as clear as it is going to be. You know. It is perfectly, spotlessly clear. Have a holiday.

HOLIDAY

You know. It can't be any clearer, but because of the momentum of beliefs, concepts and ideals impressed in your mind, you feel, "This can't be it, it must be more." Those thoughts are just habits, which create these doubts.

> *You said I don't seem clear, but I don't feel worried about it because you say the profundity will register more over time.*

I said you don't sound positive. It is perfectly clear now, but there are a lot of ideas in your head that are saying, "This can't be it." It can be something along the lines of, "This isn't the Holy Grail! I have to have a bigger aha! There must be something more than this!" It is so simple and ordinary, but the mind has many impressed beliefs saying that it is something else, something extraordinary.

> *Does it matter if I keep having doubts as long as I keep having holidays?*

Very good question and let me answer it in this way. The more you have holidays and recognize that this knowing that knows itself is your essential nature, the more you keep noticing that, the more you will recognize that this is it. You will recognize afflictions being less bothersome, the seeking ending, and you will come to rest in this peace, the knowing, who I am. This will result in fewer and fewer doubts.

Nevertheless, doubts may still appear. No problem. First of all, in this moment (forget tomorrow, the next day or even one minute from now), I want you to see, in a holiday, that you know who you are, and it is doubtless, now. It is already doubtless when you look. So, tomorrow at 3:00 PM when a doubt comes, you see the doubt is just another object that comes and goes. Nothing changes because there is a doubt. You are the same. You never change. Only some object passed before you that was called a doubt.

Have as many doubts as you like; it does not matter if you have doubts. Once the doubt passes, you, once again, know who you are. It is the same every time. This knowing does not change, and as you keep having holidays, it just doesn't matter.

This work is not about knowing any objects, now. It is about knowing thyself. Know—the knowing is who I am. Know it to the point that it is doubtless. Then go ahead and know as many objects as you like because you already know who you are.

The more you have holidays, the more natural it is to be on holidays. I am on holiday when I am speaking, and I hear the words just as you are hearing them. I don't know what I am going to say. I never know what I am going to say. In truth, and this is a good thing to know, we think that this body-mind and thoughts are the most obvious thing, but no. The most obvious is you, knowing! There can be nothing more obvious than you. The more you recognize this, the more you realize—this is the most obvious thing!

The body-mind can appear to be the most obvious, but if it can be unattended to in a holiday, then really, what is the most obvious thing? YOU ARE.

Therapy

You have spoken in the past that this work is not for everyone and some people need therapy. As a therapist, I know that most of the work involves "things from the past." How do you reconcile that with this work?

I don't reconcile it. What I mean is this work is not therapy. This is the end of working on the psychological mind. However, I am not unreasonable. Many people need therapy to get some semblance of mental health. Therapy won't result in freedom, but in an unhealthy ego sense, it can help.

I guess the question for me as a therapist is, if there is no past, what am I dealing with? Say I am working with a client on some of their childhood issues, is there a way to deal with that more directly?

What you are dealing with is people's beliefs that their mythical story is true. There is a habit of going into that story to try to resolve it. You can also be dealing with some serious traumas for people. Traumas prevent people from dropping their beliefs, and I respect that. Traumas can be significant and some need to be dealt with in a psychological way so that people can be less affected by the stories. To just tell someone who is suffering from psychological trauma to stop believing a story is not reasonable and is not compassionate. It is just arrogant.

I say a therapist like yourself is doing important work and providing a valuable service. Most people are not ready for *this* work. Even many spiritual seekers, who have been on the path for years, are not ready to drop all their stories and beliefs and be *nothing*. You do not need to conflate your therapy work with this work. It may be appropriate for some of your clients, but not all.

When you are working with a client, you may see an opportunity for them to drop everything for a moment and see something that is present. In that moment, you will know based on your training and evaluation of where a particular client is whether they may be willing and able to drop their story. I am not a therapist and I don't know much about psychology. I do know that many people can't drop their stories even for a moment because of trauma or severe psychological issues, schizophrenia being an extreme example.

> *Inquirer 2: I think the mistake is seeing psychological work as a means to liberation. When you go to a regular doctor, they are concerned with the body, not with liberation. Similarly, a psychotherapist is concerned with healing the mind, not with liberation.*

That's right. It is very true, and as I was saying, it is good to not conflate the two. Psychotherapy is not liberation. Obviously, liberation is free from the psychological, philosophical and spiritual carousels. It is free from them all and to try to mix them with this work is not realistic.

A psychologist is a doctor of the mind and they are attempting to heal the mind as much as possible. I think this is necessary and a lot of people need it.

> *Inquirer 1: It seems like psychotherapy can be a step towards liberation by freeing the mind from really obsessive thoughts and beliefs. It can prepare people to do work like this.*

For some people, it can get them ready to do work like this. They can get to a place where they are psychologically stable enough to recognize freedom. Just because they are stable does not guarantee they will come to this work. A majority won't. Just like most spiritual seekers won't come to this even though they were "prepared" by the spiritual path.

Praying Out of Fear

When I got into nonduality, I felt like I was becoming more of an atheist, and since I've been working with you, I definitely feel like I am becoming an atheist. I was reading an article about human possession (spirits controlling the body-mind) last night, and I had a scary thought, "What would I do if something like that happened to me?" Having a holiday is not really going to help me. Who would I call on?

Ghostbusters.

Right. I kept myself awake scaring myself and asking myself, "What would I believe in," because I don't really believe in anything anymore.

Oh, I see. You can't call on Jesus to help you or something like that.

Exactly, or my spirit guides.

That's the problem with this work. If something sucks, it sucks. You don't have any help.

I was sort of left hanging there thinking, "What the hell would I do?"

You would suffer through it. The thing is this, when you come to know who you are, you see your essential being is changeless and everything else is completely changeful. You come to know that not one appearance you've ever experienced in your life was ever permanent. Not one! If you go through every single experience, and there are billions throughout your whole life, not one of them has been permanent. Not one. They all come and they all go. If you really know that, then you can relax a little bit. Right?

Yes. I guess it's the same with anything like cancer, or anything bad.

True, but some things can be scary. If you're in your room and a ghost comes in and scares the hell out of you, then it scares the hell out of you. That's not going to change. If someone is coming at me with an ax, I'm not going to be on a holiday. A holiday is not going to prevent fear from arising if a train is about to hit me. Of course, there will be fear. It doesn't solve that. But it can alleviate the fear that arises by projecting fantasies about the future, which is what you are talking about.

Right. I used to pray in the mornings and the evenings. The other day, I just said a prayer, but I felt kind of silly. I thought, "Who am I praying to and why am I doing this?" I really haven't prayed since. However, if something bad happened, I'd probably pray. That's part of my conditioning.

I prayed once in my life, when I was a drug addict. I stayed up all night snorting coke and I was still up at noon the next day. When I ran out of coke and didn't have a valium, there was no doubt in my mind that I had ruined my life. I fell to my knees in prayer, not to God, because I didn't believe in God. I just prayed for help. I said,

"Help me, please help me." Then, miraculously, I fell asleep. I woke up three hours later and my whole drug addiction was finished forever, and I was a spiritual seeker.

That prayer (it was really more of a plea) was answered, but who was I praying to? Myself, obviously. I didn't believe in anyone else, God or anything. I didn't know who I was praying to. I was just saying, "Help me." It wasn't that the prayer helped me or that someone came and helped me because of the prayer. What it was is that my intention was so strong for something to change, that it changed.

The help came from me, from within. It came from the strongest intention I've ever had in my life, which was to get help or to be helped, now! That was the strongest intention I've ever had for anything— "Help!!!" Then, help came. But it did not come from someone or somewhere. It was all here.

> *And since there was no doer and no free will, was it just time for it to happen?*

I didn't choose to do that. I was literally thrust to my knees; my head hit the floor. I didn't have anything to do with that. That's just what happened. There was no God that did it either. There was a buildup of years of desperation, but you can't find a reason. There's no reason. There's no doer in that. I tried to quit drugs many times before with will power. I told myself, "I'm going to choose to quit drugs." It never worked, ever.

> *Inquirer 2: Quoting another teacher, "the only one listening when you pray is you."*

That's the way I see it too. There is only you. When people pray to God, it works occasionally just out of coincidence. But most people who pray to God never get what they want. You know why? "Because God works in mysterious ways." That is complete bullshit and just an excuse. They'll say, "That's why I didn't win the lottery, even though I prayed. I still believe in God though." God is just a children's fantasy for adults.

> *Inquirer 3: One of the things that has happened, and I can't say, "I like it," is that certain ideas have fallen away. I used to have this notion that if things didn't work out my way, something better was going to come along. That has disappeared. I was like, "Ah shit, I can't even believe in that?" But I realized for the first time, if something doesn't work out, then it doesn't work out. I have no idea what's going to happen next. The old belief created some sense of consolation. Now, I am letting go of that and free falling. That's actually freer.*

It is free. Why is there a God? Because people are afraid. God was created out of man's fear and desire. They want hope. They want some security blanket that they're going to be okay in the future, especially after they die. So, they create a God, and then they have a false sense of security. God is a teddy bear.

People haven't grown up. People who believe in that stuff are not adults, they're children. A true adult has nothing; they stand naked on their own two feet, alone, with no security blanket. Freedom is the unknown. Obviously, that's truth. Anyone who is mature can admit that's what's true.

I have no idea what's going to happen in the future. I have no idea about anything except this moment here, and if in this moment here a train is running over my foot, saying a prayer, "Help me God!" won't help. It's too late. The train has already run over my foot.

> *Inquirer 4: I used to believe in a God that wasn't separate from me, and it was all-knowing and everywhere. Now, I see that I am this aware knowing, and I can say this aware is God.*

Go one step further. I know it is blasphemous, and we're going to hell for saying it, but if this aware is God, then who else is God?

Everybody. Me. I'm God as well.

Exactly. Let's face it, you're going to hell for saying it [said facetiously]. Have a holiday, now.

HOLIDAY

Where is God? These are the words from the Bible: within everything (all-inclusive), omniscient (knows everything), and omnipresent (everywhere). Well, sounds like you to me. What did God say to Moses? Moses went to the top of the mountain and said, "What is your name, sir?" God responded, "I am that I am." Can you also say, "I am that I am?" Of course, you can. So, who is God?

It's easier to call aware God than to call myself God.

That's because you're going to hell for saying something like that. You don't need to call it God, but let's face it, the sages, on whom these religions are based, knew something. They knew: I am source, essential being, the Self, and Sat Chit Ananda. In Indian culture, they called it Brahman, and it is what everyone wants to attain. They consider it God, and you can become Brahman yourself if you're lucky. Very few people can do it of course, and very few people believe they can attain it, but at least you're allowed to believe it. You're allowed to believe it in Indian culture.

In Western culture, you're not allowed to believe that. According to the Bible, Jesus said, "I and my Father are one" (absolute and form are one, no separation). He also allegedly said, "I am the way and the truth and the life. No one comes to the Father except through Me." Jesus recognized his essential nature. Before Jesus, the original sages knew—I am source, I am Sat Chit Ananda. They put a word on it—God.

In the 4th century the originators of modern Christianity made their demands clear: "God is a thing and it's not you. Certainly, Jesus is, but not you. God is a thing to attain, and the way to attain it is by giving us a lot of money and obeying us. If you're lucky, when you die, we will put in a good word for you and maybe you'll get into the good place. In the meantime, behave and do what we tell you. And absolutely don't even consider that you are God, or you are going to hell." It's no wonder you can't say you are God.

Of course, we all feel unworthy in the West. We were told we were born with "original sin" and we are all sinners. However, when we came out of the womb, did we feel unworthy? No! When we came out of the womb, all we knew was God. We didn't have any word for it, but all we knew was God. Then, we learned that was wrong. We were told, "You are not that. You are this little fucked up person, and if you think you're anything more than that, you're going to hell."

Most people with this upbringing who later find eastern religions simply change clothing, and say Buddha is God, or Ramana is God. However, Buddha and Ramana both were saying, "No! Wake up, get enlightened. You're it!"

You see it's all just thoughts. When you see what's true, that here, now, I am all-knowing and all-inclusive (and that's the description of God), your mind says, "Don't go there or you're going to hell." You don't have to call yourself God. I don't call myself God. God is just a word, just a description of Source. That's all it is.

Enneagram

> *I came across the enneagram this week and I read about my type. It had my whole life in there. I was shocked to see the pattern and how it matched my life. I recognized the pattern was just happening and totally out of my control. Also, I realized that it is the belief in the internal dialogue and taking everything to be real that makes things so important. It felt like I saw the engine behind the inner dialog in ten pages.*

It is amazing, isn't it? And somehow, we still think we are the doer and have free will over our life. Now, we all know it's not true. I think there is some validity to the enneagram and astrology as far as this body-mind organism goes, but it is just like anything else, it is not *you*, essentially. Even though these things may have some validity, they have nothing to do with you essentially. You are watching that particular enneagram or astrology movie play out in this body. If you put value on those things, then you are right back on the carousel of mind, reifying self. There is no freedom in that.

If you don't know your essential nature, you can think this stuff means something and then you start planning your life based upon it, thinking you are accomplishing something. It is just a play. It is not you. Let it turn you around, so you see that it is just a story of your life—the myth. Let it turn you around, so you see that your essential nature is free, then it has some value.

> *Inquirer 2: I have done work with the enneagram in the past, and I recall when we were doing our individual session, you mentioned that when we come into this existence, we come in with the five senses and a blank hard drive. Is the enneagram showing another filter or tendencies that I come into life with?*

There are some tendencies we have that we don't know how they got there. For instance, my musical abilities were innate tendencies. The tendency for basketball was not there at all. I have no idea why I have one tendency or another.

When I speak about the blank hard drive, I am referring to the fact that there is no programmed data in the mind that creates a psychological story about who we are. That is what I mean by a blank hard drive. The enneagram or astrology, if true, are just innate tendencies we have and are not the result of mental input based on experiences.

The temptation with stuff like the enneagram is to aggrandize it a little bit. I honestly would give it no meaning whatsoever. It may be a fun game, but I would give nothing to it. Sort of like reading a book or seeing a movie. Once it is over, it is over. You don't carry the movie or story around with you. If you want to be free, just forget it. It doesn't even matter because if these things are true, you have no control over them anyway. So, why even consider it. It means nothing. Why limit yourself in that way? And why do you need to know? See in yourself that there is a need or desire to know in that way, as some form of security or comfort.

What I like is *no*thing—freedom, here and now. I have no idea what will happen, and I happen to like it that way. Why would I want to add this mental game onto *no*thing? The best thing is freedom. Freedom is empty-handed. I have nothing, I know nothing, and I am no one. This is freedom. If we start believing in those astrology signs and enneagram numbers, then we have something—an understanding of who I am, self, and a belief that I am that character. We know something about where we came from and where we are going. We are "someone"—an astrology sign with an enneagram number. I don't want any of that. I want less.

More and more, I want less and less. This is where the bliss of freedom is actually, Sat Chit Ananda. Sat is existence or being. We all know being is our nature. Chit is consciousness or awareness (knowing). Sat Chit equals being knowing. I always say aware and knowing are synonymous. This being knowing is you. It is all one thing, Sat Chit. What is the essence of that? Ananda, which is peace or bliss. Honestly, if you just keep having holidays more and more with the intention for freedom, you will be the knowing that is at peace.

Neti Neti

It seems to me that anything, even self-inquiry and negation (neti neti), can be used to reify the sense of self.

Neti Neti is definitely related to the negative approach that I have spoken about (see Introduction). We are not doing that approach here. We don't try to analyze or change what we are not. We see what we are, first and foremost.

Don't we see what we are not?

Just by proxy. We see what we are, then we see everything else, which is not who we are essentially. The first thing we do together is to recognize who you are, your essential being. You recognize your essential being, and you come to know that you are not what you thought you were before—all the objects. This is done in one fell swoop. Who am I? I am existence, knowing, peace. Everything else is what I am aware of.

Neti Neti is putting attention on the negative (i.e. I am not the thoughts, I am not the body, etc.) and that is endless. When you know who you are, everything else is seen as what it is, an objective appearance, known to you. I am saying let's not do the negative approach. Let's do the positive approach, which is "I know who I am," and be finished. This is a holiday and it is positive. You know who you are in a holiday.

> *I see that. It's funny because I reframed what I went through with you into a negation of everything I wasn't, and that exposed who I am. Now, I see it's not like that.*

With this work you first come to see your essential being. You go through your whole spiritual journey finding out what you are not. You seek this experience and that experience, but then you run across this message, and the first day we meet, I show you who you are. From then on out, the only thing is to have holidays and know who you are. It's a very positive approach. I never say to go in and "deny you are this and deny you are that." That is just reifying a self. I am very specific—have a holiday and know who you are, no-thing!

> *I am paraphrasing, but didn't you say, "See you're the knowing and see you're not the body?" I thought I actually had to recognize I wasn't the body,*

I don't think I say, "see you are not the body." In fact, I say you are the body. It is the wave in the ocean. Everything gets denied in a holiday, but it is not an approach that specifically goes in and denies things. Denying things would be endless because there are an infinite number of things that would need to be denied. By knowing who you are, everything is denied in one fell swoop. It gets denied by proxy. You see what I am saying?

> *Yes.*

Then, you realize in retrospect, "I am not this, I am not that, etc." You did not know this by knowing you were not those things. You knew it by knowing who you *are*.

I think I started this by bringing up the fact that even self-inquiry can reify the self.

It depends on what you mean by inquiry. To me inquiry is just being the Self. Inquiry only means one thing. It doesn't mean actually inquiring into anything. It means be Sat Chit Ananda. That's what, in my view, the highest and truest inquiry is.

Even if there is someone being the Self...

Well, there is someone being the Self. It is you. You are that. It is who you are. All of us mistakenly believe we are this body-mind, but really, *I* does exist as Self. In fact, there is only one I, that is You, essential being. The I that is called ego, is not.

What I am saying is... if it is a thought that the small self is going to be something, the mind will be involved, and the mind can't do it. There could be a subtle belief that "I am going to be the Self." It could be a mental thing.

Well, yes, if that thought is there, "I am just being," it is just a thought. Being the Self does not need any thought. No words are needed.

I am just saying it can be slippery.

You are right. It can be slippery. I see what you are saying. You can turn it into a mental thing and there can be the thought, "I am being the Self now." As others are seeing, it is not mental at all. You recognize without any thought. You cannot recognize with thought.

The word "inquiry" is not perfect because it really means stop doing anything and be who you are, which is Sat Chit Ananda. Just be consciously knowing that you exist. No words are needed and we can all know we consciously exist, now. It's just knowing, and you can probably dissect that word as well. All the words fall short. That is why many great masters taught in silence.

Let's do that now.

HOLIDAY

Any word is a word too much.

Causation

What is the cause of any event or circumstance? If we believe in the continuity of something called time, then it must be said that every single event is the result of every other event that has ever occurred throughout time, no matter how directly or indirectly, grossly or subtly connected. If, on the other hand, there is no actual time, then there is no cause for anything that is occurring now. What is, simply is, period. It has not come from anywhere and it is not going anywhere. It is simply appearing and vanishing, now, now, now. If you recognize the latter to be true, then it is good news because it means you are free from the victimization and tyranny of past stories and events. Also, it means there is no one and nothing else from the past to blame for your suffering now, or to hope for and rely upon for peace and freedom in the future. You stand alone, now. Free.

There is No Cause

You say that there is no past, and therefore, no cause for something that is right now. In my case, I supposedly had a significant accident, and now, I am permanently disabled for the rest of my life. What I am seeing is the past is only a thought and this is liberating. Also, I see I don't even really know what is right now. There is no label that I can put on right now.

That is right. Without the mind labeling things, then *what is, is.*

There are two ways you can look at this thing called "cause." One way, is to consider something called *time* real. If we do, then we see there is no one event that causes another event. When we really look, we see that countless things went into what is happening right now. In the realm of mind, the cause of everything is the Big Bang. You always have to go back to the original event to see what caused anything. In the realm of time, no event stands by itself unaffected by anything else. Everything is connected.

The problem with looking at it this way is that it causes suffering. Going into past stories and looking for reasons, and longing for resolutions in the future, creates suffering. For the work we do here, we see that time is not a real thing and actually, there is only now. However, we use time in the Play of Life to navigate in practical terms, like making plans to go to the movie or making an appointment. This use of time does not cause suffering.

To avoid the suffering caused by believing in a past and a future, it is best to know what is actually real. The truth is that there is only now. There is no past and no future. If we believe in the past experiences and the future hopes and longings, we can enter a world of suffering. This work is focused on what is true—there is only now. NOW is the end of *psychological suffering caused by the belief in time*. Let's be on holiday and notice a couple of things.

HOLIDAY

Here and now,
we see only one thing happening
which to our mind appears to be countless,
separate things.

Our mind breaks everything up into countless, separate things.

In truth, there is only one thing happening.
There is only one appearance, now,
and it is this.

Causation

The mind comes in and labels everything here—
this is a table, this is a chair, this is a body, etc.

There is nothing wrong with this;
just recognize the mind breaks up the one thing
and turns it into countless, separate things.

But,
in truth,
there is only one thing happening now,
and this is what is.

You can see it as one painting.

The other thing we notice is that if we don't use the mind,
we really don't know what this is.

All we know is that *what is, is.*

If we don't go into the mind and refer to time,
we have no idea how any of this got here
or why anything is the way that it is.

We only know what we know,
and it is very, very little.

Our minds think we know so much.

This is not true knowledge,
it is just information and description.

Knowledge is knowing this knowing which is here, now.

The knowing doesn't know what anything is, it just knows.

In the truth of now, there is no cause for anything.

The Way of Freedom

There is no time,
there is no self, and
there is no past or future.

This is freedom.

What is, here and now, stands alone.

The Concept of Moving Through Time

*I can see that all I experience is now. I can say there is
nothing behind the curtain, and if I look, I'm now, and I've
always been this now. I can see that! But there's a feeling
that the "I am" that is now, is because of what's been
before. Does that make sense?*

What's moving through time? You should be able to find something
if it's moving through time, right? If there's something about you
that is moving through time, what is it?

I would say this, just whatever this is.

Where is time? Whenever you look, when is it? Is it now?

*Yes, and there's the idea that if someone hits me on my
arm, my arm would hurt, and that hurt would continue to
be there even though the hitting was over. So, I feel there's
a causality and a connection.*

The causality happens in the mind. The analogy that is commonly
used is the movie appearing on the screen. The screen is never
moving. On the screen, there appears to be pictures that are

moving, right? They're all moving now, but the screen itself is not going anywhere. The pictures are just appearing and disappearing every millisecond, right? Every millisecond a new picture is appearing. Not in time because the screen is not going anywhere. It stays right there.

Not only that, the person on the screen isn't actually a person, is it? It's just light, but it looks like a person. There's an appearance of a person, but it isn't really there. It's appearing and dissolving on this screen now, now, now... This is a metaphor, so it's not perfect.

Consider the screen to be you, your essential being, and on the screen of you is appearing now, now, now, now... Everything is coming and going in no time. No time, not even a millisecond. It's just like buzzing. Right now, there's nothing behind the curtain, there's only this moment. This is how I see it.

In this movie of now, if the mind tries to remember previous frames, it will create something called time. That creation of time, however, is just an appearance, isn't it? It's not actual. As you see for yourself, there's only, always now. Your whole life is always now. It's always been now. From the first day you can remember, it's been now. Also, the moment you die, it's going to be now.

On the screen of now, is just this movie playing here. Then the mind says, "Okay, this indicates time," and it creates linear time, which is just a concept. Conceptually, it's fine. There's nothing wrong with having the concept of time. Conceptually, it's true. Next week, you book your flight or schedule your dentist appointment, but it's all happening now. When it comes, it's still now, isn't it? The concept of time in this manner is not at all harmful.

The harmful aspect of time is the psychological aspect of time. It is a thought that says, "Oh, when I was a child, that happened to me and that is why I am..." When we place value on these memories, it causes pain now from things that don't actually exist, now.

Okay, I do see that is totally irrefutable.

The thing we want is to be free from suffering. Having the concept that someone hit my arm and it happened yesterday, is part of the movie. It's fine, but the fact of the matter is there is only now. That's true, isn't it? There is no yesterday, is there? That's the actual truth. Truth is only what you know, now. Anything else has to be in the mind.

> *Inquirer 2: Something you said previously about the movie screen helped me see something a little bit differently. It's the idea that the current image appearing on the screen is absolutely independent of anything that previously appeared on the screen. This image can be here without it having had any previous image.*

Let's take a look. To use the—admittedly imperfect—movie analogy again, what is an image on the screen? It is just one still frame and that one frame stands alone. Alone, that frame is not dependent on the previous frame. But, when strung together, one frame after the other, it gives the appearance of movement through time and space. In truth, however, that movement is illusory. When the mind strings each individual thought together and collates the thoughts to create an illusory self, it appears that there is the movement of a "self" through time and space. The mind puts it all together to create a story, and it's not a problem. That's what makes a movie of life like that.

There are two ways to look at causality. One way is to look at the Big Bang as the cause of everything. Under this view, this moment is caused by everything else that has ever happened. What is, always has a previous event that caused it, and the causality always leads all the way back to the Big Bang. That view is in the play of mind. The second view—which is true because we can only know what is now—is that there's nothing behind the curtain, and nothing has caused anything. There is only *what is*, this one frame appearing, now. This view is hard for the mind to grasp.

You can stop the mind now, for a second, and see that the only thing you actually know is this. Why is this now the way it is? I have no idea. Where did it come from? I have no idea. All I know is that, it is.

You have to see that the feeling of traveling through time is just based on a belief that you are the body-mind, and you are going through time. When you jump out of the body-mind (metaphorically), and you're aware of yourself as just knowing, then you see that you are not going anywhere. You're here. You're aware! It's only because you relate to the body-mind as who you are that you think you are traveling through time.

> *Inquirer 2: For me, it helps a lot to see that only thinking creates time. Without thinking, there is no time. It's just a bunch of thoughts and without those thoughts, there's nothing.*

> *Inquirer 3: Something that was super helpful to me was to know that our memories are just thoughts. We may call it a memory, but in fact, it's just another thought.*

Correct. What we call a memory is just a thought, appearing now. Importantly, the accuracy of the thought (we label a memory) that appears now is very questionable. We can't even say for sure that the memory is exactly how it happened.

Recognitions & Personal Shares

There's Only Truth

This past week, a couple of times I woke up in a state of panic and freak out. I didn't even have any thoughts going on about why I was panicking and freaking out. I was just laying there noticing how I desperately wanted the feeling to stop. I kept telling myself, "I've got to get out of this. I've got to do something different. I'm obviously creating this..." And then the word "jump" just showed up out of nowhere, and I recognized there is only truth. There's only truth.

No matter what's going on, no matter what thinks it's searching for truth, there's nothing searching for truth, there's only truth. It's been such a trip to be in total angst and paranoia, just freaking out, then thinking, "Alright, whatever."

That's great. That's so wonderful, and that's the only solution. Otherwise, you get in there and think, "Okay, I'm starting to think negatively, I got to change my thoughts, if only..." I'm too lazy. It's a lot easier to jump.

I see that, and there is the insidiousness of this idea of a doer that's always on and it is labeling every feeling and sensation in my body. Whenever a feeling shows up, I realize there is label placed on it, and the label is usually something along the lines of: "This is fucked up dude. You're inherently fucked up and you have to do something to stop this feeling." This goes on even when the feeling isn't that bad. It's not like I'm getting stabbed in the stomach with knives or anything. I'm just having a sensation. With a holiday, there's just a recognition, and I am like "wow."

That's fantastic man, I love that. That's great, that's wonderful.

Convincing People About Their Essential Being

There's something about just being that sometimes makes it difficult to relate to others. It's not something painful, but it's somewhat frustrating. It's like I'm the insane one (relative to the norm), but I can clearly see it's the current state of humanity that's insane. Even as I write this, I think to myself that I have a superiority complex, but it's not even that. I see that I'm nothing.

I go to class at the university and the focus is on learning about the brain and body-mind stuff. Also, there are people in my life that I love, who exclusively ride the carousels of mind (for lack of a better term). They are constantly focused on stories of the past and fixing stuff in the future. It's really fucked up and pretty sad. Hearing it all the time makes me want to say something.

Sometimes I do, and I always seem to regret it. I say something and think, "Wait, why did I say that? What did I think I was doing? Who am I to say that?" It's probably because I think that just "being" is better, and maybe that idea will go away at some point. I don't know.

I can only speak for myself on this issue because there are no rules. Some people may be more social, and some may be more reclusive, although that is for each person to know for themselves. I am more the latter. If I look at the people I respect and feel are the most authentic jnanis, they were/are not very social, and they were/are certainly not interested in the normal mind chatter that accounts for most human interaction. Ramana Maharshi and Annamalai Swami were both mostly silent and had zero interest in normal mundane blabbering. Nisargadatta talked a lot, but it was all about self-inquiry stuff. Dolano, my teacher, is not social either, she's mostly reclusive. Siva Shatkti Ammiayar, the guru I lived with in Tiru, never speaks to anyone at all, literally. Ajja, the other master I lived with, didn't have normal discourses either. He could care less about all that worldly stuff.

Yes, I agree; the state of humanity (the human mind), is quite insane. Completely focused on self/ego, it is all me, me, me. That me of course, includes "my" worldviews—social, religious and political. That is all the "me" and it is not separate from those personally held beliefs. It is quite unreal to identify as those beliefs because in reality, you are only now, no-thing. You exist consciously here, now. To say *I am* means only that, *I am*, with nothing added. To say, "I am my name, my nationality, a boyfriend, a liberal, etc.," is adding completely arbitrary and ephemeral ideas on to reality. All these ideas are due to coincidences like where you were born and what random experiences happened to the body-mind.

You mistakenly take those arbitrary ideas to be who you are, to be so important, and value them to the point of pathology. Then, you foist it all onto the world. Yes, it's insane. Our work is about knowing who I AM, and valuing that. Ignoring the rest because it is all only a myth or fantasy, an imposter of who you are.

You put on that "me" suit and came to believe you were the suit. (You didn't actually DO that, it all just happens, but you get the point of the metaphor.) That is how almost all people think about themselves, present themselves to the world, and relate to each other. When someone comes to know who they are essentially, they see that everything else is a fantasy; they see how they suffer because of those beliefs; they see the sanity/health of knowing truth. Then, naturally the interest in those false aspects wanes. Since we don't care to relate in those old false ways (stories and illusions of past and future), we may very well become disinterested in most social discourse. I can attest to this for myself.

As far as saying something to people who still have those beliefs, it is mostly pointless and can come off as arrogant. Perhaps one in a million will hear something you say, and an interest will be sparked, but it's unlikely. I really never say anything, unless I feel there is an opening, or someone asks a question. Even then, I am hesitant. Even if "being is better," and I certainly feel it is, it is not my place to force it down other people's throats like a Christian missionary.

The only thing that needs to go is the belief that you are all those arbitrary appearances and beliefs—that suit. And that is gone every time a holiday happens. In that moment, it is all gone; you stand alone and naked. There is nothing more to do, except have holidays and know thyself. Be this knowing that knows itself as Sat Chit—existence consciousness.

In truth, there is nothing you need to know or figure out. What will be, will be. If your interest is only in truth and your essential being, then that is what you will get. If every single thing in your life falls away, then you will be okay with that too. And, if your girlfriend dumps you because you have become too boring, you will be fine. Of course, none of that may happen and you cannot plan for it. To think about it is pointless. Don't bother. Just be this knowing that consciously knows itself. Know thyself. Be thyself.

Give Up the Story

My intention for years and years, was to wake up. From working with you, I realized my true nature. It's simple and I remember you said in our first session, it's just the beginning.

The intention before was to figure it out. Well, it's been figured out. Now, the intention is going into a new place, which is practicing having holidays and being aware, here and now. Nevertheless, there's old conditioning that says, "I don't have the answer and I have to figure it out." This continues to bleed through into my consciousness.

Forget your old patterns. On other calls, you have mentioned several patterns: how you have anger; how you want to be right with your wife; and how you are addicted to jazz. It's good that you know those things. In one way it's good because you are very open.

However, I want to say something, and I want you to hear this. Now that you know those things, stop knowing them. Don't make them so precious. If you do, then you are creating a precious self (i.e. this is who I am: the guy who has to be right; the guy who has anger; the guy who loves jazz, etc.). I say you know those things, good. Now, stop knowing them. Have a holiday.

Continuing to recognize these things is what I would call the negative approach. (See Initial Comments). You recognize something which is important to know, then you keep recognizing it over and over. Don't recognize it anymore. Stop solidifying the "this is who I am" story (I am the angry guy, I am the... guy, etc.). Well no, that's not who you are.

Instead, take the positive approach. If you recognize something like that, I say good and then be done with it. Don't recognize it anymore. Take the positive approach and have a holiday. Recognize freedom.

> *That's what I'm starting to get, the realization that I'm addicted to seeking or going back to all my... whatever, all that shit.*

Good. I want to do this with you now, in this moment. Now, you recognize it. Now, stop recognizing it. Now, you know there's no Santa. Now, you know you have those addictions. Now, stop knowing them because continually focusing on them creates a personality. Now, start knowing holidays instead, take the positive approach.

> *Inquirer 2 to Inquirer 1: I know you'll know this from your days with the Landmark Forum (a personal growth group). All that stuff is your story. Wherever you go, you present your story. At some point, give up the story.*

Exactly right. Give up the story. Stop being precious about it. Like I said, there's two sides to this. The first side is that you're being honest because you expose those things fearlessly. That's great, but then the second side is you're not being honest by continuing to believe those things are who you are. That's not being honest and you're lying to yourself because that's not who you are. Be honest when you recognize your tendencies, then stop lying to yourself by reifying it over and over again. Stop lying and start telling the truth. You are free.

Be a lion. This is the Lion's Den. Really, be a lion, man. See, you are not any of those things. You are not the angry guy or the guy who needs to be right. No, you're not that. You are free. Being free is the way of freedom.

Okay With Just Being Me

I have been reflecting lately on the quote by Nisargadatta:

"If you expect any benefits from your search, material, mental, or spiritual, you have missed the point.

Truth gives no advantage.

It gives no higher status, no power over others.

All you get is truth and the freedom from the false."

It is really clear that no one cares about my recognition of truth. Nothing happened and nobody thinks I am special. I am just an ordinary guy who doesn't believe as much bullshit as he used to.

I remember you telling me at the beginning of our sessions that the benefit of this work was relief and I have been experiencing that more and more. I am okay with just being me.

That is true. Nothing new happens and nothing changes. Things just become more and more settled. I am not sure whether there is ever an end to it, and there is just this "settledness." Finished seeking is finished seeking. You have been on numerous group calls and you have continued to listen to audios. That authenticity just does it. Nothing to do. You just show up and things resolve and get settled.

All the spiritual teachings, whether they be Western (you are a sinner) or Eastern (you need to purify your mind, eliminate vasanas or transcend ego), are basically telling you there is something wrong with you. These ideas are a huge disservice.

There is great relief the more and more you just settle into being yourself. And that is a great benefit. The imperfections that are there become more benign. What we are coming to realize is the natural human condition, not some idealized state we are going to achieve some day in the future. The natural human condition is being at ease with who you are, just like an animal is at ease with who it is. Animals don't have the analytical function like we do, and they are just fine being themselves. The human mind's analytical function has been corrupted by culture and religion. There is a lot of suffering that comes along with this burden.

Intention for Freedom

I had a terrible month and I thought about all of you a lot. My daughter was in the hospital and she could have died. She is okay now, but when she was in the hospital, I knew that I could use it for my benefit and practice having holidays. It was very beneficial to go through that experience because something did happen.

Of course, I was emotional and worried, and I did react, but the holidays just kept coming back. They were brief, sometimes just seconds, but I kept having them over and over. I even had the intention to ignore feelings. I didn't know if that was the right thing to do, but I didn't want to deal with feelings. I just wanted to come back to holidays as much as I could, and it was really, powerful. I saw it's not the reaction that's really the problem because the reaction to whatever is happening is normal. Like you say, it's the reaction to the reaction that causes the suffering.

At one point, I was aware that I was thinking, "Oh well, I wasn't enlightened there; I suck." Then I was aware that thought was not true. In any event, I'm never not me. I'm never not the Self (Atman), or whatever you want to call it. Through all the madness, through the tears, and through the desperation, I still am who I am. It never changes. No event stains who I am.

It's like you're the moon. The moon has a lot of phases, but you're always, always the moon. It doesn't matter how the light is shining, you're always the moon. Through all the thoughts, feelings, and sensations, no matter what they are, you are you. It doesn't matter.

Another thing I realized is that "big events" cause me to have spontaneous holidays. Without those events, I have these petty little things to complain about and those really aren't good opportunities. By having the intention to have holidays through the tough times, something happens. I knew I was not creating them. Something happened, and they just came. They just kept coming back, coming back, and nothing was making me believe I was unenlightened for a moment.

Even though a lot of things happened, it was a pretty good month after all. I got more established in knowing who I am. It became more obvious, more "this is who I am." I now know that nothing I go through—no thought, no feeling, no sensation, no experience, no nothing can move me away from that. Nothing!

That's awesome. Thank you so much. That's beautiful, gorgeous and amazing. First of all, I'm so happy that your daughter is okay. That's wonderful. Also, I'm happy to hear that you went through that because look how beneficial it was. There are not many tougher situations for a parent to go though, and during that, you had the intention to have holidays. Why? Because you want to know what's true. You want freedom. Even in the midst of the worst thing anybody could possibly go through, holidays were happening a lot, and look at the benefit. It's so clear how beneficial that experience was for you. Let's all complain about our petty, little vasanas some more, then shut up when we hear something magnificent like this. Thank you.

Inquirer 2: I hear that this was a huge benefit for you, and I want to let you know that your sharing was a great blessing for me. Out of this amazing mystery came your beautiful share and I felt the holiday immediately just show up. Such a gift. Thank you so much.

I agree. Thank you. That's true. Wonderful. We all have these little things going on, and when they're happening, we think they're so important. But man, they aren't nothing. Something like that can happen, or worse. For most of us, we're just complaining about nothing.

And for you, it's great. You've become more doubtless about who you are because, amid that very difficult, trying situation, you recognized your essential being. That makes you doubtless. That's why it's good when difficult circumstances happen. In a way, the people who have difficult circumstances can be finished sooner than others who just have some basic silly complaints.

It's the MOST obvious thing. The MOST obvious thing is who I am: free, now, no past, no future, and no ego self. The Self (Atman), Sat Chit Ananda is the MOST obvious thing. Just keep coming to know it more and more.

It's always the most obvious thing. It's just that most of us don't know it yet because we're so used to attending to everything that's coming up. First, we have to see the value of freedom, then we have to stop attending to what's coming up so much. Ignore. Ignore. Ignore. It's not just me saying it. It's Ramana saying it, it's all the Tamil saints saying it, and it's all the great sages saying it: IGNORE whatever's appearing and recognize the truth that's here.

Recognize that. And the more you do that, the more this truth becomes obvious, until it can't be more obvious. Even then, keep going, keep going, keep going, and more and more, things get resolved.

> *Inquirer 3: The extent to which we value truth or have the intention to have holidays on some level is completely out of our hands. I notice that within myself there can be a tendency to say, "I'm not having enough holidays." I seem to use it as a stick to beat myself. That's a bit dramatic, but...*

Yes, exactly. We beat ourselves up because we think we're not having enough holidays and we're so unenlightened.

Inquirer 3: Actually, when I have a holiday, really what happens is, a holiday just happens. The intention comes or doesn't come.

That's exactly right. Holidays happen. That's why I don't say take a holiday. Holidays happen. The intention comes or doesn't come, AND you know when it comes? When you get extremely fed up and you get tired of suffering, or something extremely strong happens.

Inquirer 1: For me, the intention has switched from waking up to recognizing that I am free because I realize I am already awake. The intention now is to keep recognizing it, to keep seeing it over and over. The intention is not to wake up because I've never been not aware.

Let's prove what was just said. We've always, always, only been awake. Let's have a holiday.

HOLIDAY

Here and now, you know you exist, don't you?

I am, here and now.

This knowing, aware, now, is not separate from who I am.

It *is* who I am.

This knowing of existence, here and now—Sat Chit.

Knowing is being. That's awake.

I know I am, here and now. That's being awake.

We don't know the profundity of that, until we start to know the profundity of that and how it can change everything. That simple thing which is always true leads to liberation of the mind. And that simple thing, which is always true and unknown for most people, can become our dominant condition most times.

Beyond Holidays

> *I don't feel like I'm going into holidays anymore. It feels like a natural state. It feels strange because I can see, feel and hear. There's been a lot of drama at my job, and I participate, but I don't care. I participate because I have to. I'm not angry with the person who is doing the bad thing, and I just don't care. At home, I'm not looking for anything and I'm not thinking it's bad. I am just wondering, why am I not having holidays? It feels like it's just in my heart, you know?*

You don't have to have holidays. Once you know who you are, you don't have to have a holiday again.

> *In Liberation IS, you expressed everything I feel. I'm not attempting to describe it, and I'm not speaking about it to anyone. That's why I am very happy to be with all of you on these group calls. I feel peaceful. I don't have any goal, and I'm not looking for anything. A few months ago, I lost my job (I'm not rich), and in the first few hours, I was going into panic, then it just dropped. I realized, "Everything comes to me. I don't care. I have what I need,*

and I'm not asking for much. I don't want to be anything."
It feels strange when you speak about holidays.

I speak about holidays a lot because I want people to become doubtless. Just go about your life. Know what's true, and if you come to rest in that, that's it.

If some things are troubling, holidays can come in handy, especially in the middle of something that may be stressful. If you get the message, you get the message. The only point of holidays is to get the message. That's why I always say you don't have to keep looking up the chimney to know there's no Santa Claus. You know there's no Santa Claus. Why do you have to keep looking up the chimney if you know there's no Santa Claus? That's the analogy I use. Sounds like you're doing fine.

Okay, thanks.

Limitless Aware

I noticed that when I have a holiday, nothing is being recognized. Aware is "no thing." The movement of attention seems to be the movement of conscious focus. This movement of the focus of attention from one thing to another is also seen, but it is subtle and sometimes it is not seen.

You always know the movement of attention, but you are not always conscious of it. You always know everything except in deep sleep. You are always aware of everything. You may not be consciously aware that you are aware, yet you are still aware. Even in deep sleep, you must be aware because you wake up when your alarm clock goes off.

> *In a holiday, the focus of attention becomes so wide it just becomes borderless and there is no movement of attention, it is just all-inclusive.*

That's right. There are two states (not a great word) of aware. One is aware of objects—focused attention. Another is aware of itself. When aware is aware of itself, it is self-evident, and this is borderless or objectless. You could say there is still attention, but it is just attention attending to itself.

> *It is not attention that turns around and looks back because there is nothing to look at.*

That is right. Aware, aware of itself. This knowing is self-evident. In this knowing, this whole manifestation appears. When aware is focused on objects, it appears more limited. When it is aware of itself, it appears limitless.

Attention is a function of the brain. It is non-dual, even when it is focused on an object. Aware is still all-inclusive, even when attention is consciously aware of one object exclusively. Aware is always limitless.

Limitations of Thinking

> *The thing I'm starting to get is that I can't think my way to this. I realize in my approximately forty years of searching that's how I've been trying to get there, by*

*thinking my way to it. It's not "figure-out-able" because
what it is, is not in the realm of thinking. I have been
following what you said a couple of weeks ago about just
ignoring the thoughts. I've just been having holidays. I see
that if I am trying to think about it, it isn't it. It's just in the
moment, just here I am.*

It's a very good point. Don't think about it, just have holidays,
period. I've never said that before [said facetiously]. I'll say it for
the first time—have holidays. Finally, after five years, I'm finally
saying it, have a holiday.

*For me, a holiday comes and I say to myself, "I am having
a holiday. I am aware now. I'm aware of my
surroundings." The more I do that, the more something
happens. I'm not even sure what that is.*

The more things get resolved. You come to know yourself as this,
instead of all the mental stuff. You have a mistaken identity. You
believe you're this body-mind. After more and more holidays, you
just come to know yourself more as this. The more you know
yourself as this, the more it becomes your natural default condition
to be this way. You know this knowing is who you are, and you no
longer believe you are all this other stuff. It takes time.

Being on a Retreat vs. Normal Life

*It seems like it is easier in the Indian culture to be more
relaxed, to do nothing, and to be liberated, than in other
cultures.*

That is because as a foreigner in India, you are not engulfed in its culture or in your own hectic, mundane life. It is like being on a retreat the whole time and it is easier to relax. Also, the culture in India is nowhere near as intensely oriented towards striving for success and achievement. Just being in India, whether you are a seeker or not, relaxes a lot of that intense success vasana that westerners have. You feel good to just be here, without all the striving.

> *I went on a retreat for two weeks and there was a feeling that I was really getting it. When it was over, it seemed like I went right back to the way I was.*

Yes, that happens on retreats. We get fooled into thinking we are getting somewhere. Then, the retreat ends and the peace that was elicited ends with it. It's true, there is a lot of benefit to having plenty of free time, but there is no excuse for not knowing who you are at any time. Even in the midst of work, you can have a holiday. Everyone can take time out of their day and be on holiday. In America, some people think they have to work sixty hours a week, so they can make more money than the next person and be more successful. If that is what you want, then that is what you want. If you want freedom, then life will have a way of arranging things for you to have time.

> *I don't have a job and I am on holiday a lot, but it seems like the retreat is still a different environment.*

Yes, it is, but you don't live on a retreat. You live where you live and there is plenty of time in your day to be on holiday. It doesn't matter where you are or the circumstances. You don't need silence, quiet, or anything. To know requires no particular circumstance. Of course, it is more pleasant to be in silence than having construction equipment working right outside your window, like my current situation. However, the noise does not prevent me from knowing who I am. You don't need a meditation retreat to know who you are.

You could be in a very unpleasant situation and still know who you are. It only depends on what you want. If you want to be on holiday and know peace, you will. If other things are more interesting, you will have that. No judgment, it is simply scientific.

Just know who you are whatever the circumstances are. Know, now.

> *When we are on these calls together, it seems like it is different.*

Jesus said, "When two or more people come together in my name, there I'll be." What he's really saying is that when a group of people come together in truth, there truth will be. It is called a satsang—meeting in truth. Of course, it is easier here to recognize your essential nature. That is why we have these group meetings. It is really valuable when people come together for the purpose of recognizing truth. It is also very beneficial to listen to the audios from past groups.

Even without these calls, you have to have the authenticity to want freedom for yourself. You can't be dependent on coming to these group meetings or listening to audios. You can't be dependent on anything. They are helpful as a reminder. The rest of the time, your own authenticity for truth will keep you free. There is no other way.

We want a lot. Many people say they want freedom. Let's get real and be honest. Many people really want a lot of other things. If you want freedom, it is done. It is over. A big part of the work is to be honest and recognize that maybe you want other things. Maybe you are only saying you want freedom. It is fine and there is no judgement about it, but get real. The more you see this, the more you will notice that you do want freedom, but there are many other things you actually want as well. There is nothing wrong with wanting things. However, if you only wanted freedom and nothing else, it would be finished.

Be honest and have a look. You can sit around for a long time with thoughts coming and going and be on holiday, BUT you have to get real. The more holidays you have, the more the mind will calm down. It is just scientific. What do you want? Right now, it is already finished. There is nothing—just peace, Sat Chit Ananda.

Soul and Death

What is Soul? Is There Anything After Death?

My father-in-law passed away yesterday and the question arose if there was a soul? My wife and different people talk about the soul. How would you speak about that?

I am sorry for your loss, and to be honest, I don't speak about it. I don't believe there is a soul or anything that carries on after death.

Okay. Let's forget about heaven and that. What about a soul in daily life, before you die?

I don't find anything called a soul myself.

So, being aware is not soul?

Well, in my understanding of the word soul, it is a very personal, individualistic thing. My soul, your soul, his soul, etc., and when I die, my soul will continue on and go somewhere, heaven or reincarnation, or wherever. To me, that is just an extension of the belief in ego. I only know what I know, here and now. That is—I am here, now, aware, free, and unborn. To think there is a soul gets into the realm of philosophy and belief because no one can prove there is a soul. In that case, I don't have any beliefs.

I certainly have not found something called a soul. There is the sense of an individual "I" here, but it is just a sense, and it is very fleeting and ephemeral. There is no solidity to it and it is mostly not even here.

Based upon religious ideas and fear, and in the interest of a "me" never dying and living forever in Heaven (or an afterlife), we have created something called a soul. My "soul," which is the highest part of me, will continue after the death of this body. This belief somehow allays the fear of utter non-existence, which we can neither fathom nor bear.

One thing I would say is, if your wife or mother believes in a soul, I would never offer my opinion to the contrary. I say let them believe. They are not coming to you to know what is true. I let people have their beliefs unless they specifically ask me to do the inquiries with them.

If you would summarize, is it just another concept?

How can it be otherwise if there is no actual knowing of it? See for yourself. If you don't know it for yourself, in actual, real knowing, then it has to be a concept. Anything other than this knowing that is now has to be a concept or a belief. I'm very stubbornly skeptical. I just don't hold beliefs anymore. I really don't believe anything. Not even that there is a soul. Why is that? Because I only know what I know, here and now. Anything I don't know, I don't know and don't care to believe. This is just being honest. I happily don't know, and I like it that way.

Most people need some kind of security, which is why all of these concepts about what happens after death have been created. If belief in a soul gives your family some comfort during this time, I would support them in that belief. This stark sense of not needing to have that false security is not for everyone.

When I was a spiritual seeker and thought I knew so much, I may have felt the need to put my opinions out there in order to be the one who "knew." That way of being, however, is aggressive and not compassionate. Coming to know you lack nothing means knowing you don't need to be the one who knows or the one who is right. Also, it is too tiring to try to convince true believers of anything. I'm too lazy for that.

Inquirer 2: One of the benefits of believing in the soul is that it helps make it easier for people to let go when someone dies.

Yes, that is the exact reason there is something called heaven in the first place, to make it easier to accept one's own death or the death of a loved one. Most people do need that belief to comfort them in the face of death, or when thinking of their death in the future. For most people that is fine, but none of us here get to have that luxury because we want to know what is true and what is freedom. Well, in truth and freedom, we have no idea what is going to happen after death.

I don't need that crutch at all. You don't either. I have no idea what will happen after death. It could be that this consciousness ends and there is no one to know anything at all. In that case, there is nothing to fear because there will be no one there to know it. It could be that we die and go to heaven. That's a pretty good scenario, and in that case, there is nothing to fear either. It could be that we will be reincarnated and come back to life, so we won't even really die. It sounds like there is no problem any way you look at it.

We are just coming to know what's true, and what's true is we have no idea what is going to happen after this body dies. Let's be honest. That is all we are doing here together anyway, being honest. When we see this whole concept of me (this self story that we think is going to die), is just a story, then there's not much fear about it dying.

Consciousness After Death

In some of the Advaita teachings, there is consciousness, with a small "c" and Consciousness, with a capital "C." Consciousness (small "c") is usually what people talk about when speaking about their own thinking consciousness. Consciousness (capital "C") is what is always there and continues after you die.

How would they know that? I say no one can know what happens after death because they haven't died yet. It is just philosophical thinking and more egoic hopes of continuing forever. What can I actually know for myself, now? It is actually very little. What I can know is this—here and now, this knowing is present. I don't mean that I know anything about this moment, like the meaning or the why's and how's of it. I simply mean this present *knowing*. When you stop attending to objects for a moment and have a holiday, you recognize this aware-knowing that simply is. This is the only true knowing and it is just here and now.

What I can only really know is that I exist, here and now—I am whole and complete, and I lack nothing. These are obvious. If I refer to some psychological aspect of this thinking mechanism and a so-called historical story, then I could say, "I am lacking something." However, I don't refer to that as who I am. Who I am, essentially, is this present knowing, here and now, only. Therefore, I am free and lacking nothing. This is obvious and I know this. After this body drops, how can I possibly know anything about that?

A lot of Advaita stuff is philosophical. Freedom is not needing to know anything like that at all. It is the end of all that type of questioning. The only thing that is really needed is to be honest. If I am being honest, I have to say there is no past, there is no future, and there is no self. Also, if I am being honest, I have no idea what will happen when this body dies. This kind of honesty is the end of beliefs and the end of philosophies.

Near-Death Experiences

There are a lot of accounts of people dying and coming back. I recently saw one where a woman with cancer died. She saw herself outside of her body and realized the cancer was caused by fear and stress. When she came back, she healed herself. I am wondering if this is just something happening in the brain?

I don't particularly like this concept of "near death." We are all "near death" every moment of our lives. I mean, I could walk out of my house now and get hit by a car. These people who have had these experiences didn't die, because if you die, you are dead. To say that an out-of-body experience is "out of consciousness" is not true. She was there knowing the experience.

Previously, I had a lot of mystical experiences, including an out-of-body experience. In each one of them, I was there knowing the experience.

In essential mind, all experiences arise and pass, even the subtlest transcendental experiences and all of them are known to you.

Obviously, her cancer was cured, and I am not implying it wasn't the result of the experience she had. However, as we all know, she did not do anything. There is no doer. It just happened and she was the knowing of the cure happening.

> *Inquirer 2: A lot of books are written based on the author's personal experiences. People who read them tend to think that if they do the same thing the author did, they will get the same results. However, I think we each have our own experiences, and following someone else's path will not lead to the same place.*

That is true and that is why I stress from the very beginning of our work together that you have to come to your own knowing. It doesn't matter what I know. What is important is what you know for yourself.

> *What I used to think is that someone else knew more than I did.*

I wonder why? Many religions say the leaders are the ones who know. In the education system, there are teachers at the front of the room who have all the answers. Our cultural and religious systems instill ignorance and subservience.

Actually, religions don't want you to know for yourself. If people know, then they don't need the religion anymore, and it cuts off the religion's income. Constantine is often credited with converting the Roman Empire to Christianity, and he decided that only Latin would be spoken in the churches (it stayed like that until the 1960s). This prevented people from really understanding anything and it forced them to go to the priests to get answers. Also, Constantine specifically told people—don't do self-inquiry, and don't look within, come to us for answers.

My teacher told me she did not create sheep, she created lions, and this she got from Papaji. Religions create sheep. When you know for yourself, you are your own authority. You don't need any confirmation. Who cares what I or anyone else knows? Be a lion. Once you know who you are, God is not going to convince you of anything different.

We are all equals here. We all know who we are.

To find out more about **The Way of Freedom**

and Salvadore's other writings, inquiries and events

visit:

www.liberationis.com

www.salvadorepoe.com

Made in the USA
Monee, IL
07 July 2024

61393774R00260